Educating the Global Village

Including the Young Child in the World

Second Edition

LOUISE BOYLE SWINIARSKI
Salem State College

MARY-LOU BREITBORDE
Salem State College

Merrill
Prentice Hall

Upper Saddle River, New Jersey
Columbus, Ohio

Library of Congress Cataloging in Publication Data
Swiniarski, Louise Boyle.
   Educating the global village : including the young child in the world / Louise Boyle
Swiniarski, Mary-Lou Breitborde.—2nd ed.
      p. cm.
   Includes bibliographical references and index.
   ISBN 0-13-098176-1
      1. International education—United States. 2. Multicultural education—United States. 3.
Early childhood education—United States—Curricula. I. Breitborde, Mary-Lou. II. Title.
LC1090 .S86 2003
370.116—dc21

                                                                     2002025461

Vice President and Publisher: Jeffery W. Johnston
Executive Editor: Kevin M. Davis
Associate Editor: Christina M. Tawney
Editorial Assistant: Autumn Crisp
Production Editor: Sheryl Glicker Langner
Production Coordination: Rebecca K. Giusti, Clarinda Publication Services
Design Coordinator: Diane C. Lorenzo
Photo Coordinator: Kathy Kirtland
Cover Designer: Jeff Vanik
Cover Illustration: "Earth" © 1998 Lauren Van Woy; Courtesy *Kids-Did-It! Designs*® www.kidsdidit.com
Production Manager: Laura Messerly
Director of Marketing: Ann Castel Davis
Marketing Manager: Amy June
Marketing Services Coordinator: Tyra Cooper

This book was set in Zapf Humanist by The Clarinda Company. It was printed and bound by R. R. Donnelley &
Sons Company. The cover was printed by The Lehigh Press, Inc.

Photo Credits: AP/Wide World Photo: p. 163; Betsy Bergman: p. 90; Michael Bergman: p. 192; Mary-Lou
Breitborde: p. 190; Anne Crouch: p. 12; K. Deter Empacher: pp. 70, 71; Jo Ann Murphy: pp. 9, 41, 116; Ann
Murray: pp. 36, 101; PhotoDisc: pp. 29, 39, 61, 82; Evan Richman/The Boston Globe: p. 167; Louise Swiniarski:
pp. 3, 6, 15, 17, 21, 34, 46, 48, 57, 68, 79, 83, 107, 118, 127, 138, 143, 152, 159, 165, 172, 175, 179, 187, 193, 213,
219; Linda Vogenthaler: p. 123; Tom Watson/Merrill: p. 51; Carol Wolter-Gustafson: p. 93.

Pearson Education Ltd.
Pearson Education Australia Pty Limited
Pearson Education Singapore Pte. Ltd.
Pearson Education North Asia Ltd.
Pearson Education Canada, Ltd.
Pearson Educación de Mexico, S.A. de C.V.
Pearson Education—Japan
Pearson Education Malaysia, Pte. Ltd.
Pearson Education, *Upper Saddle River, New Jersey*

Merrill
Prentice Hall

10 9 8 7 6 5 4 3 2 1
ISBN 0-13-098176-1

To Andrew, Max, and Peter,
my hope for the world's future is with you — L.B.S.

To Reuben, Micah, and Jonas,
with pride and gratitude for who you are, and with my
love — M.B.

Preface

Since the publication of the first edition of *Educating the Global Village*, world events have called for the book's revision. Today, the realities of the global village are more evident to all of us in our daily lives. The challenge of today's schools is to define and implement new directions that address global concerns, issues, and needs that face educators and parents in this 21st century. The intent of this edition is the same as that of the first, to help children live effectively in the global village. To that end, we have revised the text with up-to-date information, learning theories, teaching practices, and home/school/community partnerships that protect, promote, and provide for all of the world's children.

Children's attitudes are formed in the beginning years of life. Many texts ignore the early years in the teaching of global or international education. We feel that young children should be included in the discussion and decisions about their world; thus, another goal of this text is to approach global education with a background and strategy that educators and families can use for effecting a proactive and positive influence on young children. The text intends to help those working with children from their earliest social interactions through their elementary school years.

New to This Edition

We have made many changes to this new edition.

- We reorganized the book into 10 chapters that integrate teaching exceptional children in an international context throughout the text to reflect the inclusion philosophy of special education.

- We expanded on teaching practices for global education to include several innovative approaches and international models such as multiple intelligence schools, Reggio Emilia schools, the Montessori method, standards-based schools, and full service schools.

- We considered the roles that distance learning, the Internet, and web designs play in outreach, collaboration, and conferencing in a global community. Readers also are directed to pertinent references and websites at the end of chapters for greater depth and breadth of information.

- We added the importance of a sustainable environment for the future needs of children and the new imperatives to support the spiritual side of teaching and learning.
- We extended the definition of global education from 10 to 12 principles.
- The appendixes are updated and revised as resources for further study and implementation by teachers, families, and children.
- Finally, we have revisited the state of childhood and the UN Convention on the Rights of the Child in context of the new directives the United Nations is taking in its campaign to better the lives of all children around the globe.

Organization

A major theme of this text is unity in diversity. The theme expands the usual definitions of global education and multicultural education. It perceives the world as community while recognizing the world in the local community. With that dual purpose, the book is organized into three parts:

- Part I: The Need for Global Education Continues
- Part II: Including Diverse Learners
- Part III: Implementing a Global Education Curriculum

Topics covered include the ever-changing definition of global education, the state of the world's children, UN mandates, comparative education practices, the importance of culture, multicultural America, creating community, placing the world in the curriculum, teaching themes, and the role of the globally literate educator.

In conclusion, we wrote this book to serve families, educators, and children as a text that puts theory into practice. We hope to provide our readers with a knowledge base for understanding the issues and concerns of global education. We offer teaching-learning strategies that are inclusive of all children in a diverse array of learning styles, that infuse global education into the child care center, school, home, and community, and that help children solve today's problems so they can face the challenges of tomorrow.

Acknowledgments

We would like to thank our editors, Ann Davis and Allyson Sharp, and Salem State College for financial and academic help. We would especially like to thank the following reviewers for their helpful insights and suggestions: Jacob Mayala, St. Cloud State University; Lorna H. Greene, Skagit Valley College; Cheryl W. VanHook, Ohio University; and Sandra B. DeCosta, Indiana State University. We owe a great debt of gratitude to our former coauthor, Jo-Anne Murphy, for her contributions to this edition. We thank Allan Shwedel and Michelle Pierce, who aided in the photo selection, and Phyllis Arouth, who is always a crucial support. We appreciate our families, friends, and colleagues who loved, listened to, and lived with us throughout the revision of the book. Dr. Swiniarski wishes to acknowledge the memory of her parents, Bernice and Charles Boyle, for encouraging her to be a lifelong learner, and her husband, Joe, for his constant help and encouragement. Dr. Breitborde would like to acknowledge the memory of her mother and father, who gave her a sense of her own history and of her responsibility as a citizen of the world, and extend a special thanks to sustaining friends and the three sons who have blessed her life.

Discover the Companion Website Accompanying This Book

The Prentice Hall Companion Website: A Virtual Learning Environment

Technology is a constantly growing and changing aspect of our field that is creating a need for content and resources. To address this emerging need, Prentice Hall has developed an online learning environment for students and professors alike—Companion Websites—to support our textbooks.

In creating a Companion Website, our goal is to build on and enhance what the textbook already offers. For this reason, the content for each user-friendly website is organized by topic and provides the professor and student with a variety of meaningful resources. Common features of a Companion Website include:

For the Professor—

Every Companion Website integrates **Syllabus Manager™**, an online syllabus creation and management utility.

- **Syllabus Manager™** provides you, the instructor, with an easy, step-by-step process to create and revise syllabi, with direct links into Companion Website and other online content without having to learn HTML.

- Students may logon to your syllabus during any study session. All they need to know is the web address for the Companion Website and the password you've assigned to your syllabus.

- After you have created a syllabus using **Syllabus Manager™**, students may enter the syllabus for their course section from any point in the Companion Website.

- Clicking on a date, the student is shown the list of activities for the assignment. The activities for each assignment are linked directly to actual content, saving time for students.

- Adding assignments consists of clicking on the desired due date, then filling in the details of the assignment—name of the assignment, instructions, and whether or not it is a one-time or repeating assignment.

- In addition, links to other activities can be created easily. If the activity is online, a URL can be entered in the space provided, and it will be linked automatically in the final syllabus.

• Your completed syllabus is hosted on our servers, allowing convenient updates from any computer on the Internet. Changes you make to your syllabus are immediately available to your students at their next logon.

For the Student–

• **Topic Overviews**—outline key concepts in topic areas
• **Web Links**—general websites related to topic areas as well as associations and professional organizations.
• **Read About It**—timely articles that enable you to become more aware of important issues in early childhood education.
• **Learn by Doing**—put concepts into action, participate in activities, complete lesson plans, examine strategies, and more.
• **For Teachers**—access information that you will need to know as an in-service teacher, including information on materials, activities, lessons, curriculum, and state standards.
• **Visit a School**—visit a school's website to see concepts, theories, and strategies in action.
• **Electronic Bluebook**—send homework or essays directly to your instructor's email with this paperless form.
• **Message Board**—serves as a virtual bulletin board to post—or respond to—questions or comments to/from a national audience.
• **Chat**—real-time chat with anyone who is using the text anywhere in the country— ideal for discussion and study groups, class projects, etc.

To take advantage of these and other resources, please visit the *Educating the Global Village: Including the Young Child in the World,* Second Edition, Companion Website at
www.prenhall.com/swiniarski

Contents

Contents

Note: Every effort has been made to provide accurate and current Internet information in this book. However, the Internet and information posted on it are constantly changing, so it is inevitable that some of the Internet addresses listed in this textbook will change.

Part I

The Need for Global Education Continues

1 What Is Global Education?

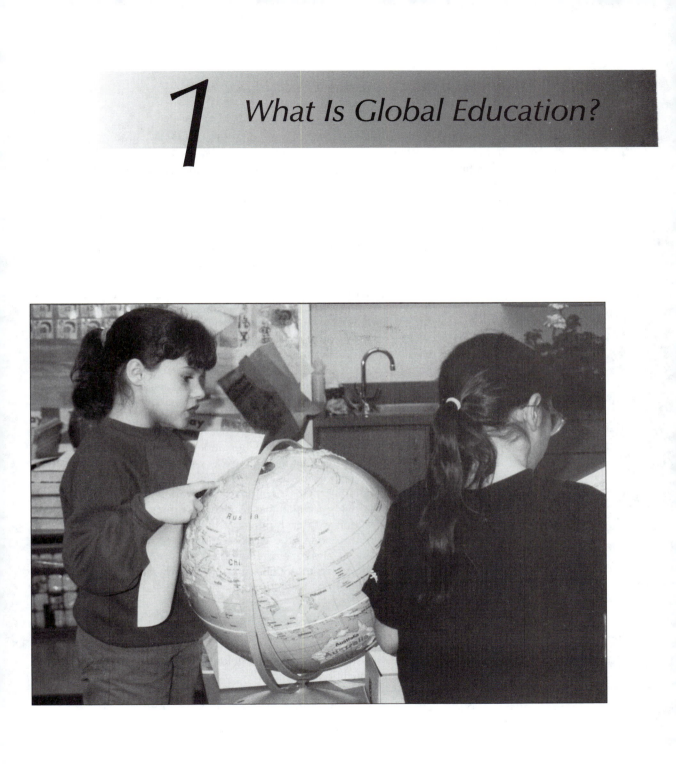

Introduction: Defining Global Education

Global education involves teaching perceptions of the world in terms of unity within diversity. The goal of this type of education is to promote the knowledge base, skills, and attitudes that permit young children to see the world as a community while appreciating the mosaic of cultures in their immediate neighborhood, town, or city. Children need to feel that they are part of the world community and to be able to accept differences among cultures. The connections that children make with other peoples and the appreciation that they have for other cultures will stem from an activity-based curriculum of hands-on experience with the universals of childhood and a study of the "interconnectedness of systems . . . ecological, cultural, economic, political and technological" (Tye, 1990, p. 5).

Global education is multifaceted and embraces a broad scope. It has been defined as "seeing things through the eyes and minds of others and it means the realization that while individuals and groups may view life differently, they also have common needs and wants" (Tye, 1990, p. 5). It can also be defined in further contexts concerning global issues, world cultures, and world systems that are interconnected and interdependent.

Global education promotes basic skills for living and interacting in today's world. It is for people of all ages, starting with the early childhood years. Its scope includes all people as it calls for a moral commitment to responsible social behavior.

Interdependency is a key concept of global education (Ellis, 1995, p. 298; Fortson & Reiff, 1995, p. 276). Fortson and Reiff maintain that "the interdependency of people immediately highlights the urgent need for better understanding among persons and nations" (1995, p. 276). This interdependency exists worldwide and, if understood, can lead to constructive relationships (Fortson & Reiff, 1995, p. 276), such as that among educators collaborating across national boundaries to develop effective schools. The purpose of studying comparative education systems is not to rank schools and place them in competition with each other. Rather, global educators must join in alliances to study the different models the world community offers, to share effective measures for reaching children, and to reform schools with approaches that are appropriate, tested, and feasible. Access to equal and equitable education extends beyond national considerations as a right of all children.

The Twelve Principles of Global Education

Global education is based on 12 principles that guide educators to develop a comprehensive view of a global education program:

1. Global education is basic education.
2. Global education is lifelong learning.
3. Global education is cooperative learning.
4. Global education is inclusive of all.

5. Global education is education for social action.
6. Global education is economic education.
7. Global education involves technology.
8. Global education requires critical and creative thinking.
9. Global education is multicultural.
10. Global education is moral education.
11. Global education supports a sustainable environment.
12. Global education enhances the spirit of teaching and learning.

Global Education Is Basic Education

Traditionally, global education numbered among the social studies teachings of the school's curriculum and did not appear in the curriculum's scope and sequence until the later years of childhood. However, current definitions of such education are more inclusive, extending the field beyond the social studies. Global education now is an interdisciplinary subject that traverses the curriculum array of academic areas. It provides a continuum of study and thought provocation from early childhood throughout an individual's education. Global education promotes the basic skills necessary for young and old to live and work in today's global village. In this context it can be considered basic education (Evans & Myers, 1995, p. 7). It involves the development of the cognitive domain in the academic areas of the language arts, mathematics, science and technology, politics, geography, economics, and history. It promotes the affective skills involved in moral development and artistic expression by cultivating the understanding needed for decision making and the appreciation of community life. Such skills are essential to all curricula and provide a mode for infusing global education in all the disciplines.

Global Education Is Lifelong Learning

Social theorists have maintained the importance of promoting a world view in the early social education of children. Elise Boulding, an educator and a sociologist, labels her approach to global education as the "sociosphere, a term . . . for learning and teaching about the worldwide society that is a reality of today" (King, Chipman, & Cruz-Jansen, 1994, p. 201). Boulding contends that children have a right to learn about the world as it exists today, with all its multiple facets, so they can assess the range of possible roles they can play in today's society (King, p. 202). Margaret Mead's prophetic work of the 1950s emphasized the need, created by our changing world, for teachers to teach beyond today for tomorrow (King, p. 200). Effective schools begin teaching global education to the young child.

Children do not come to school as tabulae rasae onto which knowledge is imprinted, nor as empty vessels into which learning is poured. Research has established that attitudes and cultural identity are formed in infancy. As children grow and develop, the socialization processes continue (Derman-Sparks, 1993, p. 6). Educators cite studies indicating that children's attitudes become "more consolidated" during the early years, so that by the time children are 9 years old their racial views are "constant unless the children experience a life changing event" (Derman-Sparks, 1993, p. 7).

Furthermore, to study today's society without including young children would constitute an incomplete analysis, according to Judith Evans and Robert Myers, co-directors of the Secretariat of the Consultative Group on Early Childhood Care and Development. They point to the growing importance of young children in the world based on reports from UNICEF/UNESCO's 1990 World Conference on Education for All (Evans & Myers, 1995, p. 7).

Global Education Is Cooperative Learning

Global education shapes the young child's role in the world through a process-oriented curriculum of learning experiences that provide connections with other children from diverse cultures. Cooperation is central to the universal themes of global education. The curriculum requires learners to work together identifying and resolving global concerns and issues. Children form small groups in which they listen to and value each other's opinions, brainstorm ideas, and formulate action plans. The cooperative approach begins with concerns immediate to the well-being of the children and spirals as they grow older. To appreciate another's culture, children must know about their own. We all gain insights

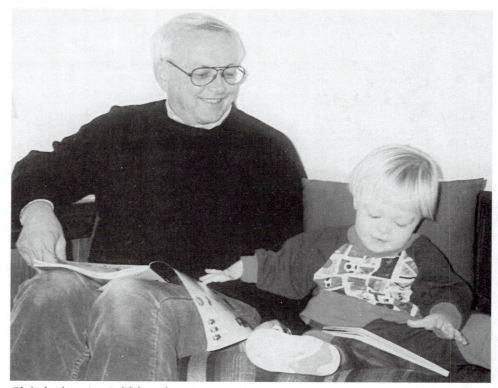

Global education is lifelong learning.

about ourselves through studying about and comparing ourselves with others. Cooperative learning situations promote both activities simultaneously.

Cooperative experiences are not limited to working with peers. Children can bring the skills gained in cooperative learning to joint ventures with parents and professionals to learn about worldwide agencies and organizations that serve their needs. By studying children from other nationalities and national schools, both children and adults encounter a multitude of model programs for schooling and parenting. With involvement in international agencies, they examine mutual concerns about world peace, safe environments, equality, and equity.

The goals of global education are to instill in learners of all ages the motivation to grapple with worldwide issues for a common gain, to promote common ventures, to celebrate each other's accomplishments, to define bonds that connect, to appreciate differences that make the world interesting, and to protect and preserve the world's resources. One might say these goals mirror the outcomes desired in any cooperative learning strategy.

Global Education Is Inclusive of All

The World Conference on Education for All underscored the need to begin the study of global issues early in the lives of all children. The conference set forth the challenge of "reaching children before the age of 3 . . . particularly in situations where children are at risk" (Evans & Myers, 1995, p. 13). We agree with the conference's charge and include children and parents who are challenged by physical and cognitive impairments or emotional and social problems. Global education speaks directly to the child with special needs in its pursuit and implementation of the rights of the child.

Global Education Is Education for Social Action

The overall purpose of global education is to educate children, parents, and teachers to be socially responsible for the world they inhabit. This global responsibility involves the rights and duties of national as well as world citizens and mandates an action plan for the protection of these rights. Knowledge of what is happening in our world and the exploration of reasonable resolutions to problems frame the content of the global education curriculum. And the directives for social action plans in global education include avenues that ensure peaceful resolutions to conflicts, protection of the world's natural resources for future generations, and guarantees of social justice for all societies.

While global education is not peace education, it embraces the same goals of harmony, equity, and justice for the world's citizenry. As in peace education, those involved in global education look for resolutions to disputes and encourage listening and negotiating skills as alternatives to disruption and war.

Global Education Is Economic Education

The difference between today's interest in global education and that of years ago is due to the support of businesses. The world's economy is a prime example of an element of society linked by interdependence. Multinational corporations recognize the urgent need for a workforce that can interact collaboratively around the globe. In addition to requiring employees who are competent in basic skills areas, businesses want personnel who are knowledgeable about the world and its people, cultures, and dynamics. Businesses also require individuals with a world view not bound by parochial limits. Workers of the future will have to utilize collaborative and cooperative measures to engage in an international economy. Some of the qualities that today's employers value in their workers include multilingualism, experience of a diversity of lifestyles, an openness to different perspectives, and proficiency in a specific area or career path. Additionally, the future workforce in a global economy has to appreciate its own worth and protect the tenuous role that labor contracts and agreements will play in the expansive workplace. The goals of global education are to promote the rights of all workers for equitable and livable wages, to ensure that working conditions are in safe and healthy environments, and to protect children from all forms of exploitation as laborers. It is reasonable to assume that these insights will continue to be important in future economic circles.

Changes in the workplace call for versatile workers with the flexibility to transfer knowledge and skills from one field of expertise to another. Global education seeks to stretch the imaginations of young children to construct new concepts of and solutions to issues in their own and others' lives. Global education prepares children to see the world as a whole unit with interconnected events. Understanding the impact that an event in one part of the world has on others hundreds or thousands of miles away is crucial for the citizen of today and tomorrow. Working in a global economy requires an understanding of one's personal role in interdependent societies. Individuals form consortia, produce alliances, and create alternative resolutions to conflicts and disputes.

Families immigrate for economic gain. The movement of families with young children is commonplace around the globe. Mexicans seek a better lifestyle in California; Turkish families take advantage of job opportunities in the European marketplace; Asian workers settle in New Zealand and Australia, where their professional skills are welcomed. In all such instances, the work skills, training, and adjustments that families make in their new residences impact the early educational practices of the child care center, preschool, and primary school. Global education is sensitive to parenting matters and to maintaining the delicate balance between long-held family traditions and newly acquired social skills and practice.

Alternatively, the immigrant families impact the culture and economy of the new homeland. While their lifestyles enrich a culture, the economy accommodates changes. New foods appear in the marketplace; restaurants offer more diverse menus. All forms of entertainment, such as music, the theater, and the arts, reflect new motifs in an appeal to a wider audience. Multiple forms of media are presented in a language that acquires an expanded vocabulary.

Global Education Involves Technology

Computers are an important component of any global education program. Young children are comfortable with technology as they use it in their play and work. The computer facilitates analysis and communication of information. With the aid of computers, children can create their own knowledge base with the world literally at their fingertips. Access through technology is open-ended. The Internet links children through electronic mail and webpages. Children can create their own webpages and communicate with each other through email so that pen pals can easily be email pals. Distance learning, daily conferencing with satellites, mapping the world and beyond with remote sensing, as well as probing the mysteries of the universe are some of the tasks technology addresses in a global curriculum.

Much has been written about the negative impact of television on young children. Yet this media is also open-ended in the possibilities it offers children to learn about their world and its people, places, and concerns. Through television and videos, children can travel the world with documentaries, drama, concerts, and films. They in turn can make their own television and video productions to be shared with children around the world.

Personal production of webpages and television programs, frequent communication with email, and the creation of videos take away the mystique of technology and allows children to discern the differences between the physical world and virtual reality. These forms of technology can be used for assessment as well as instruction. They allow children to see themselves and evaluate their own performance, knowledge, and attitudes.

Teachers can use the Internet as a communication device with families. Teacher or class webpages invite home/school partnerships as a way of communicating what's happening in school. Parents and teachers with access to computers can readily email

Global education involves technology.

each other with concerns or comments on daily events, homework, or a global education collaborative.

Global Education Requires Critical and Creative Thinking

Throughout this chapter we have underscored the interdisciplinary nature of global education. Curriculum development is defined in a holistic approach that is extended to include a world perspective. Central to this perspective are critical and creative thinking skills. In a global education curriculum, children are required to develop at an early age what John Dewey termed "habits of mind," noted in Chapter 2. Children are encouraged to be open to new ideas and options, analyze and synthesize information, compare and contrast data, make decisions, evaluate events, and formulate moral imperatives.

This approach requires educators of young children to value the teaching of global education as an intellectual process. Teachers need to be informed of world events, to be able to cull what is important to the lives of their children, and to be savvy enough to assess what is valid to the teaching/learning processes. Such teachers need to possess in-depth appreciation for world happenings to avoid the superficial and stereotypical. If children are expected to provide solutions to world issues or at least predict feasible alternatives, teachers must be able to meet those challenges. Again, research into assessing current American educators' grasp of these major areas of global education is discouraging. Audrey Wright's comparative study of Swedish and American teachers found American educators lagging behind their Swedish counterparts in grasping the major issues of global education as well as the strategies for addressing these issues (1994, p. 55). This study supports the need to provide in-depth teaching of global education and to assist educators in authentic applications of this knowledge in their daily teaching.

Global Education Is Multicultural

Cultural awareness is the core of both global education and multicultural education. Both disciplines perceive unity in diversity. Global education and multicultural education are parts of a continuum: global education looks at the world as a community, while multicultural education sees the world in the local community.

Factors of immigration, global economics, technology, transportation, and transnational endeavors impact the emergence of the global village in the same way they account for the growing multicultural populations present in all nations. No longer is any one nation as homogeneous as it was a decade ago. The study of global education is inclusive of these multicultural populations. These factors make it impossible for serious scholarship to separate global education from multicultural education.

Fortson and Reiff, in their "Open Structures Approach to Social Awareness," cite their "basic R's as Reasoning, Responding, Relating and Responsibility" 1995, (p. 281). They interpret responsibility as a "hyphenated concept, response-ability, meaning the ability to respond" (p.281). Surely, these "basic R's" are intertwined equally in both global education and multicultural education. A world perspective is critical in responding to diversity in any neighborhood, school, or family. Similarly, the global village is composed of these neighborhoods, schools, and families. To live effectively in their local milieu as well as in the world community, children need to respond appreciatively to differences in language, lifestyle, dress, race, and belief.

Many families themselves are multicultural and multiracial. The growing number of international adoptions and interracial and international marriages mirrors a microcosm of the world in the family. Children recognize differences among family members; perhaps they identify more with one parent than another, or maybe they feel different from other family members. Global education in its support of parent education is open to various family styles and options. Teachers and families can work together to promote a sensitive global education curriculum that fits all families' needs. Likewise, teachers need families for mediating needs in any institution.

Global Education Is Moral Education

Global education develops the moral domain of the child. It requires that choices be made that reflect the ethical code of a responsible citizen with a commitment to the well-being of the citizen's own nation as well as of the world. Decisions need to be made based on a value system that considers the implications that certain courses of action have for oneself and others. Families join with educational institutions to develop moral exemplars through a code of conduct and belief systems. Global education allows open discourse on belief systems along with support of world peace, provisions for human rights, and protection of the environment. Like character education, global education requires reflection and introspection by each individual to develop a code that will promote the well-being of the planet.

Global Education Supports a Sustainable Environment

Earth Day in its international celebration symbolizes the commitment of global education for a sustainable environment. Global education encourages children to relate to their natural setting, to care for their world, to preserve their natural resources, to protect wildlife, and to engage in responsible social actions for maintaining a safe environment.

As Maria Montessori included practical life experiences in her curriculum, a global education curriculum presents environmental issues as practical life experiences that are infused in all of the academic areas. Support for a sustainable environment is not limited to just one activity such as planting a tree or making an Earth Day poster. Worthwhile as these experiences are, environmental learning experiences should be a continuous study, project, or research program.

All curriculum areas address the care and concerns for the environment. The language arts skills of speaking, reading, writing, and listening are central to the study of environmental issues. These skills help children collect their information, share it, and communicate their findings and concerns. The social studies disciplines of history and political science examine governmental responsibilities and historical precedents for

An English child cares for a kangaroo during her visit to Australia.

protecting the environment. These disciplines offer children the knowledge base to make decisions and plan social action. The sciences also provide the necessary foundation and competencies to probe issues such as toxic wastes, reforestation, recycling, pollution, and population. The universal language of mathematics offers the tools for analysis of such issues. Each academic area is included in the rubric of global education. Each discipline develops informed citizens who will maintain their environment for future generations.

There is a rich variety of resources that teachers can draw upon for developing an environmental education curriculum, including environmental atlases, posters, videos, and computer software, as well as books, journals, and children's magazines. Some materials are free and sent to educators from governmental agencies. They include population studies made by the Population Reference Bureau (PRB) (Population Reference Bureau, 1997) and publications of the U.S. Department of the Interior and the U.S. Geological Survey. Likewise, free or inexpensive curriculum packets of materials and teaching ideas are also provided to educators by private nonprofit organizations such as the National Geographic Society, its state alliances, and the Massachusetts Global

Education Consortium. Many of these resources are linked to national curriculum standards or designed for meeting state curriculum frameworks (Massachusetts Global Education Consortium, 2001). National Geographic Society produced kits for the 2000 Annual Geography Awareness Week on conservation (National Geographic Society, 2000) and care for water resources and rivers as the theme in 2001 (National Geographic Society, 2001). These programs were joint ventures between the state alliances, the Massachusetts Consortium and National Geographic to disseminate all of the materials.

Global Education Enhances the Spirit of Teaching and Learning

Parker Palmer's work on teacher formation (1998) has focussed on the spiritual side of teaching and learning. In the recent rush for educational reform, there is a de-emphasis on the human side of schooling; yet Palmer's work resonates with many students and teachers. With the increased rhetoric for more standards and high-stakes testing in schools, many teachers, students, and family members feel that the heart and soul of the educational experience have been overshadowed by the teaching-to-the-test mentality and a narrowing definition of curriculum. Concerned parents and educators call for a caring humane school with a safe, violence-free environment where children feel connected, secure, and fulfilled.

Consistent with Parker Palmer's work on educational spirituality is the mission of global education. The mission endorses the goal for schools and centers to be places where teachers and children experience a sense of belonging, a freedom of expression, and a connection to others. The mission supports a school climate where teachers and students can engage in cooperative study with open points of view. Lastly, the mission seeks to provide opportunities for teachers and children to network and celebrate the common bonds of educators and learners worldwide.

Often spirituality is confused with religion. While a spiritual experience can be religious and embedded in one's belief system, the spiritual aspect of teaching and learning is the recognition of one's inner self and the respectful acceptance of one's own personal voice. Rachel Kessler calls it "the Soul of Education" in her book with that title. She feels schools can honor the United States' First Amendment of separation of church and school and at the same time support the "rights of our children to freely express their own beliefs" (Kessler, 2000, p. xiv).

The revival of character education in the professional literature and school mandates exemplifies recent efforts for providing humane practices in schools. Programs such as Matthew Lipmann's Philosophy for Children have been translated, adapted, and implemented in countries from all corners of the globe (Reed & Johnson, 2000, p. 205). Such programs aim at creating children who think for themselves and are nurtured with a methodology that permits self-reflection and self-correction along with respect for others (Reed & Johnson, p. 205).

Care must be taken in institutions or in countries where there is no separation of church and state. Spiritual education can embrace religious education, but the spiritual side of teaching and learning is not to be limited by or confused with the study of a particular dogma or set of rituals. The spirit of teaching and learning not only implies the discovery of an inner self but it speaks to those moments of transcendence, an "epiphany", or insight, that comes when you are totally immersed in the teaching/learning process. The spirit of global education challenges you to take an educative journey of ideas and to ask the cosmic and metaphysical questions.

Global Education Needs a Core of Globally Literate Educators

Teachers' voices:

> "It is interesting to discuss and share ideas and experiences and no doubt this influences how we all develop."

> "It is interesting to view our institution from an outsider's perspective. It helps to take a fresh look at how and why we do things in a certain way and avoids introspection."

> "The exchange of information regarding the two systems was useful. It was interesting to note that many of the pressures in the educational systems were the same."

> "I feel it is very important to be open to other ideas and cultures and to learn from them. The children have gained a lot from discussion of our similarities and differences and hope to keep talking via the Internet."

> (Interviews of British teachers)

Teachers are key to the success of implementing global education in early childhood programs and with families. They need to be sensitive to the diversity of the world's cultures and knowledgeable about world issues and the interdependent nature of world affairs and events. Some research has indicated that American teachers are less attuned to global education issues in their instruction than their counterparts in other nations (West, 1994, p. 66). But ongoing case studies that follow the professional and personal growth of American pre-service teachers involved in an international student teaching program indicate that such opportunities change perceptions (Swiniarski & Breitborde, 2001).

In these case studies, American education majors shared an international perspective about the role of education not previously held before having taught in the British system. In exit interviews and reports, the student teachers noted changes in their personal outlooks. They also shared an appreciation of the common bonds and universal traits of childhood. They recognized the central role families play in the education of all children, regardless of national origins. They acknowledged the professional commitments competent teachers everywhere share. They described in their portfolios an expanded view of education by comparing their American practicum with their British experience and evaluating cross-cultural projects (Swiniarski & Breitborde, 2001).

Exchanges and student teaching abroad programs can make a difference even years later, as follow-up study also reveals (Swiniarski & Breitborde, 2001). Former students still credit their student teaching experiences for broadening their understanding of the

An American student teacher helps British children develop literacy skills.

world, global events, and the interdependent nature of people in their social institutions. They cite their student teaching experiences as having a profound impact on the kind of professionals they are today, the way they (those who have children) parent their own children, and the subsequent life choices they have made (Swiniarski & Breitborde, 2001). Such evidence supports the need for continued provision of international study in teacher education.

Other professional development programs for teachers at both the pre-service and in-service levels confirm these findings by infusing global education issues, practices, and concerns in a variety of formats. Such programs offer teachers opportunities to conference with each other globally, study together in exchange programs, review and resolve common concerns, and explore innovative approaches that effect positive learning experiences. Programs can include workshops, conferences, seminars, study tours, lecture series, curriculum projects, or Internet conferencing, sponsored by the local school authorities, institutions of higher education, or professional and governmental agencies.

It is incumbent upon teachers to become involved with national and international agencies that sponsor these efforts. The range of staff development opportunities for teachers cuts across the entire spectrum of the curriculum and schooling levels and is provided by agencies both within and outside the profession. The National Geographic Society is a case in point. Through grants, it supports geographic alliances in most of the fifty states in the United States and in Canada. These geography alliances host summer institutes, travel study seminars, conferences, and workshops and produce a range of multimedia materials that identify issues common to both geography and global education.

Teaching organizations that specifically address international and global education include the Comparative and International Education Society, the Society for Educational Reconstruction, and Educators for Social Responsibility. Other curriculum-specific organizations have broadened their agendas to reach out to an international membership. One such organization is the Association for Childhood Education International, which is rediscovering its original international focus. Similarly, the National Association for the Education of Young Children searches worldwide for appropriate early childhood educational practices to share with the world's teachers as well as its own national constituency. In the arena of administration and supervision, the Association for Supervision and Curriculum Development has a framework for global education and publishes works on global education topics. All these groups network with teachers worldwide to identify common concerns and share effective practices. Indeed, when teachers come together, they immediately recognize the similarities in their tasks as educators. These teacher exchanges result in a bonding of professionals across borders.

Complementing the work of professional organizations, some states have established centers for global education. These centers serve the local school districts as outreach agencies for staff development of teachers from prekindergarten to grade 12. In the Commonwealth of Massachusetts, the Massachusetts Global Education Consortium is a network of six centers based in private and public colleges and universities as well as in a public school setting. They are located throughout different regions of the state to ensure access for all of the Commonwealth's schools. The centers provide a variety of services, including a lending resource library, traveling exhibits, a speakers bureau of experts in fields related to global issues, consultation on curriculum design, school-based global education projects, professional development for educators, international student teaching opportunities, school exchange projects, lecture series, and acknowledgment of the Massachusetts Global Educators of the Year annually at the State House in Boston. These centers are conduits for change in the schools and serve as models that promote the global context in the local community. The Northeast Global Education Center at Salem State College is one such center. It has enjoyed working with teachers in its district, enhancing pre-service opportunities for teacher education at Salem State College, working directly with children in school-based international projects, and engaging local area businesses in the promotion of global education ideals.

Consistent in all these programs is the goal to develop what some researchers have described as "globally literate educators in the US workforce" (Mahan & Stachowski, 1994, p. 19). Globally literate teachers infuse global education in daily teaching. They encourage their students to filter the world through the lenses of personal daily experiences to relate to other children's lives. Rather than presenting "others" as exotic and unusual or being superficial in their representation of the world and its complexities, globally literate teachers focus on the common bonds, present concepts in a global context, open the curriculum for divergent thinking, and encourage participation in a global society.

In conclusion, the definition of a globally literate teacher is multifaceted. The following definition summarizes the many roles of a globally literate teacher. These roles are inclusive but not limited to those presented for consideration.

The globally literate teacher

- views the curriculum from an international perspective
- is able to make connections and identify universal implications
- is knowledgeable of world issues, affairs, and happenings
- is sensitive to the unity and diversity issues
- is active in social issues
- is involved in local and international happenings
- is open to new ideas
- is willing to share expertise with others
- employs critical and creative approaches to problem solving
- performs on the basis of a personal moral imperative
- exhibits a positive spirit in teaching and learning
- is reflective (Swiniarski & Breitborde, 2001).

Summary

Global education involves a view of the world that requires an open perception of oneself and others. It is an inclusive and integrative area of the curriculum that ties together many strands, life skills, attitudes, and appreciation. It is focused on world

Mentor teachers pass on the spirit of teaching and learning to the next generation of educators.

systems, issues, and cultures. Global education programs are based on 12 guiding principles.

Formerly, global education was in the sole domain of the upper levels of schooling. Current theorists, based on research on the affective and cognitive development of the young child, place an emphasis on the importance of beginning the study of global education during the earliest years of childhood. Young children are the decision makers and leaders of tomorrow. They will continue to live in a world that is ever shrinking because of changes in technology, transportation, communication, and the world economy. To resolve world issues, protect the environment, seek viable means of employment, and ensure peace and tranquility both within and between nations, tomorrow's citizen will need to be comfortable working cooperatively in settings with a diverse membership.

Global education is interdisciplinary in content and purpose. It integrates its numerous and changing themes across the curriculum. Global education is framed around the twelve principles. It is basic, lifelong, inclusive, economic, multicultural, and moral. It requires critical thinking, calls for social responsibility, utilizes technology, protects the environment, and seeks the spirit of teaching and learning in its quest for a better world.

Reflection Questions

1. How can you infuse global education into your curriculum? Make a web of your core curriculum, and note where you can infuse the twelve principles of global education. Draw up a curriculum that meets the challenges of the principles and addresses the standards of your state or school community.

2. What does it mean to teach with a world perspective? With a collection of newspapers from different localities, national or international, note treatments of the same story: the differences and likenesses in the reporting and the tone of the different papers. Develop international news coverage into your daily current events.

3. What is your definition of a *globally literate teacher*? Use the Principles of Global Education to define a globally literate teacher. Hold a recognition ceremony for teachers who meet your criteria. Share the spirit of global education.

4. How can your class help sustain the environment for future generations? How can you involve your community?

References

Derman-Sparks, L. (1993, Winter). Revisiting multicultural education: What children need to live in a diverse society. *Dimensions of Early Childhood,* 6–10.

Ellis, A. (1995). *Teaching and learning elementary social studies.* Boston: Allyn & Bacon.

Evans, J., & Myers, R. G. (1995). A call to action: Improving the situation of children worldwide. In Karen Menke Pacieorek & Joyce Hiurth Munro (Eds.), *Annual editions, early childhood education 95–96* (pp. 6–14). Guilford, CT: Duskin.

Fortson, L., & Reiff, J. (1995). *Early childhood curriculum: Open structure for integrative learning.* Boston: Allyn & Bacon.

Kessler, R. (2000). *The soul of education.* Alexandria, VA: Association for Supervision and Curriculum Development.

King, E. W., Chipman, M., & Cruz-Jansen, M. (1994). *Educating young children in a diverse society.* Boston: Allyn & Bacon.

Mahan, J. M., & Stachowski, L. L. (1994). The many values of international teaching and study experiences for teacher education majors. In Jean L. Easterly (Ed.), *Promoting global teacher education: Seven reports.* Reston, VA: Association of Teacher Education.

Massachusetts Global Education Consortium. (2001). *The Massachusetts social studies framework.* Framingham, MA: Framingham State College.

National Geographic Society. (2000). *Here today, here tomorrow*. Washington, DC: National Geographic Society.

National Geographic Society. (2001). *Rivers*. Washington, DC: National Geographic Society.

Palmer, P. (1998). *The courage to teach*. San Francisco: Jossey Bass.

Population Reference Bureau. (1997). *World population and the environment: A data sheet from the Population Bureau*. Washington DC: Population Reference Bureau.

Reed, R., & Johnson, T. (2000). *Philosophical documents in education* (2nd ed.). New York: Longman.

Swiniarski, L. (1998, March). Interviews with British teachers, Sacred Heart Primary School, Ilkley, England.

Swiniarski, L., & Breitborde, M. (2001, April). *Teacher formation: Beginning with oneself, changing the world*. A presentation for the 2001 Annual ACEI Conference on Education Odyssey: From Froebel to the Internet, Toronto, Canada (Case Studies by L. Swiniarski).

Tye, K. (1990). Introduction: The world at a crossroads. In Kenneth A. Tye (Ed.), *1990 ASCD yearbook, global education: From thought to action*. Alexandria, VA: Association for Supervision and Curriculum Development.

West, B. (1994). A look across the reports to a global horizon: Concluding comments. In Jean L. Easterly (Ed.), *Promoting global teacher education: Seven reports* (63–68). Reston, VA: Association of Teacher Education.

Wright, A. (1994). Implementation of global education in the classroom: A comparison of Swedish and American educators. In Jean L. Easterly (Ed.), *Promoting global teacher education: Seven reports* (53–62). Reston, VA: Association of Teacher Education.

Further Readings for Research

Anderson, C. (1994). *Global understandings*. Alexandria, VA: Association for Supervision and Curriculum Development.

Becker, J. (1979). *Schooling for a global age*. New York: McGraw-Hill.

Bracey, G. (2001). *The condition of public education*. *Phi Delta Kappan, 83(2)*, 157–169.

Breitborde, M. & Swiniarski, L. (1999). Constructivism and reconstructionism: Educating teachers for world citizenship. *The Australian Journal of Teacher Education, 24(1)*, 1–15.

Derman-Sparks, L. (1993–94). Empowering children to create a caring culture in a world of differences. *Childhood Education, 70(2)*, 66–71.

Hirschland, R. (Ed.). (1996, February). *Update*. Washington, DC: National Geographic Society.

McLuhan, M. (1964). *Understanding media: The extensions of man*. New York: McGraw-Hill.

Websites

Ben's Guide to the U.S. Government for Kids: *http://bensguide.gpo.gov*

Federal Resources for Education Excellence (FREE) for Students: *http://www.ed.gov./free/kids.html*

Globe (global education): *http://www.globe.gov*

Massachusetts Global Education Consortium: *http://choosefsc.org/global.htm*

National Geographic Society *www.nationalgeographic.com*

Northeast Global Education Center at Salem State College: *http://www.salemstate.edu/ngec*

PBS Kids: *http://www.pbs.org/kids*

Who Are the World's Children?

Introduction: Examining the Conditions of Children's Lives

The goals of global education call for reaching children around the world in their early years to nurture in them what Dewey (1979) called "habits of mind." These habits involve considering the perspectives and welfare of others within what Noddings refers to as an ethic of caring (1992). We would like to engage children in growing toward becoming the "world citizens" that Brameld (1956), a global educator before his time, thought was the ultimate goal of education. Any effort to provide children with a global perspective and help them understand global issues must be based on a thorough understanding of the children themselves, including the conditions of their lives. While educators know that habits of mind and heart form early in life, we also understand that children's understanding of concepts and experiences is limited by their age, their cognitive abilities, their culture, and the physical and social conditions of their immediate life experience.

Ideally, young children are fed and sheltered by families and communities who care for them, who have knowledge of what they need and the resources to provide it. Ideally, they have time to play, a world rich in learning experiences, emotional support, and intellectual guidance. Within a physical and social context that nurtures their bodies, minds, and hearts, young children are capable of growing toward responsible world citizenship, armed with knowledge, a caring heart, and competence. However, too often their economic, political, and social circumstances do not support the ideal. This chapter describes some of the conditions and limitations affecting the welfare and education of the world's children—in particular, their relative wealth, their health, and their access to schooling and thus their ability to learn. Subsequent chapters will describe the effects of culture on how children think, what they know, and what they value.

The Health and Wealth of the World's Children

Abraham Maslow told us in *Toward a Psychology of Being* (1968) that humans operate according to a "hierarchy of needs" that filter our experiences so we can pay attention and understand information that will satisfy what we require. He convincingly argued that we first look for ways to satisfy our basic physiological needs for food, clothing, and shelter. Only after these needs are satisfied can we attend to satisfying our need to feel loved and respected. Once we feel secure that those needs have been fulfilled, we are free to learn and care about others. Finally, when those first levels of physical and emotional needs are satisfied, we attain the highest level of need, which is "self-actualization." At this highest level, we look for ways to satisfy a need to feel fulfilled—for example, through meaningful work or creative endeavors.

Too many of the world's children are trapped at the most basic level of this hierarchy, searching effortfully for sources of food, clothing, shelter, physical safety, and health care. Too many live where these basic needs are unavailable or inadequate, where governments do not care well enough or equitably enough for their children. Because the world of the very young child is experienced through the immediate world of the family, these children will not understand larger political or economic issues that affect their physical welfare. They know only that they are hungry or cold or hurt or afraid. If they live in a war-torn nation, their parents may have disappeared. If they live in an unstable community, they may not have the security of strong, supportive, loving parents who are physically and emotionally secure enough themselves to love and care for their children well.

Worldwide, children's health is affected by conditions of poverty. The United Nations Children's Fund (UNICEF) estimates that tens of millions of children have poverty-related health problems. Infant mortality rates for poor African children are double that of children in industrialized nations (Hellinger & Hammond, 1994). The World Bank contends that parents' access to basic education has important effects on improving children's health. It estimates that every year of schooling results in a 10% decrease in child deaths and a 10–20% increase in wages (Murkowski, 1994).

UNICEF reports that, despite continued progress in improving the health of the world's children, nearly 13 million children die every year of preventable malnutrition and disease. Immunization programs have resulted in 3 million fewer child deaths each year, but still, 1 million of the world's children die of measles and half a million newborns die of tetanus (in Murkowski, 1994). Diarrhea still kills 3 million children each year in places where parents do not know that affected children need rehydration or where the water supply is contaminated. More than 1 billion people have inadequate and unsafe drinking water, which causes more than 80% of the diseases in the developing world and millions of fatal cases of childhood diarrhea (in Murkowski, 1994).

The World Health Organization reports that 1.4 million children had been infected with HIV by December 2000 (Report on the Global HIV/AIDS Epidemic, 2001). Six hundred thousand were newly affected or infected in the year 2000. In some African cities, where as much as one third of the young adult and adult population is HIV infected, 60% of new infections are among the child-bearing age group of 15–24-year-olds. In eastern Africa, on average, every mother who dies of AIDS leaves three children (*UN Chronicle*, 1994). Successful prevention programs, including education and condom distribution, have reduced the rate of infection in sub-Saharan Africa in recent years; however, infection rates are growing elsewhere in the world, including Eastern Europe, Central Asia, and Latin America (Report on the Global HIV/AIDS Epidemic, 2001).

It is sadly ironic that, as Jim Grant, executive director of UNICEF, points out, UNICEF could accomplish its 1990 10-year goals of controlling childhood diseases, cutting malnutrition in half and child deaths by a third, and providing a primary school education for at least 80% of the world's children with an expenditure of only $34 billion a year, less than the $40 billion the world spends each year playing golf (in Murkowski, 1994). Statistics for children living in the United States, which prides itself on its standard of living and its humane concern for individuals and social groups, hardly depict a country that takes adequate care of its children and their families.

Health statistics for Americans vary by race and ethnicity. According to U.S. Census Bureau figures, in 1988, 88.5% of white Americans were covered by health insurance, while only 74% of Hispanic Americans were so protected (cited in Sleeter & Grant, 1995, p. 7). For this and other reasons, the U.S. Department of Health and Human Services found large gaps in the life expectancy rates for whites, blacks, and Hispanics, with black males living 10 years less than white males and Native Americans living 6 years less than other people of color (cited in Sleeter & Grant, 1995, p. 8). One would expect that the country that touts itself as the home of the world's best medical facilities would support excellent medical care for children. In comparison with other developed nations, however, infant mortality rates and child deaths in America, though declining, are still embarrassingly high (Annie E. Casey Foundation, 2001). The decline in infant mortality has been affected by a similar decline in births to teenage mothers, rated at 37 per 1,000 females in 1990 and 30 per 1,000 females in 1998. While infant mortality and child death rates (CDRs) for children ages 1 to 14 have declined in recent years, these rates varied widely by race and geography. In 1998, the CDR for African American and Native American children was 42 per 100,000, twice that of all other racial groups. According to the *Kids Count Data Book*, "poor minority children, especially African-American children, are often isolated in dangerous neighborhoods where the chances of life-threatening mishaps are highest" (Annie Casey Foundation, 1995, p. 11). Of twenty-five industrialized nations, the U.S. ranked 23rd in the number of child deaths, many of them due to automobile accidents.

The city of Boston, home to some of the world's finest hospitals, is a troublesome example of the failure of an advantaged locality to take care of its own children. In 1994, the infant mortality rate (IMR) for Boston was 9.1 per 1,000 live births. Of those deaths, 48% were black non-Hispanic infants, while 27% were white and 18% were Hispanic. Black infants died at a rate of 12.2 per 1,000 births, the IMR for Hispanic infants was 8.2, and the rate for white infants was 7.1. Although the infant mortality rate for blacks had improved from the previous year, for which the rate was 14.9, great racial differences are obvious in Boston's IMR figures. Low birth weight, associated with problematical child development and a range of health problems, also differs greatly by race in Boston. In 1994, 13% of black infants had low birth weights, compared with 7.8% of newborn Hispanics, 5.6% of Asians, and 5.8% of white babies. Many of the causes of infant mortality and low birth weight involve inadequate prenatal care for expectant mothers. Statistics show that in 1994, in a city teeming with hospitals and doctors, only 71.5% of expectant black mothers received adequate prenatal care, compared with 87.3% of white mothers (Boston Department of Health & Hospitals, 1994).

According to the Kids Count data-collection project, mothers' and infants' health and access to health care at birth have improved in the past decade as the economies of the state and the nation have improved. The state of Massachusetts has aggressively enrolled pregnant mothers and newborns into public health insurance programs. The result is improved prenatal care, lower teen births, and a decrease in the number of pregnant mothers who smoke. But the state also mirrors national increases in the percentage of babies born before thirty-seven weeks, in the rate of low-birth-weight babies, and in the percentage of children born to unmarried women (45%) ("Study Sees Good Start," 2001).

The health and welfare of children correspond closely with the income levels of their families. Twenty percent of our children live in poverty (i.e., in families whose incomes fall below $13,000 for a family of three) (Annie E. Casey Foundation, 2001; Bennett & Lu, 1999), a rate significantly higher than that of child poverty in Sweden, Switzerland, Norway, the former German Federal Republic, Canada, and the United Kingdom (all under 10%). Of 17 developed (industrialized) nations, only Russia has a child poverty rate higher than our own (cited in Annie E. Casey Foundation, 2001). It is worth noting that most of these other countries have some form of nationalized health insurance, government-supported early childhood education, and other family support programs, policies lacking in our own nation. While the number of children living in families totally dependent on welfare is dropping, the number of working poor families has risen, a result of reform in national welfare policies that limits the duration of welfare eligibility and mandates that parents (including single mothers) work. The rates of "near poor" children (with incomes below $26,000 for a family of three) are at an alarming 40%. The problem is especially acute for children under the age of 6. Reflecting the correlation of child poverty with race, poverty rates varied from a low in New Hampshire of 10% to high rates in the District of Columbia and New Mexico of 25% and 28% respectively (Annie E. Casey Foundation, 2001). Differences across cultural groups are clear: approximately 36% of African American children, 34% of Latino children, and 11% of white children are poor. The Census Bureau projects that by the year 2006, 16.4 million children, including 7.6 million black children and 3.4 million Hispanic children, will be living in poverty, a steady increase in real numbers since 1975 (cited in Garcia, 1994, p. 14).

Factors statistically associated with child poverty include single parenthood, parental unemployment, and low levels of parents' education. Twenty-seven percent of our children live in single-parent households, increasing from 5.8 million in 1960 to 19.8 million in 1999 (Annie E. Casey Foundation, 2001). Indications are, however, that the rate of single-parent families will decline due to a decline in rates of divorce and in teenage births. Young children living with single mothers were five times as likely to be poor (56%) as those living with two parents (11%) (Bennett et al., 1999). In 1996, 25.4% of American children lived in father-absent families (Rodriguez, 2001a), a dramatic increase from the 6% who lived in father-absent families in 1950 (Annie Casey Foundation, 1995). The 1996 census figures document substantial differences in the rates of children living with single parents across cultural groups: figures stand at 16% for Asian children, 21% for white children, 32% for Latino children, 38% for American Indian children, and a high of 62% for African American children (Rodriguez, 2001a), where many young males grow up in whole neighborhoods without live-in fathers and where adult males often do not earn enough to support a family.

Children and Violence

Too many of the world's children are innocent victims of war. The *U.N. Chronicle* (in Seufert-Barr, 1995) reports that by the year 2005, wars will have killed about 2 million children and physically disabled another 4 to 5 million. Countless other children in war-torn nations such as Sierra Leone and Sri Lanka have been orphaned and displaced. In Guatemala since the mid-1980s, where 50,000–100,000 Guatemalans have been killed in civil war, another 40,000 have disappeared, and some 400 rural villages have been destroyed, children have suffered the loss of their parents and their homes (Lykes, 1994). Kabul, Afghanistan, is a city full of orphans (Burns, 1995). And in the city of Srebrenica in Bosnia-Herzegovina, 1,000 children died of hunger and disease in 1993. One 10-year-old witness to the violence in Sarajevo kept a record of her experiences, published in book form as a diary of fear and sadness ("Child of War," 1994).

Children are not only forced victims of war but forced perpetrators as well. When families do not have enough food, clothes, or money for schooling, children often quit school to join rebel groups. In Colombia, where UNICEF estimates that about 6 million of the nation's 16 million children live in absolute poverty, as many as 6,000 children under age 18 are fighting in the two main guerrilla factions or in right-wing paramilitary forces (Penhaul, 2001). According to a 1998 government study, in some units nearly a third of the soldiers were minors (under 18). International groups have condemned these groups for "press-ganging children as young as 10 into service." The Colombian Revolutionary Armed Forces has pledged not to sign up any more fighters under 15 and to allow other teenagers to return to their villages to study, but in places where schools have few books and children have no futures, "most students drift back to their family plot to wield a machete, rope cows, and tend maize, yucca or coffee." One 17-year-old says, "I went to the FARC and they gave me boots, clothes, food, and drugs if I got sick" (Penhaul, 2001, p. A11). UNICEF's Colombia director, Carel De Rooy, avers, "If the state does not come up with responses to provide vulnerable children in rural areas with a real alternative, rather than just drug crops and the war, then we're looking at a latent potential force for recruitment of around 2 million" (Penhaul, 2001, p. A11).

Children have been used for direct combat and in other war-related roles in Liberia, Sudan, Mozambique, and other countries in civil war around the world (Minter, 1992; *Index on Censorship*, 2001; Moszynski, 1994). UNICEF estimated that half the soldiers fighting in Liberia's civil war have been children under age 15, forcibly recruited (Whitman & Fleischman, 1994). Captured "soldiers" as young as 9 years old have told stories of atrocities committed both on them and by them, including torture and murder (Shiner, 1992).

Psychological research into the effects of war on children yields sad and frightening pictures of children beset by constant fear, bleak expectations of the future, and little vision for themselves beyond merely surviving (Melville & Lykes, 1992; Zivcic, 1993). In a review of the research on the mental health status of child victims of war, Elbedour, Ten Bensel, and Bastien (1993) report that the degree of psychological suffering depends on several factors: the child's own psychobiological makeup; the disruption of the family unit; the breakdown of community; the intensity, suddenness, and duration of the war; and the culture of the child. For example, children whose culture includes the belief that negative experiences in life are to be expected and accepted may see war and hardship as necessary parts of life, recurring in each generation and, with luck and effort, surmountable. Moreover, the culture may assume that the children's extended family and village share in the responsibility for their welfare and upbringing; therefore, if their parents die as a result of war, the children know that others will care for them.

Young children's cognitive immaturity and innate adaptive capacities may also shield them somewhat against the full implications of their experience of violence and displacement, which adults might understand (Jensen & Shaw, 1993). After all, children's worlds are small, and their understandings immediate. If their basic needs are met, they may have a sense of disruption and certainly will respond to the anxiety of adults around them, but they probably will not understand what is happening far from their view or what might be the future local consequences. Children are also adaptable. To a degree, they are capable of accommodating to new places and faces. However, when they are constantly or abruptly disrupted, when those they depend on are taken away, or when formerly dependable adults become unresponsive or despondent, children will be hurt.

America's children are not exempt from the experience of violence. Many have been directly involved. In 1992, 11,383 teens died violent deaths, the percentage having increased 6% from 1985. Our rate of juvenile arrests for violent crimes increased from 305 per 100,000 in 1985 to 483 per 100,000 in 1992, rising in every state but Vermont (Annie Casey Foundation, 1995). These figures vary with ethnicity and color; in 1990, the Department of Justice reported that 47.4% of national prison inmates were black, while 34.5% were white (cited in Sleeter & Grant, 1995, p. 8).

The increasing violence in this country includes growing numbers of reported cases of child and domestic abuse. More children these days are victims of physical abuse by parents, adults (e.g., their mothers' boyfriends), and older siblings. More of them witness beatings inflicted upon their mothers and siblings. Too many learn by watching their elders that anger and frustration are expressed in immediate violence; too few learn alternative models for expressing these feelings.

The classic research of Albert Bandura (1973; Bandura, Ross, & Ross, 1961) supports the link between children's disposition to violent play and the availability of violent toys and violent images on television and in movies and videos. Bandura studied children playing with inflated "Bobo" dolls. Children who played in the presence of toy guns or who had previously watched live or taped adults exhibiting violent behavior were more likely to play violently with (i.e., strike) the dolls than children whose environments did not contain these stimuli.

More children today watch more television than ever before, especially in inner cities, where outside play is restricted because parents fear for their children's safety. And child-accessible programs on daytime and early evening television are rife with images of violence. Local television news broadcasts compete for sensational reports of outrageous and heinous murders, robberies, and rapes, at times covered "live." Television shows that simulate actual crimes abound; programs such as *America's Most Wanted* blur the line between reality and fantasy, especially for viewers who are young children, cognitively and experientially unsure about what is real and what is not. Furthermore, the once passive act of watching violence-laden cartoons has been enhanced by interactive video and computer games, which involve the players in graphic, though vicarious, violent acts. The toy industry, building on the popularity of violent cartoons, series, and movies, expands the imaginary world of the child with a host of "action figures" and accessories that allow them to play out the violence-ridden story lines they have seen on television. Loath to compromise First Amendment rights to free speech and free press, the media and the government call for parental oversight of children's television and video watching, yet it appears that too many children are left alone with the remote control to decide for themselves what they would like to watch.

As we prepare this second edition of *Educating the Global Village*, the nation is coping with the aftermath of the September 11, 2001, attacks on New York City's World Trade Center and the Pentagon. Some 3,000 people have died as a result of those attacks, some of them children, leaving behind countless sons and daughters, nieces and nephews, and grandchildren of financiers, governmental officials, pilots and flight attendants, firefighters and police officers, and innocent airline passengers. All the children of America have seen televised images and heard radio broadcasts of the news. Parents and teachers, troubled by their own grief and fear, are trying to find ways to speak to children about this unimaginable horror. In some schools and child care centers, staff have met with experts who guide them in their conversations with children. In other sites, psychologists have been available to counsel children and teachers. In our campus preschool, teachers placed toy airplanes among the toys in case children wanted to enact the attack and talk about it. One boy built the World Trade Center using Bristle Blocks and made himself Superman in an attempt to rewrite history. It remains to be seen what will be the long-term effects of this incident and the international conflict that results. One real effect is that American children are no longer physically or psychologically safe from the direct experience of massive destruction that has long been the fate of children in many other nations.

Children and Education

Some 950 million people in the world are totally illiterate, meaning that they cannot read, write, or understand simple facts. If we were to add to that figure the number of "functional illiterates" worldwide, meaning those who can read and write at a simple level but for whom reading and writing are not part of their everyday lives, the number would reach more than 1 billion (United Nations Educational, Scientific, and Cultural Organization, 1994). Great strides in literacy education have been made in the past 50 years by governments of developing nations; however, illiteracy figures are still abysmally high in many countries of Asia, Africa, and South America. Three quarters of the world's illiterates live in the 10 countries of India, China, Pakistan, Bangladesh, Nigeria, Indonesia, Brazil, Egypt, Iran, and Sudan. Some two thirds of India's population is illiterate, while in some areas of Mali, Afghanistan, Benin, Togo, Guinea-Bissau, and Liberia the figure tops 80%. Two thirds of the world's illiterates are women. Even the industrialized nations are part of the statistics; in America, one in eight persons cannot read, a rate similar to that found in Canada, France, and the United Kingdom.

Primary schooling for children in most nations is mandatory, but 20% of the school-age population does not attend school (United Nations Educational, Scientific, and

Cultural Organization, 1994, p. 13). Statistics from the Organization for Economic Co-operation and Development demonstrate that even among wealthier nations, opportunities for four-year-olds to attend preschool are unequal, ranging from universal attendance in France, Belgium, Japan, New Zealand, and the United Kingdom to a 26% attendance rate in Switzerland. Fifty-four percent of American four-year-olds were enrolled in preschool in 1996 (Organization for Economic Cooperation and Development, 1996).

The problem of lack of access to school is not always a matter of government neglect. Schooling is problematical in places where large numbers of refugees flee from place to place within countries or from one country to another. In countries affected by famine, war, or rampant population growth, available government funding understandably is funneled to those crises first. In sub-Saharan Africa, an area of great demographic growth and economic strain, there are not enough seats in schools for the children who need them (United Nations Educational, Scientific, and Cultural Organization, 1994, p. 16). Civil wars in Afghanistan, Somalia, Angola, Lebanon, Mozambique, and Liberia have severely compromised primary education (United Nations Educational, Scientific, and Cultural Organization, 1994, p. 19).

Who are the "missing children"? According to the United Nations Educational, Scientific, and Cultural Organization (UNESCO), most live in remote rural areas or in

Chinese students show playful side of the preschool day.

urban slums. Most are girls. Most belong to population groups outside the mainstream of society; they pass their days in overcrowded refugee camps, displaced by manmade or natural disasters, or wander with their herds. Often marginalized by language, lifestyle and culture, they do not enjoy a basic human right: the right to education (1994, p. 13).

Access to schooling often depends on whether one lives in an urban or a rural area, whether one is male or female, and whether one has the money necessary for tuition and books or, in many cases, the bribes that it takes to buy one's place in overcrowded schools. Illiteracy is demonstrably associated with conditions of poverty. For example, in South America, great disparity exists between those who acquire college-level educations and those who are totally excluded from school at all levels. Rural poverty may create conditions where young children are forced to work to supplement their families' incomes. The agrarian Somalian economy demands that children help with farming. Families are large, with five, six, or seven children, and women, especially, are discouraged from schooling. Civil war in Somalia has caused the death of many fathers, leaving uneducated women and children refugees without skills or schooling. The executive director of Somali Development Center in Boston estimates there are at least 15 homeless Somali families in Boston, most headed by uneducated women with children who have spent most of their lives in refugee camps in Kenya (Rodriguez, 2001b).

In many nations of Africa and South Asia, a young girl's basic right to education is limited by the idea that she is an economic liability and fit for little more than an early marriage. Sometimes girls are married off for their families' economic gain, sometimes in the belief that an early marriage will protect them from unwanted sexual advances. Besides being denied schooling, child brides are at risk for sexual oppression, premature pregnancies (a leading cause of death in girls under age 19), and a life as a domestic servant. They are also more susceptible to AIDS, as in some countries there is a false notion that a man who sleeps with a virgin will be cured of the disease (Leopold, 2001). Researchers in India, for example, report that "the fate of the female infant. . . has been getting progressively worse, despite state efforts to combat sex stereotyping" (Lakshmi, 2001, p.12). The government has been giving small stipends to every girl born in poverty for her education and marriage dowry. To reduce the possibility of female infanticide, it also has banned prenatal gender testing; however, this rule is often violated by clinics. Half the young girls in India drop out of school by age 12, half marry under the legal age of 18, and 130,000 die each year in pregnancy or childbirth. It is possible, in fact, that the national goal of two children per family in this heavily overpopulated nation has worked against girls and contributed to the illegal abortion of female fetuses (Lakshmi, 2001).

There is some evidence to suggest that the education of girls in developing countries may be more limited by family income levels than by cultural practices restricting women. For example, "in Kuwait, where 1990 GNP per capita was $16,150, a female has a better chance of being educated than a Moroccan male where GNP per capita equals $950" (Heyneman & Esim, 1994, p.168). Children's schooling may be compromised by their having to work to help support their families. In a rural province of

China, for example, primary school students have been forced to make firecrackers. They attend school in the morning and make firecrackers in the afternoon. The Official New China News Agency proudly reported in 1996 that "campus businesses," enterprises run by primary and high schools, generated $37 billion from 1991 to 1995. Ninety-three percent of China's schools had launched such businesses, encouraged by the central government to supplement available financial resources. Because the percentage of China's gross domestic product earmarked for education has fallen below 2.4, among the lowest in Asia, there is pressure on teachers to boost their pay with financial schemes. Tragically, in Wanzhai county, where as much as one fifth of the population is employed in fireworks factories, 40 children were killed in 2001 when the firecrackers they were making during their lunch break exploded (Pomfret & Pan, 2001).

Many studies cited in this chapter indicate that significant correlations exist among women's educational levels, fertility rates, poverty, and their children's health. Illiterate mothers may not have access to the knowledge necessary to make informed, healthful decisions for their children, including decisions regarding the provision of clean water and balanced nutrition, the availability of training programs, and the long-term economic importance of schooling. Educated women have fewer babies, keep them healthier, and have more resources to provide for them.

Yet one out of three of the world's women is illiterate, with figures as high as two thirds in sub-Saharan Africa, the Arab states, and South Asia. While the percentage of girls in primary schools worldwide grew 3% from 1980 to 1990, in the Arab states the percentage dropped, and in South Asia the percentage stayed the same.

Domestic violence, a worldwide problem, compromises the education of women and children. In an "unheard-of" act of protest, 1,000 Ethiopian women marched on the capital in Addis Ababa Square in February 2001 to demand greater police protection and harsher sentences for offenders. Most abuse is unreported, yet "the conspiracy of silence is frightening when the violence is against toddlers, and it is time that we spoke out," said Konjit Fekade, chairwoman of the protest committee (Andualem, 2001, p. 8). With increased poverty, the dearth of jobs for young men, and frustrations fueled by alcohol and drug abuse, violence against women and girls, as well as the incidence of rape of very young girls and teenagers, is on the rise in Africa. Most vulnerable are street children, domestic workers, and the handicapped (Andualem, 2001).

Complicating the gender differences are cultural factors, including lesser status accorded to girls and women and inordinately more household responsibilities for them, which limit the time they have available to attend school. Following their religious beliefs, the fundamentalist Taliban government in Afghanistan has outlawed schooling for girls. According to UNESCO, "The illiteracy disadvantage [of girls] will not just 'go away' in the course of general educational development" (1994, p. 12).

Schooling may be available but may be inappropriate, providing children with experiences of failure rather than learning success. In schools in many developing countries, children enter school overage. This poses a problem for teachers, who are confronted with large numbers of children of various ages and developmental levels and who are usually without the training or the materials to address the students' disparate needs. The World Bank reported that in Nigeria it is not unusual for 50 children to share one book, and in Peru and Paraguay two thirds of the school-children have no books at all (cited in United Nations Educational, Scientific, and Cultural Organization, 1994, p. 34). Too many teachers are neither knowledgeable nor trained to teach, especially where they have been recruited to staff schools in areas with rapidly growing populations. In Uganda, Zimbabwe, and Nicaragua, for example, little more than half the teaching force is trained. In Haiti, the figure is 10%.

In many nations, schools are conducted in the official state language, while people within the country speak a variety of native tongues. Most developing nations are multicultural and multilingual, with indigenous populations living in rural areas in ethnically isolated communities and sometimes in a geographic terrain whose physical barriers create linguistic and dialectical differences, making it impossible for one group to understand another. National governments committed to common schooling and official languages do not provide instruction that is understandable and meaningful to their diverse peoples.

Finally, children around the world may have special learning needs not addressed by their nation's schools. Victims of prenatal, perinatal, and postnatal events, often brought about by conditions of poverty, malnutrition, lack of education, lack of health care, and/or substance abuse, may have physical, cognitive, perceptual, and neurological disorders that compromise their learning or school attendance. Some learning exceptionalities are the result of childhood traumas—accidents, head injuries, poisoning (for example, by lead paint exposure), and domestic violence. Inadequate medical help with perinatal conditions such as anoxia, caused perhaps by breech birth or an umbilical cord wrapped around a fetus's neck, and inadequate facilities for the neonatal care of premature infants compromise normal cognitive and physical development. Unsanitary conditions, including water contamination and lack of immunization, are prevalent in developing countries with undereducated populations and without the funding and personnel necessary to implement adequate health care programs. Children in unhealthy environments are, then, subject to infections and diseases that can seriously damage their cognitive and physical functioning.

Nations vary greatly in their willingness to meet the needs of children with exceptionalities. In many cultures, exceptionalities are unrecognized, ill-defined, or hidden behind cultural preconceptions. In Japan, a child with serious special learning needs may bring shame upon the family (Fulton & Dixon, 1993). In China, where extended families take responsibility for the care of children, parents or grandparents without an understanding of the nature, needs, or potential of children with special needs may in fact limit their access to effective interventions (Piao, 1994). In Latino cultures, as well, the family takes care of its own and may not accept outside help. It does not help that in some Latino families, the fact that a school or agency identifies a child as having a special learning difference may be a sign that the agency considers that child "loco" (Harry, 1992).

Even where learning exceptionalities are recognized, nations may vary in their ability to respond with effective programming. Political philosophies, social welfare policies, and economic priorities impact the education of children with disabilities. The Nordic countries of Sweden, Finland, Norway, and Denmark, along with the United Kingdom and New Zealand, have strong social welfare programs and/or socialized medicine and can offer equal education opportunities to all children regardless of disability, with support from several sectors of the government. On the other hand, countries with unstable economies are focused on the basic feeding of their people and working toward universal primary schooling for as many children as possible. In agrarian, rural nations in which people live on subsistence farms isolated from one another by rough terrain or lack of transportation, the government may not see special education for some (indeed, even any education for all) as a major priority. In areas of the world experiencing war or civil strife, the number of children with disabling conditions increases with war-related injuries such as loss of limbs, blindness, and emotional trauma. Understandably, despite this increase, such nations are more concerned with returning to normalcy and maintaining regular schooling than they are with the specific concerns of the exceptional learner.

Under the conditions described above, many children fail. Grade-retention data for Latin America and Africa range from 15% to 20% (United Nations Educational, Scientific, and Cultural Organization, 1994, p. 33). Many children leave school before they are fully literate. In sub-Saharan Africa, Latin America, and South Asia, fewer than two thirds of children finish fourth grade. In industrialized nations, social expenditures, including money for schools, have diminished. At the same time, the educational needs of children in these countries may have become more complex because of increased numbers of immigrants and refugees, linguistic-minority students, and children with special needs brought on by physical problems or problems associated with the traumas of escaping war, poverty, family breakdowns, or neighborhood violence. With reductions in remedial programs and programs that address the needs of minority students, and with larger classes, fewer materials, and more burdens on teachers, reduced commitments to public schooling often result in greater school failure and higher dropout rates.

The 1990 World Conference on Education for All was held in Jomtien, Thailand, to survey the status of worldwide primary education and to formulate plans to ensure for all children the right to an education. As a result of the conference, 121 countries have begun to implement the Education for All (EFA) initiative. The 1994 UNESCO report describes efforts in Costa Rica, Mexico, the Dominican Republic, Mauritius, India, Nepal, Pakistan, and Ireland, among other nations, to secure additional funding for schools, plan effectively and collaboratively, train teachers, and reach more women and young children in both formal and nonformal educational settings. These laudable efforts are being waged in the face of great odds. In Malawi, for example, the initiative to expand primary education has led the government to hire thousands of young people who will undergo a six-week "crash program" of teacher training. Textbook shortages mean that six students might have to share one book. Insufficient and inadequate school buildings mean that children may be schooled outdoors, under the trees (Chombo, 1997). With increasing attention and support from the United Nations and other international agencies, however, both developing and developed nations are

A British mother reads to her children.

waking up to the fact that national welfare depends on an educated populace and that the effort must begin with young children.

Education in America

In a nation of universal free public schooling, and despite laws mandating education for all, there are still children in the United States who do not attend school, including those whose access to schooling is limited by the migratory patterns of their families or their lack of a permanent residence. Children who are homeless or whose families move frequently in search of temporary work (e.g., as farm laborers) do not have consistent, stable schooling. Too many adolescents leave school before graduation, and they do not necessarily go to work. Dropping out is likely to lead a teen into poverty; statistically, high school dropouts are three times as likely to be poor as those who have finished school (Annie Casey Foundation, 1995, p. 13).

School attendance and success are particular problems for the numbers of children without homes in the United States, most of whom live without fathers. Female-headed single-parent families with children account for a large percentage of the nation's homeless, seriously impairing children's access to schools. The National Center for Children in Poverty concluded the following in 1990:

> The escalating visibility of single mothers with preschool and school-age children living on
> the streets, in welfare hotels, and in emergency shelters is perhaps the most distinguishing

attribute of contemporary homelessness. The National Coalition for the Homeless estimates that between 500,000 and 750,000 children in America were homeless in 1990 and that fewer than half of those attended school regularly. (cited in Quint, 1994, pp. 11–12)

Among all U.S. teenagers, 10% leave high school before graduation, which is certainly a low rate compared with that of other nations of the world. But dropout rates are not standard among various socioeconomic and cultural groups. The figures are much worse, for example, for many minority adolescents. American Indian youth have the highest national dropout rate, followed by Hispanics and African Americans. The 1990 national census revealed that, while the dropout rate for whites was 8.9%, the rate for Asian/Pacific Islanders was 9.6%, for African Americans, 13.6%, for Hispanics, 35.3%, and for American Indians/Alaska natives, 44.5% (cited in Bennett, 1995, p. 16). The general categorical labels mask great differences within these designated groups (e.g., between the high educational attainment of Japanese and Korean Americans and the low educational attainment of native Hawaiians, "second wave" Vietnamese, and Samoans, and between the relatively high educational attainment of Cuban Americans and the low educational attainment of Puerto Ricans).

A new concern is the impact of high-stakes testing on the dropout rates of students who do not pass the test by tenth-grade benchmark points. In states such as Texas and Massachusetts, which have tied passing scores to graduation effective in the year 2001, educators and parents are anticipating a surge in the number of students who fail the test leaving school early, assuming they will never be able to pass and obtain their diplomas. Passing rates on these tests are disproportionately low for Latinos whose English is substandard and for students with special needs.

A comparison of aspirations and educational achievement of black and white children in America yields sad results. It seems that black children at high school graduation have the same occupational aspirations as do other American children: similar percentages look forward to professional, managerial, service, and other careers. Actual school experiences differ markedly, however, with black children having attended and graduated in significantly lower numbers. Their achievement levels as measured by standardized tests and Scholastic Aptitude Tests have been significantly lower. The reading gap between white children and children of color in the United States persists. The National Assessment of Educational Progress (Belkin, 2001) found that while average reading scores for white students from 1990 to 2000 increased one point, scores for black students remained low and scores for Latino and Native American students dropped. Sixty-three percent of black students and 58% of Hispanic students have less than basic reading skills. They will enroll in colleges and graduate schools in significantly lower proportions than will whites. And when it comes time to train for the professions (e.g., medicine, dentistry, pharmacy, and nursing), their numbers will be tiny as compared with those of whites (U.S. Bureau of the Census, 1994). While black students' visions for their academic and professional futures are governed by the same ideals as those of white children, American schools, for a variety of reasons, have failed them.

Eight Cousins

Summary

The troublesome picture of the facts and figures presented in this chapter demonstrates that we are a long way from helping children to achieve their rights as described by the United Nations declaration. Physically, economically, and educationally the children of our nation and the world still do not receive care adequate to their needs. Those battling on their behalf in world organizations such as UNICEF and UNESCO are working against powerful deterrents in the form of unavoidable natural environmental conditions and avoidable political and social conditions. While as adult world citizens we must expect and accept the havoc created by drought-induced famine and natural disasters such as earthquakes and hurricanes, the disabling effects of "people-caused" problems such as international and civil wars and disrespect for minority cultures, problems that bar children from family support, income guarantees, universal health services, and free appropriate schooling, are quite surmountable given the financial and intellectual resources of the world. The authors of this book agree with child welfare organizations that there is no fundamental reason not to safeguard the world's children against the debilitating effects of poor health, inadequate shelter, the absence of a stable family and community, and lack of a basic education. Our global commitment is weak and inconsistent, and too many children are needlessly hurt. Advances in areas such as immunization demonstrate the immediate effects of positive intervention. We hope that such trends continue. We hope also that educators who understand, as Maslow did, that learning and psychosocial development rest firmly on a foundation of adequate health, wealth, and physical safety will lobby beyond individual schools, classrooms, and local communities to achieve the basic levels of need. The time is past when we need take care of only the children in our own families, our own schools, and our own communities. The health, welfare, and education of our children are inextricably linked to events and conditions elsewhere in the world. In this chapter, the authors have attempted to lay bare these events and conditions, including the "darker side" of the condition of America's own kids.

Reflection Questions

1. From your reading of national newspapers and magazines, what themes do you see related to the condition of the world's children currently addressed? Are there both positive and negative trends? Is there evidence of effective interventions and responses to these problems? (It might be interesting to share these findings with classmates or colleagues in the form of "poster sessions" and to brainstorm with them possible solutions.)

2. How do the sources of the problem of inadequate schooling in the United States differ from those in developing nations?

3. How do children's health, wealth, and education interact in causing some of the problems mentioned in this chapter?

References

Andualem, A. (2001, February 11). Ethiopian women, in unheard-of march, demand rights. *The Boston Sunday Globe*, p. A8.

Annie E. Casey Foundation. (1998). *Kids count data book 1998: State profiles of child well-being*. Baltimore, MD: Author.

Annie E. Casey Foundation. (2001). *Kids count data book 2001: State profiles of child well-being*. Baltimore, MD: Author.

Bandura, A. (1973). *Aggression: A social learning analysis*. Upper Saddle River, NJ: Prentice Hall.

Bandura, A., Ross, O., & Ross, S. A. (1961). The transmission of patterns of self-reinforcement through modeling. *Journal of Abnormal and Social Psychology, 63*, 575–582.

Belkin, D. (2001, April 7). Growing divide noted on best, worst readers. *The Boston Globe*, p. A3.

Bennett, C. I. (1995). *Comprehensive multicultural education: Theory and practice*. Boston: Allyn & Bacon.

Bennett, N.G., & Lu, H. (1999). *Child poverty in the states: Levels and trends from 1979 to 1998*. New York: Columbia University Mailman School of Public Health, National Center for Children in Poverty.

Bennett, N.G., Jaili, L., Younghwan, S., & Yang, K. (1999). *Young children in poverty: A statistical update*. New York: Columbia University Mailman School of Public Health, National Center for Children in Poverty.

Boston Department of Health & Hospitals. (1994). *Natality and infant mortality data for Boston residents*. Boston: Author.

Brameld, T. (1956). *Toward a reconstructed philosophy of education*. New York: Dryden Press.

Burns, J. F. (1995, April 2). City of orphans. *The New York Times Magazine*, p. 58.

Child of war: The diary of Zlata Filipovic. (1994, February 28). *Newsweek*, pp. 24–28.

Chombo, G. M. (1997, February). Conversation with author. Annual meeting of the Eastern Educational Research Assocation, Hilton Head, SC.

Dewey, J. (1979). *Experience and education*. New York: Collier-Macmillan.

Elbedour, S., Ten Bensel, S., & Bastien, D. T. (1993). Ecological integrated model of children of war: Individual and social psychology. *Child Abuse and Neglect, 17*(6), 805–820.

Fulton, L., & Dixon, V. (1993). Interviews with mothers of severely handicapped children: School leavers in Japan. *The Viewfinder: Expanding Boundaries and Perspectives in Special Education, 2*, 3–6.

Garcia, E. (1994). *Understanding and meeting the challenge of student cultural diversity*. Boston: Houghton Mifflin.

Harry, B. (1992). Making sense of disability: Low-income, Puerto Rican parents' theories of the problem. *Exceptional Children, 59*(1), 27–40.

Hellinger, D., & Hammond, R. (1994, November–December). Structural adjustment: Debunking the myth. *Africa Report, 39*(6), 52–55.

Heyneman, S., & Esim, S. (1994). Female educational enrollment in the Middle East and North Africa: A question of poverty or culture. *Educational Horizons, 72*(4), 166–169.

Index on Censorship (2001, October). State critics "Threaten place." www.indexonline.org/news/2001/1015_sudan.shtml, accessed 1/2/02.

Jensen, P. S., & Shaw, J. (1993, July). Children as victims of war: Current knowledge and future research needs. *Journal of the American Academy of Child and Adolescent Psychiatry, 32*(4), 697–709.

Report on the Global HIV/AIDS epidemic. (2000). Joint United Nations Program on HIV/AIDS (United Nations and World Health Organization). www.unaids.org/epidemic_update/report_dec01/index.html, accessed 9/10/01.

Lakshmi, R. (2001, April 4). Gender prejudice in India still against daughters. *The Globe and Mail*, p. 12.

Leopold, E. (2001, March 8). Child marriage is widespread, harmful, UN report says. *The Boston Globe*, p. A10.

Lykes, M. B. (1994, February 15). Terror, silencing and children: International, multidisciplinary collaboration with Guatemalan Maya communities. *Social Science and Medicine, 38*(4), 543–553.

Maslow, A. (1968). *Toward a psychology of being.* New York: Van Nostrand.

Melville, M. B., & Lykes, M. B. (1992, March). Guatemalan Indian children and the sociocultural effects of government-sponsored terrorism. *Social Science and Medicine, 34*(5), 533–549.

Minter, R. (1992, September 28). Children at war and play. *Africa News, 37*(1), 5–6.

Moszynski, P. (1994, September 2). Letter from Nairobi. *New Statesman and Society, 7*(318), 11.

Murkowski, F. L. (1994, July 19). UNICEF progress of nations report: Child nutrition needed as part of foreign aid. *Congressional Record*, S. 9187.

Noddings, N. (1992). *The challenge to care in schools.* New York: Teachers College Press.

Organization for Economic Cooperation and Development. (1996). *Lifelong learning for all.* Paris: OECD Publication Services.

Penhaul, K. (2001, March 4). Colombia's force of child warriors. *The Boston Sunday Globe*, p. A11.

Piao, Y. (1994, April). *Special education and family in China.* Paper presented at the national conference of the Council for Exceptional Children, Denver, Colorado.

Pomfret, J., & Pan, P. P. (2001, March 8). Fatal blast tied to child labor. *The Boston Globe*, p. A11.

Quint, S. (1994). *Schooling homeless children: A working model for America's public schools.* New York: Teachers College Press.

Rodriguez, C. (2001a, April 13). Lineup shifts in US family portrait. *The Boston Globe*, p. A16.

Rodriguez, C. (2001b, February 10). Somali refugees fall victim to housing squeeze in Mass. *The Boston Globe*, pp. B1, B5.

Seufert-Barr, N. (1995, March). Children often bear high cost of armed conflicts, poverty. *UN Chronicle, 32*(1), 85.

Shiner, C. (1992, December 7). Liberia's children coming back from war. *Africa News, 37*(6), 1–3.

Sleeter, C. E., & Grant, C. A. (1995). *Making choices for multicultural education.* New York: Macmillan Publishing.

Study sees good start for Mass. children. (2001, February 20). *The Boston Globe,* p. B2.

UN Chronicle. (1994, June). *31*(2), 40–53.

United Nations Educational, Scientific, and Cultural Organization. (1994). *Education for all: Status and trends.* Paris: EPA Forum Secretariat, UNESCO.

U.S. Bureau of the Census. (1994). *Statistical abstract of the United States* (114th ed.). Washington, DC: U.S. Government Printing Office.

Whitman, L., & Fleischman, J. (1994, July–August). The child soldiers. *Africa Report, 39*(4), 65–67.

Zivcic, I. (1993, July). Emotional reactions of children to war stress in Croatia. *Journal of the American Academy of Child and Adolescent Psychiatry, 32*(4), 709–714.

Websites:

Kids Count Data Book 2001, Annie E. Casey Foundation: *www.aecf.org*

Oxfam: *www.oxfam.org*

World Health Organization: *www.who.org*

United Nations Program on HIV/AIDS: *www.unaids.org*

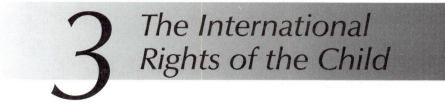

3 The International Rights of the Child

Introduction

Many nongovernmental organizations (NGOs) serve children around the globe. Each has a special focus and philosophy; many have nonprofit charters, some have religious foundations, and others are nondenominational philanthropies. All agencies that serve children and families worldwide need to work in concert with educators. Likewise, teachers need to be aware of these agencies and their specific goals and agendas. Such organizations include Save the Children, Care, Oxfam, National Council of Churches, International Red Cross, and Inter-Faith Hunger Appeal, to name a few. Each organization provides direct services to children and families; many produce and/or disseminate instructional materials on their particular causes and concerns.

The United Nations (UN) is a worldwide organization representing 184 independent countries that services children and their families. The UN charter gives the people of the world a voice through the UN system, which establishes and enables NGOs to address the needs of its members. The United Nations Children's Fund (UNICEF) is a UN agency that supports children's causes and rights. Indeed, UNICEF has sponsored the Convention on the Rights of the Child in the United Nations at large.

The Convention on the Rights of the Child

To appreciate the Convention on the Rights of the Child (CRC), it is important to understand the meaning of the word *convention*. Simply put, a convention is a binding agreement, a "covenant" (Castelle, 1990, p. 3). Regarding the United Nations, a convention is "a legal document setting out universally acceptable standards, agreed among nations by consensus" (Castelle, p. 3). Nations must note their compliance with the convention by ratifying it and making it a binding law, which they agree to enforce and comply with (Castelle, p. 3). Likewise, the UN has recognized human rights as "the rights we are all born with" and promulgated in the UN Declaration of Human Rights and two covenants, namely, the International Covenant on Economic, Social and Cultural Rights and the International Covenant on Civil and Political Rights (Edmonds, 1992, p. 205). The CRC is a further extension of the human rights documentation.

Human rights are generally organized into three types: the rights of protection, provision, and participation, commonly called the "three p's" (Edmonds, 1990; LeBlanc, 1995). Plan International, a private foundation with consultative status with UNICEF, categorizes the rights into three groups as well, namely, the rights of survival, protection, and development (Castelle, 1990, p. 5). In particular, Plan International categorizes the rights of the child as follows:

1. The Right to Survival through provision of adequate food, shelter, clean water and primary health care.

2. The Right to Protection from abuse, neglect and exploitation ... [and] special protection in times of war.

3. The Right to Develop in a safe environment, through the provision of formal education, constructive play, advanced health care and the opportunity to participate in the social, economic, religious and political life of the culture free from discrimination. (Castelle, 1990, p. 5)

Historical Antecedents

In 1959, the UN set forth its Declaration of the Rights of the Child, which emerged from the 1948 Declaration of Human Rights and its two subsequent covenants. Nearly 20 years later, in preparation for the 1979 UN Year of the Child, Poland proposed a convention of the rights of the child. This initiative prompted the Commission on Human Rights to draft a working convention. The convention proposal underwent many changes and revisions. In 1989, it was put forth for ratification and further debated and refined at the 1990 World Summit for Children and again at the 1993 World Conference on Human Rights. By September 1995, 179 countries had ratified it (United Nations Children's Fund, 1996). Debate still ensues as the Commission on Human Rights seeks full ratification. To date, the United States is one of the countries whose ambassador to the UN has signed the CRC but whose government has yet to ratify it.

All children have a right to an education.

Future Directions

Following up on the 1990 World Summit for Children are mid-decade and end-decade reviews of the outcomes of the 1989 Convention on the Rights of the Child and the Summit. These reviews resulted in the call for UNICEF's Special Session on Children for 2001 and the outcome document, *A World Fit for Children*. The 2001 Special Session on Children was slated by the UN General Assembly to meet at the United Nations in New York with the following goals:

to reaffirm commitments to the Convention of the Rights of the Child,

to expand on movements of support for the rights of children

to examine better means for attaining goals and meeting challenges,

to encourage governmental adoptions of the document, *A World Fit for Children*. (UNICEF, 2001, *A Briefing to Educators*)

While *A World Fit for Children* documents strides made since the 1990 World Summit, it admits that many aspirations have not been attained. The conditions and effects of poverty, disease, violence, war, hunger and gender inequalities on children still need attention and action. The document addresses challenges still facing the world and outlines its solutions in "Ten Principles," namely:

1. Put children first
2. Leave no child behind
3. Care for every child
4. Educate every child
5. Stop harming and exploiting children
6. Protect children from war
7. Combat HIV/AIDS
8. Fight poverty: Invest in children
9. Listen to Children
10. Protect the earth for children. (UNICEF, 2001, *A Briefing to Educators*)

The document also proposes an action plan that endorses resources and support for monitoring progress to bolster the goals for "creating a child-friendly world" (Preparatory Committee for the Special Session of the General Assembly on Children, March, 2001). Taking the goals and opportunities of the Special Session to the next level is the Global Movement for Children with its "Say Yes" to Children campaign, spearheaded by world leaders such as Nelson Mandela (UNICEF, 2001, *A Briefing to Educators*). Detailed information about these movements and updating of current accomplishments can be found on the Internet and in UNICEF publications.

While the UN convention is not the only declaration for children's rights, the CRC has received worldwide support and deserves study and recognition by all countries and their children. Teachers need to be cognizant of the CRC's implications for the children they teach and need to explore strategies for informing their children of their rights.

In 2001, UN Secretary General Kofi Annan and the United Nations were the recipients of the Nobel Peace Prize. *The Boston Globe* reported that the "Oslo-based panel hailed Annan for 'bringing new life to the organization'. It was the first time the entire 189-member United Nations, and not one of its affiliated agencies, had won the peace prize" (Neuffer, 2001). Such an honor affirms the important mission of the United Nations, and surely the cause to better the lives of children as a part of that mission is worthy of study in school, support from professionals in the field of education, and endorsement from families of young children. While so many children suffer from poverty, hunger, abuse and exploitation, inequity due to race, gender, ethnicity, or social class, and health issues such as AIDS, the school can no longer afford to ignore their plight. The 21st century school must put children first in support for implementation of all social policy, educational endeavors, and political decisions. The schools and child care centers of the world need to keep the cause of children's rights in the limelight to protect the future of their constituents, the children.

Teaching the Rights of the Child

Can Children Learn About Their Rights?

Why teach the rights of the child to young children? Considered from the perspective of the child, the question becomes relatively rhetorical: "Should I, the child, know about my rights? When am I too young to know?" The level of knowing and understanding, of course, will vary with each child. Just as the ability to make moral decisions is developmental, influenced by gender, culture, learning style, and personal experience, the quantity and quality of knowledge of one's own rights is influenced also by these factors. Furthermore, children can be empowered by knowing about themselves as world citizens with defined rights. Howard Gardner's (1983) research on multiple intelligences and Carol Gilligan's (1996) work on the "inner voice" both point to the early emergence of intrapersonal skills as well as the interpersonal development of the child. Through experiences appropriate for the child, insights and understandings about one's rights become evident. It is incumbent upon teachers, parents, and child care providers to create situations, implement activities, and encourage autonomy in children.

There is debate about the optimal age to begin teaching children about their rights. In Canada, Katherine Covell and R. Brian Howe, founders of the Children's Rights Center at the University College of Cape Breton in Sydney, Nova Scotia, recommend beginning with children in sixth grade (Smith, 2000, p. 44). Their programs are designed for children in Canadian schools beginning in grade 6 (Smith, p. 44). Arguing for teaching the rights at an earlier age is Anne Smith, who convened the 1999 Children's Rights Conference in New Zealand. She contends that since the rights of participation by children are often overlooked and that young children's insights and understandings are underrated, early childhood education is the time to begin (Smith, p. 201).

Preschool as well as primary school can offer opportunities for children to learn and decide about their rights. Working with young children from prekindergarten to grade 5 in the United States, this author supports Smith's position. I have found that children can appreciate the notion of rights and responsibilities. They use the concepts of rights and responsibilities as bonds they share with a diverse population of peers. Yet it is fair to note that not all educators are in agreement as to the best age for teaching such complicated concepts as the meanings of rights.

Implications for Teaching the CRC

First, you as an informed educator might want to know about the CRC and the impact it has on the child, the family, and the community. Cultural values, family attitudes, and social manners and mores influence one's perception of the CRC. At all times, the rights must be considered in these contexts. Start with a simple summary of the rights. Glean from your parents and children their understanding of children's rights and their comfort levels of acceptance. Then, proceed to a more in-depth study and interpretation as proposed by the UN. Invite families and children to interpret for themselves the meanings of the rights. Allow them to have an open discourse and critique of the implications these rights have on their lives.

Not all people agree about the interpretation and implications of the convention. There are voices of disagreement on the rights of "participation." Some feel "participation" implies children are given a "control" and an "autonomy" that diminish parents' rights. Others counter that position by defining "participation" as an opportunity for children to "make a contribution to the decision making process" (Marshall, 1997, p. 2), not a challenge to parents. Such different interpretations cause concerns over the implementation of the CRC. Care needs to be taken in the explanation of the CRC principles to effect an equilibrium in the "tension between respect for children's rights to participate, and their right to have their interest protected" by adults and family (Marshall, p. 2).

Respectful balancing of parents' rights with children's rights and the family's role with respect to governmental agencies should be made. The sovereignty issues between nation-states and a worldwide agency such as the United Nations pose challenges to the United States' ratification of the rights in Congress. Likewise, sensitivity to religious concerns, family values and sense of control, and social and cultural factors of a nation's citizenry need to be recognized and factored into any dialogue concerning the convention.

All rights imply responsibility. Often, the issue of responsibility is missing from the discourse on rights. To internalize rights, people need to act accordingly in responsible, prosocial behaviors. They need to understand the consequence of their behaviors, accept responsibility for their actions, and seek outcomes that are respectful of themselves and others.

Teaching about rights and responsibilities has to be implicit in all behaviors throughout the child's day. For example, as children learn about the right to an education, they must recognize that they have a concomitant responsibility to take advantage of the opportunities an education offers. Likewise, the right to play is a simple right to implement in an early childhood program. Children can learn that the right to play means that they must engage in play activities with a sense of fairness. For older children, fairness might mean playing according to the rules; for younger children, it might mean sharing equipment. Fairness in play requires participation of special needs children, the physically and mentally challenged, both boys and girls, and children of all ethnic/racial backgrounds. While children are empowered to make choices, arrive at resolutions, and put ideas into practice, they need to do so in a way that ensures the integrity of everyone involved.

The School's Role

To teach the rights of the child, the terms for framing and defining the rights have to be meaningful to the children and their families. You might start with your children's personal declaration of rights, which you can compare with the UN document to determine any universal characteristics in both. In one child care center, the youngsters set forth their own "Bill of Rights" and posted it proudly at the entrance to their room for all to see. In one school of education, early childhood education majors held a Celebration for the Rights of the Child, at which UNICEF speakers were invited to present the CRC to the college and local area residents. Then the students designed lessons around a variety of themes, which they showcased in a day-long Lesson Plan Jamboree. Subsequently, these lessons were published in a series of guides for teaching the rights. One edition's interpretive summary was based on the Declaration of the Rights of the Child. Accordingly, it proclaimed that every child has the following rights:

the right to affection, love, and understanding

the right to adequate housing, nutrition, and health and medical care

the right to a free education, reflective of his or her own culture

the right to play

the right to a name and nationality

the right to provision for special needs when appropriate

the right to be among the first to receive relief in times of war and disaster

the right to be a useful member of society and to be able to develop individual abilities

the right to be brought up with tolerance and protected against all forms of neglect, cruelty, and exploitation

the right to be protected from practices that may foster any form of discrimination. (Swiniarski et al., 1996)

The wording might differ from the formal document, but the major message of the CRC is contained in the interpretation. Understanding personal ownership of rights is

The right to affection, love, and understanding. . .

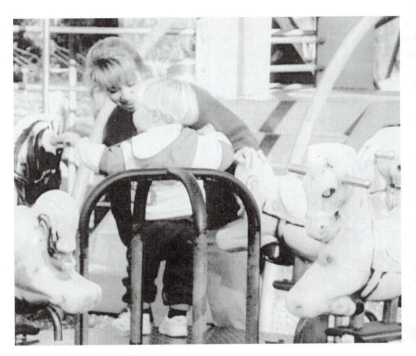

an essential first step for ensuring the rights. In creating this list, critical thinking skills are applied to a relevant, authentic learning situation.

Activities are limitless. UNICEF offers a host of resources for ideas, materials to use, and background information for in-depth content. Its publication *Reaching the Children* is an activity-centered unit on the rights of the child, written and classroom tested by a teacher, Marilyn Stroud. As part of the UN campaign for human rights, a helpful booklet entitled *ABC Teaching Human Rights* provides valuable content material and specific instructional strategies for teaching human rights, starting with the preschool level and continuing through secondary school. One of its recommendations is teaching human rights through the use of picture books (Centre for Human Rights Geneva, 1989, p. 12). So it is no coincidence that there is no better picture book for teaching the rights of the child than another UN-endorsed publication, *For Every Child*. This edition presents fifteen illustrators' artistic interpretations of CRC principles. The text adapts and defines these principles in language that children can understand. Archbishop Desmond M. Tutu, a staunch supporter of human and children's rights during his struggle against apartheid in South Africa, restates his commitment to children's rights in the preface of the book. This edition is published in association with UNICEF as an update of an earlier work, *A Chorus of Children*.

Just as the authors and illustrators of these editions adapted the text and communicated in illustration the meaning of the convention, young children can render their own interpretations of the rights in words and illustrations. They can design posters and bulletin boards based upon their readings to advocate and promote the convention. Librarians can use picture books and materials from UNICEF to support the theme of children's rights in story-time programs. Teachers can share information on the rights in newsletters, email, or webpages for parents, at community assemblies, in staff-development presentations, at professional conferences, and in journal publications.

Technology offers an array of options for dissemination. Children, along with their teachers, can use the Internet for advocacy and outcomes of research on their study of the rights. Classrooms can produce and exchange slide tape and/or video programs that can be accommodated for viewing not only in schools and centers nearby but across national boundaries as well.

Children across America use Halloween as a time to collect contributions to UNICEF. They could also include in their solicitation information on the CRC. Local area cable TV can cover the children's cause. Additionally, with the help of teachers, children could disseminate information by developing a webpage on CRC as an international movement or an issue for voters to consider in upcoming elections.

Using published materials from UNICEF, the kindergarten supervisors of the Horace Mann Laboratory School at Salem State College infused the teaching of the rights of the child in a thematic unit. They reinforced the teaching of the rights in all areas of the curriculum. For a math activity, they had the children design and make a peace quilt. The children used UNICEF symbols for peace and then geometrically designed their quilt. For language arts, a "big book" in the shape of the globe was authored by 10 children, each child selecting one of the rights and illustrating an interpretation of the right. Another group of 10 children performed a readers' theater enactment of the rights. Again, borrowing UNICEF's universal pictorial symbols for each right, the children gave a "reading" of the rights. The rights were put to song and chants, linked to the study of the alphabet, and depicted in posters and class murals. As a culmination to the unit, each child illustrated a personal book on the rights to bring home to share with other family members as part of a home library.

To prepare for teaching the rights in your own setting, collect materials, books, and resources on the rights of the child for a reference center in your classroom or child care facility. UNICEF is but one resource for free and inexpensive materials. Invite libraries, colleges, universities, families, and community and professional organizations to contribute to the collection.

Find information on the Internet to keep your references up to date. We have provided United Nations' websites at the end of this chapter to further your own knowledge base about the rights and ensuing concerns. Some of the websites provide resources and lessons for you to adapt to the age level in your classes or centers.

Starting in the preschool years, any study of the rights is ongoing. As the child develops, a spiral approach to various implications of the CRC has to be presented in concrete experiences, connected to what is currently important to the child. Some educators focus on one right at a time, lending an in-depth analysis through a variety of activities. Other schools and centers carry the theme of the rights in a year-long timetable throughout their buildings as a term project. In all instances, the children need to relate the rights to their own lives, to see the impact the convention has on their daily activities both in and out of the classroom.

The right to have basic necessities. . .
United Nations Children's Fund, A Children's Chorus: Celebrating the 30th Anniversary of the Declaration of the Rights of the Child. *New York: E. P. Dutton, 1989.*

Keep us warm and sheltered. Give us food to eat and a place to play. If we are sick, nurse and comfort us.

Advocacy Roles for Teaching the Rights

Once children formulate a clear and personal vision of their rights, they, along with the important adults in their lives, should implement an action plan that recognizes responsible outcomes. Such a plan needs to solicit support from all facets of the community. Children can petition officials to clarify the protective measures that the U.S. government is taking in adapting or adopting the CRC for its citizens.

As an initial step to recognition of children's rights, teachers and administrators can energize their communities to be involved in the adaptation or adoption of the convention. The educational process does not end with the children. Rather, it is necessary that we, as educators, model appropriate leadership roles that citizens can take to make governments work for important causes. Children learn the role of citizenship through the models that adults provide.

Joining adults in such an endeavor, children become involved in a cooperative effort in the real world that lends credibility to their work. Adult participation in the action plan sanctions the worth of the study and implies approval of the solutions the children resolve to put in place.

In her paper given in November 1991 at the Forum of the Japanese National Committee of OMEP, Jadwiga Kopczynska-Sikorska extolled as timely in today's world the early work of the Polish child rights crusader Janusz Korczak. (OMEP [Organization

Mondiale pour l'Education Préscolaire; World Organization for Early Childhood Education] has ties with UNESCO. As the only NGO for young children, it represents 60 nations to promote the child's well-being and education.) Korczak was a physician who wrote passionately on the rights of the child before his death in 1942; his writings laid the foundation for later declarations. Supporting the recommendation of joint child/adult advocacy, his "catalogue of the rights due to children" begins with "the right to dialogue and cooperation with adults" (Kopczynska-Sikorska, 1993, p. 64). Surely, families, professionals, community leaders, and interested world citizens of today can join in the "Say Yes" to Children campaign for that dialogue and cooperation.

Implications for Learning and Development

The Rights Require Thinking Skills for World Citizenship

As in any action plan, the analysis and advocacy of the convention requires critical thinking skills, necessary for participatory citizenship in a democratic society. In a constructionist, activity-based approach, children compare situations, contrast conditions, clarify their feelings, and listen to and evaluate the ideas of others before they apply their convictions in the promotion of their decisions. Following in the tradition of Theodore Brameld's social reconstructionism, children enact their rights as citizens and reconstruct their world. Refer back to Chapter 2 for more information on Brameld's calling for schools to be at the forefront for social reforms.

Children engage in intellectual inquiry during brainstorming sessions in which they express their perceptions while attentively listening to those of others. As they formulate solutions to the problems the convention poses, children are "encoding, combining and comparing," abilities that Robert Sternberg and Janet Davison identify as mental processes required in developing "insight" (Ellis, 1995, p. 157). The cooperative nature of collectively and jointly drawing up an action plan enhances in children the group process skills of respecting other opinions, behaving in a responsible and tolerant manner, and gaining confidence in their own beliefs through reflective actions.

Developing the Moral Domain

Before his death, Lawrence Kohlberg worked diligently to put into classroom practices his theory of moral development. His approach evolved into the vision of seeing each class as a "Just Community" (Murphy, D. 1998, Feb; 427) in which moral and social problems were identified by the students, discussed, and resolved by having each member of the class share thoughts at a class meeting. The goal of class-meeting time was for each student to acknowledge a just decision and course of action. Worldwide efforts to replicate this approach have been made, beginning with the early childhood level.

In the United States, first-graders would meet at circle time to discuss a class issue, which could range from concerns involving missing items from the cubbies to health and safety measures, combative behavior, and sharing or taking turns. As in King Arthur's court, each member had a chance to share in or pass on the discussion of the issue, but all individuals voted on the course of action. The purpose of the "just community" was to engage children to seek justice and to behave responsibly with an understanding of the moral implications their actions held. Unlike King Arthur's court, in today's schools both genders have equal voice in the vote for social justice.

Framing problems in terms of dilemmas, Kohlberg posed situations to children and noted the kind of responses they gave to a set of prepared answers for the dilemmas. He then evaluated the responses according to his fixed levels and stages of moral development, which he had based on Piaget's theory of cognitive development. Kohlberg placed young children at an egocentric level and postulated that they did not act out of moral convictions but from fear of punishment or for reward and recognition (Sunal, 1990).

Questions as to the reliability and validity of Kohlberg's theories have ensued (Sunal, 1990, p. 148). One of his critics, Carol Gilligan, a psychologist and colleague at Harvard University, noted that Kohlberg's subjects for his study were all boys and that he had disregarded gender differences in his scheme of moral development. She contends that girls resolve issues using a "different voice" and are empathetic and nurturing to others as well as resilient to adversities in the early childhood years (Gilligan, 1996). Some educators dispute her claim of gender differences (Ellis, 1995, p. 327; Sunal, p. 148). Arthur Ellis suggests that both boys and girls are caring and that "boys could just as well be taught to be more cooperative and supportive of the feelings and needs of others" (Ellis, p. 327). He further maintains that moral development varies and is not solely determined by age (p. 326).

Putting the debate of gender difference aside, the important point is that many psychologists and educators observe that young children, both girls and boys, extend themselves to understand, appreciate, and care about other children as well as themselves (Fortson & Reiff, 1995). Studying the CRC offers children an opportunity to express their inner voices and enhance an appreciation of themselves and others. The teaching of the rights in an early childhood curriculum implies that teachers believe young children can act responsibly. Teaching the rights supports teachers' expectations that children can make moral decisions and embrace the rights as their own.

The Rights of the Child Promote Inclusion

Special Education   Building on the 1979 Declaration of the Rights of the Child, the 1989 convention spells out the rights. The right to education and the right to special care for special-needs children are specifically addressed in Articles 28 (the right to "free and compulsory primary education"), 29, and 23 ("a mentally or physically disabled child has the right to a full and decent life. . . . The state. . . . ensure[s] that the disabled child receives education, training, and services leading to the fullest possible social integration") (Castelle, 1990, pp. 19, 22).

Unfortunately, even in countries that have ratified the convention, "progress is too slow in providing universal basic education" (United Nations Children's Fund, 1994, p. 5). On the other hand, the U.S. federal mandate and individual state initiatives provide the world with some effective models for inclusion of special needs children. The

*The rights of the child protect
and include all learners.*

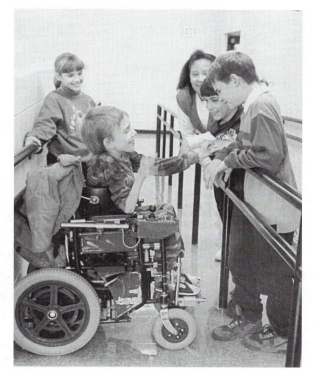

convention endorses these efforts and supports future directives that the United States and other countries must take for equal opportunity for all children to learn under the best circumstances, in schools that offer experiences inclusive of everyone's learning styles and needs. In Chapter 4 there is more discussion of individual nations' support for special education that is consistent with the principles of global education.

Indigenous Peoples   Similarly, the convention includes the rights of indigenous peoples to an education that reflects their language, culture, and learning styles. The mandate for indigenous education is being met around the globe. In New Zealand, for example, strides are being made to offer the Maori educational options within the national school system. Maori language is taught in all schools, beginning in the early childhood years, as New Zealand forges a new identity in the community of nations. In Wales, Welsh is being reinstated in the British National Curriculum for children. Likewise, the native peoples of the United States and Canada are demanding equitable and equal education for their children. Such demands are consistent with the philosophical contentions of educators worldwide and are deemed sound pedagogy.

Bringing It Together   Within the immediate social structure of the school, child care center, or community, an atmosphere of appreciation of the rights of all children can project a mind-set that encourages children and adults alike to be inclusive of differences. Once children recognize the rights as being universal, they become connected to others. Building upon this connection, parents and teachers can join with their children by engaging in caring and tolerant behaviors that are accepting of diversity.

Summary

The Convention on the Rights of the Child grew out of a history of declarations and mandates for universal support for human rights. To date, the convention, an agreement based on the 1959 Declaration of the Rights of the Child, has yet to be ratified by all member nations of the United Nations. The rights are in the moral domain of development of young children. They empower children to be effective, participatory citizens of their own nations and the world. The CRC is a document intended to protect, provide for, and allow participation of all the world's children.

It is incumbent upon educators to be informed of these rights and to bring them to the attention of their students, families, and communities. Numerous resources are available for teaching the rights of the child. Action plans to advocate for the rights are most effective when educators take a leadership role and model participatory citizenship. Teaching the rights of the child has to be a joint effort of the adults in their communities as well as the school.

Rights cannot be separated from responsibility. Any discussion or teaching of the rights of the child would be incomplete without attention to the promotion of responsible behavior in children. Rights cannot be taught in isolation. They must form an integral part of the curriculum, practiced by teachers, families, and children.

Support for initiatives that promote the CRC continue to be mandated, but the United States Congress has not ratified the convention. The purpose of the UN's Special Session on Children, 2001 is to expand on the Convention in the document *A World Fit for Children,* in the action plan Global Movement for Children, and in the campaign "Say Yes" to Children. The intent of UNICEF is to continue the cause through the 21st century.

Reflection Questions

1. What would you include in a Bill of Rights for all children? Think of how you could publicize your class's bill.
2. How can you advocate for the rights of the child in the United States and elsewhere with the use of technology? Explore websites for further information. Think about the kind of class or teacher webpage you can create to publicize the Convention on the Rights of the Child.
3. How might you implement a thematic unit on the rights of the child that is inclusive of diverse learning styles and needs? How would you include the indigenous people of your part of the globe?
4. What issues are involved in the ratification of the CRC in the United States? Host a public forum at your school for your community to air its concerns.

References

Castelle, K. (1990). *In the child's best interest: A primer on the U.N. Convention on the Rights of the Child*. East Greenwich, RI: Plan International.

Castle, C. (2001). *For every child: The UN Convention on the Rights of the Child in words and picture*. New York: Phyllis Fogelman Books in association with UNICEF.

Centre for Human Rights Geneva. (1989). *Teaching human rights: Practical activities for primary and secondary schools*. New York: United Nations.

Edmonds, B. C. (1992). The Convention on the Rights of the Child: A point of departure. *Social Education, 56*(4), 205–207.

Ellis, A. K. (1995). *Teaching and learning elementary social studies*. Boston: Allyn & Bacon.

Fortson, L., & Reiff, J. (1995). *Early childhood curriculum: Open structures for integrative learning*. Boston: Allyn & Bacon.

Gardner, H. (1983). *Frames of mind: The theory of multiple intelligences*. New York: Harper Collins.

Gilligan, C. (1996). Presentation made at the Distinguished Author Series of Harvard University Graduate School of Education's Principals' Center.

Harris, R. L. (1994). Voices at the United Nations: The role of non-governmental organizations. *Social Education, 58*(7), 420–421.

Kopczynska-Sikorska, J. (1993). The rights of the child: Reflected in the life and works of Janusz Korczak. *Journal of Early Childhood, 25*(1), 64–66.

LeBlanc, L. J. (1995). *The Convention on the Rights of the Child*. Lincoln, NE: University of Nebraska Press.

Marshall, K. (1997). *Children's rights in the balance*. Edinburgh, UK: The Stationery Office Limited.

Neuffer, E. (2001, October 13). Annan, UN recipients of Nobel Peace Prize. *The Boston Globe*, p. 1, A5.

Smith, A. (Ed.) (2000). *Advocating for children: International perspectives on children's rights*. Dunedin, NZ: University of Otago Press.

Stroud, M. (n.d.). *Reaching the children*. New York: UNICEF.

Sunal, C. (1990). *Early childhood social studies*. Upper Saddle River, N.J: Merrill Publishing Company.

Swiniarski, L., et al. (1996). Teaching the rights of the child. Unpublished booklet of lesson plans of early childhood education studies majors, Salem State College, MA.

United Nations Bureau of the Prepatory Committee for the Special Session of the General Assembly on Children. (2001, March). *A world fit for children*. Revised draft outcome document. New York: Author.

United Nations Children's Fund. (1989). *A children's chorus: Celebrating the 30th anniversary of the Declaration of the Rights of the Child*. New York: E. P. Dutton.

United Nations Children's Fund. (1994). *The state of the world's children 1996*. New York: UNICEF.

United Nations Children's Fund. (April, 2001). *A briefing to educators UN special session on children, September, 2001 and The global movement for children*. Presented at the Association for Childhood Education International 2001 Education Odyssey from Froebel to the Internet, Toronto, Canada.

Further Readings for Research

Barricklow, D. (1995). Can a "school-in-a-box" hold the key to Rwanda's future? Unique UNICEF program educates more than 700,000. *Educational Horizons, 74*(1), 10–12.

Greenberg, P. (Ed.). (1996). Calling all children's champions …. An opportunity to stand for children. *Young Children, 51*(3), 34–35.

Limber, S., & Flekkoy, M. (1995). The U.N. Convention on the Rights of the Child: Its relevance for social scientists. *SOCIAL POLICY REPORT Society for Research in Child Development, 9*(2).

Morrison, D., Roma, D., & Bazar, R. (1986). *We can do it! A peace book for kids of all ages*. Vancouver, BC: Namchi United Enterprises.

Murphy, D. (1988, Feb.). The just community at Birch Meadow Elementary School. *Phi Delta Kappan, 69*(6), 427–428.

Nawwab, N. (1995). The children's kingdom. *Aramco World, 46*(6), 18–27.

Rodham, H. (1973). Children under the law. *Harvard Education Review, 43*(4), 487–514.

Websites

Convention on the Rights of the Child: *http://www.unicef.org/crc*

UN System: *http://www.unsystem.org*

UNICEF: *http://www.unicef.org*

UNICEF Language and Literature Lesson Plans: *http://www.unhcr.ch/teach/tchlang/tchlang.htm*

Part II

Including Diverse Learners

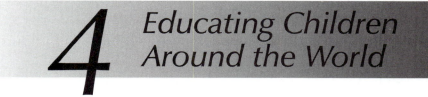

4

Educating Children Around the World

Children's Voices Define Education

Cape Town, South Africa

"Our family has moved to District Six and now I am going to a city school." Sheena and her siblings live in the uprooted sixth district of Cape Town. Before apartheid, this district was noted for being a successfully integrated community. The former all-white South African government demolished most of the neighborhoods and sent people off into segregated areas. Now the present government is trying to reverse directions. Sheena no longer attends an all-black school in a township. She now represents the district's hope for its future at a local school.

Spain

"We would love to live all year on our family's *finca*. We could go to the little primary school seven miles away in the village and help with the crops, game keeping, the dog kennels, and the lodge. But we live in a big city to attend school and visit the *finca* when our parents help with the business," explain Cara and Carlos, twin eight-year-olds. The *finca* is in central Spain. It is a family business of two generations, which provides employment for the local communities in the La Mancha area of Spain. The *finca*, a working ranch, markets its game and harvest around the globe and provides a lodge for international visitors to the area. Each family member has a role with the daily supervision of the *finca* or with the management of its finances. While the twins' formal education is urban, their grandparents and parents hope to pass on the family land to them. As Spain becomes a major player in the economics of the European Union, the children are preparing to assume responsibilities for the *finca* with each visit, where they receive their informal education.

United States

"Auntie, come and see our new playhouse," invited a small band of four-year-old native Hawaiians to a class visitor. "We're painting it green." Native Hawaiians are looking to infuse more of the indigenous culture in their schools. The terms *Auntie* and *Uncle* are extended to all adult community members as a social greeting. While the elite private Kamehameha schools, generously endowed by the Bishop Foundation, serve a percentage of native Hawaiian children, statewide movements are campaigning for a broader base of native education as a right of indigenous people.

New Zealand

"Today's my birthday!" exclaims Fiona. "I'm five years old. Mummy says now I can go to school." Fiona is about to begin the First Entrants class in a state school of New Zealand. Like all her counterparts in this two-island nation, Fiona can begin her school career on her fifth birthday in a full-day-equivalent reception, or kindergarten, class. The staggered admission policy of the First Entrants classes in New Zealand underscores the highly individualized approach this national school system provides. In this class, Fiona will develop her early literacy skills in English and Maori. She will proceed at her own pace through a literacy-based curriculum in a print-rich environment, engaging in hands-on integrated learning experiences. A running record of her skills and performance will carefully monitor her achievement. Should she need intervention for reading when she moves on to the six-year-old class, she will be tutored by the Reading Recovery teacher and benefit by the one-on-one individualized attention.

Canada

"Je m'appelle Lisa. J'ai sept ans. J'aime parler français." Lisa is a young Canadian child whose first language is English. She attends a French immersion school in Vancouver, British Columbia. The school is one in a Canadian province that does not have a dominant French-speaking population but is committed to the call for all children to be bilingual.

In an immersion classroom, children learn the same curriculum as their peers, but they do so in a "foreign" language (Checkley, 1996a, p. 7). Canadian researchers point out what teachers of world languages have always known, namely, "having the experience of learning a second language helps you better analyze and reflect on your own" (Checkley, 1996b, p. 2).

France

Claude is four years old. Like all his age mates in France, he attends his village's École Maternelle during the school year, but in summer he likes to join with friends of all ages at the beach on the Baie de Pampelonne for a varied physical education program of swimming, boating, sports, and games.

The Mimi Club des Trop-Kids is sponsored by a national association, with programs situated on beaches along all the coasts of France. The Union Française des Clubs de Plage et de leurs Amis (l'UFCPA) is the umbrella organization that seeks corporate and community funding for the equipment and administration of the programs. Staff members are primarily experienced teachers who work at the sites from July 1 to August 30 each year. The children can participate in both a three-hour morning program and the later afternoon events. Claude goes daily to the program as his family lives in this coastal area, but many of his friends in the program are visitors to the beach from throughout France and participate during the family vacation time. So Claude meets new friends weekly and has connections with children from all corners of France.

Children tell us about themselves and what school means to them. As adults, we need to heed the child's perception of school. In any analysis of schools, near and far, the children's voices must provide the framework for selecting effective practices from a variety of international models. Their voices offer a filter through which to view different systems. They need to be reflected in the world community's definition for world-class standards of excellence in education.

Adult Memories of School

Also important to defining early education are adult memories of early schooling. Recall the early experiences that shaped you to be the person you are today. The following vignette illustrates one young adult's perceptions of her early years.

Japan

"My favorite memories of kindergarten are playing in school. I went to a private kindergarten. I was glad I went to this school, because many preschools in Japan are very academic. We were allowed to play in kindergarten, but in the upper grades, school became a lot of work. We went to school on Saturday as well.

"I remember in my public primary school, all of us wore the same uniforms and had to have the same hair cut. I went to an all girls' private middle and high school that required a dress code similar to those of the public co-ed schools. In Japanese schools no student was to stand out or to look different!"

These are recollections of Famiko, a Japanese international student, studying in the United States for her bachelor's degree. She often shares childhood reminiscences with her American peers.

Early Childhood Education: An International Movement

Professionals in the field of early childhood education agree that the ages served in this area range from birth to eight years. However, the manner of delivery of services and the title given to schools for this age range bring into question many different political, cultural, social, and class values. In the classical Greek writings, Plato guaranteed all three- to six-year-olds the right to an education in what he named a "sanctuary" for children. In his utopian scheme in *The Laws*, Plato prescribed that each community provide a "sanctuary" for children beginning with age three, with a focus on the enhancement of language and socialization skills (trans. 1960, p. 176). Historically, early education has been seen in the context of the family, with the prime responsibility resting on the mother. This antecedent is evident in France's École Maternelle. In 19th-century Prussia, Friedrich Froebel established the kindergarten, which was disseminated by his disciples to become a global practice. Maria Montessori contributed her Casa dei Bambini (Children's House), and the English McMillan sisters initiated the nursery school movement for international export.

Shakespeare's Juliet asked whether a rose is a rose by any other name. This question aptly applies to the world view of early childhood education. Some countries place all early education in multiple age groups under one rubric, while others cluster children in a single age bracket. Kindergarten can be for children from age three to six or for just five-year-olds. The British Infant School is for children from five to seven, with the reception class being for the youngest children as they are received into school. If child care is delivered in the home, it can be called *home care* or *family care*. If the care is in a center, it can be referred to as a *crèche*, a *day nursery*, or *group care*. Inclusion class-

Parents and teachers want their kindergartners to be happy. A child who is nurtured blooms!

rooms, early intervention programs, and special schools are some early childhood settings for the special child. Professionals are known as teachers, nursery nurses, directrices, child minders, or child care providers. For the age-old practice of child care at home, the British *nanny* is a popular term. Whether a program's philosophy is the social development of children or the academic preparation for formal schooling, the approach is expressed both in the curriculum and in the name. *Preschool* has an academic ring, while *playgroup* and *playschool* suggest socialization and activity-based programs. For six- to eight-year-olds, school can be a primary grade, a first school, an elementary school, or a grammar school (except in British-dominated systems, where *grammar school* is a term for the secondary level). In all instances, the early childhood program is evolving according to community needs. Opportunities are more available in some parts of the world and are restricted by financial and political factors in other regions.

International Mandates for Standards-Based Curriculum and School Reform

The world community protects the child's right to an education, including special education, through the UN Convention on the Rights of the Child (CRC). As each nation examines its own national education system, the challenges from the global community herald a call for reforms. The combined impact of technology, global economics, and the changing worldwide workforce places new demands on the school's curriculum. As nations fret about the future of their citizens in this global marketplace, they define new expectations for their schools. The demands for school reform and restructuring resound around the world. Some nations are meeting the demands by national standards for curriculum and assessments; other nations are open to local control of curriculum and standards definition. In either case, countries are concerned about how their educational systems can meet the challenges of the undefined "world-class standards".

In this postcolonial age, emerging nations are restructuring their own national identity through school initiatives. Countries such as India, Kenya, Pakistan, and Trinidad are weaving national trends with former colonial practices. South Africa is in the process of implementing its reform known as *Curriculum 2000*, an outcomes-based education approach, which is attempting to transition practitioners from using teacher-centered approaches to using active, constructionist, learner-centered practices (Tiley, 2000). The reform measures of *Curriculum 2005* contend that "Every learner has some skills-no learner has all skills" in a lifelong educational process "that begins before birth and ends only with death" (Tiley, 2000, p. 8). "The ten or twelve years in school are only a small part of this process" (Tiley, p. 8). In this scheme, the early childhood years are "the first four years, Grades 0, 1, 2 and 3, … called the Foundation Phase" (Tiley, p. 8).

Limited resources restrict the availability of equal education for all children, and social-class practices often inhibit educational opportunities, particularly for girls. In some instances, primary education takes precedence over preprimary endeavors, but even the picture for primary education is discouraging in countries torn by civil strife and exploitation.

Many school reform initiatives have been top-down directives. Great Britain is a case in point. In England, much of the resistance to school change came from the lack of ownership felt by both the educational professional and the local authorities. Great Britain's Department of Education and Science has adapted its 1988 mandate for a national curriculum to accommodate the complaints of these segments of the community. Yet there is still a disgruntled constituency in Great Britain.

While many industrialized nations such as Great Britain are looking for common standards and centralized approaches to education, Morocco's Ministry of Education is attempting to modify its central control of education by seeking routes to decentralization. During July of 2000, *World Boston* hosted representatives of the Moroccan ministry in a seminar on decentralization of education. Select models of American schooling in the private and public sectors, such as charter schools, pilot programs, and alternative schools, were examined for possible adaptation.

Other nations that mirror Morocco's move to less central control include Israel and South Korea. Israel is small geographically, but it has a school population of "immigrant children from more than 70 countries" (Kalbus, 2000, p. 78). To meet the schools' diverse needs, Israel is resisting the standards movement by establishing experimental pre-K to grade 8 schools. One such school is charged with the special mission to "give all students an education consonant with their parents' worldview" and another is a bilingual school that "received a peace funding award from a Japanese foundation" (Kalbus, p. 79–80).

South Korea hopes to establish an "Edutopia" as its vision of an educational system deemed "excellent by world standards." To ensure that level of excellence, the control of education is shifting from the "national Ministry of Education to local and individual schools" (Diem, Levy, & Van Sickle, 1997, p. 87).

People closest to the schools need to have their vested interests aired in any reform measure. A grassroots approach to school reform gives ownership of the school to the community. Along with the children's voices, parents and teachers need to express their vision for the schools of today and tomorrow. To support the notion that there are many scenarios that work best for children, Peter Moss, professor of early childhood provision at the University of London, argues against international guidelines or standards for early education. He feels such guidelines are too problematic. He contends that local culture and identity need to be valued. There is no single way to teach or learn. He cites the position of educators in Reggio Emilia, where choices are made among many possibilities for effective teaching and learning situations (Moss, 1999, p. 23).

Family Issues and School Expectations

Parent and Teacher Expectations

Parents' and teachers' expectations deserve joint consideration in developing the best learning situations for young children. Educators worldwide recognize the importance of home/school partnerships (Swiniarski, 1994b, p. 4). To cement a sound foundation for the entire educational process, parents must feel confident about their children's schools and must feel in harmony with the expectations the schools hold for children. In the "schoolhome" model of Jane Roland Martin, effective schools respect parental needs and concerns and invite parent input (Martin, 1992).

One good recipe for an effective school came from the voices of parents in Great Britain and the United States when they were both surveyed as to their expectations for their children's kindergarten and reception class year (Swiniarski, 1994b). Responses from the two sides of the Atlantic differed in accents but were similar in their message. Some common goals held by parents were for their children to experience the following:

to be happy at school

to learn how to learn

to cooperate

to develop social responsibilities

to develop a sense of security

to promote confidence in mixing with other children at play and work to be able to cope with the new life at school

to stimulate interest in reading, writing, and number work

to succeed at his/her own level

to be allowed to go at his/her own pace

to build a foundation for later education

to communicate with other children and teachers

to read (Swiniarski, 1994b)

When the parents' responses were compared with kindergarten and reception class teachers' responses, agreement on most issues was also consistent. Additionally, teachers from both countries expressed identical expectations. The implications of this study point to the fact that there are universal issues and some common ground in educational programs for young children. While still respecting diversity, school reform agendas have to seek common venues for building home/school partnership. Matching expectations of the home with school outcomes ought to be a goal of the reform effort (Swiniarski, 1994b).

In some instances, voices of dissent exist in school/home relationships. Although the British teachers and parents agreed on matters regarding the reception class, parents are less than pleased with arrangements in nursery school education. In Great Britain, nursery education has been traditionally part of the state schools. Currently, about 20% of four-year-olds are accommodated in these settings, with private playschools servicing other families. British parents look to continental Europe, where four-year-olds are provided with free state education. The École Maternelle of France, the Italian Reggio Emilo, and the German kindergartens are exemplary models of state education for four-year-olds. As Great Britain looks to the future with its membership in the European Community, British parents are concerned about the "head start" these continental children have. They have demanded that the British government provide similar offerings.

In 1997 the government's voucher system for private and state nurseries changed. In September of that year, the Labour Party declared that all four-year-olds had a right to an education, and that has been the policy since then. Parents can choose to send their four-year-olds to reception classes for a full- or part-day program. For some parents, this government offer is "too little and too late." These parents are crusading for more appropriate nursery education for all four-year-olds in Great Britain, since all children are required to be in full-time education by the term after their fifth birthday.

Great Britain is also experiencing a growth in private child care. While the state sector provides for some preschool opportunities, many two-parent working and single-parent households are seeking adequate care that coincides with their work day and work year calendar. Some families select child minders who care for preschoolers and infants in the child's' home (nannies); others find care in the providers' homes (playgroups); most families seek professionally managed day nurseries.

Since such options can be costly, choices are restricted by the families' financial means. In all cases, British early childhood educators encourage parents to look for placements that reflect the government's guidelines recommended by the Department of Education and Employment for the optimum development of children in their "Foundation Years" of three to five (*Kangaroo Club Parents Handbook,* n.d.). Many parent guides for understanding these "Foundation Years" are available in community bookshops, agencies, and libraries, at nurseries, and through the Qualification and Curriculum Authority or Department of Employment websites (*Kangaroo Club Parents Handbook*).

An example of parent/school tensions lies with the Japanese schools. Ethnographic studies contradict the myth that parents have an influential voice in Japanese preschools (Lewis, 1995; Peak, 1991). While some private preschools cater to the parents' demands for academic curricula, most schools in Japan work to discourage parent involvement. These schools promote a sense of community in which children are seen as friends, mentors, and group members responsible for each other. According to Lewis, Japanese educators see parents as too focussed on their own children and thus too egocentric and indulgent for the school's mission. Parents in Japan traditionally defer to the teacher, whose role it is to motivate the children to learn and be responsible for their education (Lewis). However, Japanese teachers routinely make home visits, play a personal role in the lives of the children, and, in essence, become extended members of their children's families (Lewis).

Both educators and parents can learn lessons in the study of other national models for early education and child care. Any examination of comparative education can glean effective practices and draw parallels. Many common threads weave through the reform movement globally, including limited monetary support, frustrations in striving for excellence, equity and equality issues, declining academic standards, inconsistent moral behavior, and violence in society and social institutions. Dealing with these concerns requires that parents and teachers form concerted alliances across national boundaries. Rather than compete with each other, it is more productive for educators and parents to explore and investigate avenues for adapting and adopting successful measures (Swiniarski, 1994a).

Educating Educators and Families

Gaining firsthand knowledge is the best approach to evaluating practices that are effective and identifying the factors that account for their success. For American teachers, the Fulbright Teacher Exchange Program invites candidates to apply each academic year. Its annual booklet catalogs the host countries and their available positions. Colleges and universities offer practica and internships for teachers who are in training or are seeking professional development. The Council for Basic Education provides professional development in science and math for teachers of nine nations to exchange successful models of teaching and learning in its Schools Around the World program. Likewise, individuals in local school systems can informally arrange teacher exchanges. Embassies and consulates also recommend avenues to explore for research of educational practices in their homelands.

Parents can access information about teaching practices and standards through local community agencies, libraries, governmental websites, schools, the media, and the Internet. Through both governmental and non-governmental organizations (NGOs), free and inexpensive literature in parenting and educational issues abounds in many countries. Community programs that promote adult literacy skills help parents avail themselves of these materials to support their children's learning opportunities and to enrich the entire family's lifestyle.

Effective Exemplars of Early Education

Investigations into effective exemplars of early education uncover similar themes that resonate around the globe, along with unique approaches that prompt proactive practices. No school has all the answers, and not all models transplant well from one community to another. When teachers are involved in an educational exchange, it is comforting to learn that others are grappling with similar problems, facing dilemmas but still striving for authentic teaching situations. It is also energizing to share with each other our quests for resolutions and solutions. The following models are offered in the spirit of an open exchange to strategize uncharted leadership roles necessary for the global village. The models visited include different national schools and child care, community play facilities outside the sphere of schools/centers, and the private sector of international schools around the globe.

Italy: Reggio Emilia

The Reggio Emilia schools of Northern Italy have captured the attention of early childhood educators globally. These municipal preschools have pioneered their unique philosophy of early education based on constructivism. Several features distinguish these schools, beginning with the belief that all children can learn. These schools also believe that children construct their own meanings to experience. Children express what they learn in many "languages", that is, different ways of knowing. The arts are the core of the curriculum (Brewer, 2001; Jalongo, 2000).

The teacher is the *pedagogista*, the art director is the *atelierista*, while the school environment or the community is "the third teacher." The curriculum involves projects that are extended over a long period of time and continually revisited for further study and investigation. Documentation of the children's work is comprehensive and measures all areas of development. The history of the child's growth and development is evident in multiple assessments such as exhibits, performances, demonstrations, and productions (Brewer, 2001; Jalongo, 2000).

The children's work is often on display for years so that alumni and older siblings on return visits to the school can point to their contributions with pride. The children's investment in their own learning and in the school is valued as they grow into adult members of the municipality. Other principles of Reggio include

- Integral community involvement
- Collaboration among and between the community, teachers, children, and families
- A child paced sense of time

- Teachers as learners
- An emergent curriculum (Brewer, 2001).

Nordic Models

Typically in Nordic nations, youngsters begin their formal education at age seven. They attend a nine-year scheme of compulsory education, after which they enter a career path or prepare for higher education at a gymnasium-style secondary school. All forms of preschool education, be it nursery school or kindergarten, are subsumed under the umbrella of child care.

Sweden   A unique feature of Swedish primary education is its nongrading group pattern. Swedish children stay with the same teacher for three to four years. The time frame allows the teacher and child the opportunity to bond, develop long-term goals, and implement learning experiences at a pace that matches the learning style and rhythm of the child's personal development.

The Swedish classroom is a window on the world. All primary teachers are trained to teach in another language, usually English, as second languages are routinely part of the core curriculum. Also, their teacher training experiences require an emphasis on global education and its inclusion in the primary school day (Wright, 1994). Swedish children also have a grasp of geography and are credited with placing first in comparative studies of achievement in this field.

Supporting the schools and the families in Sweden are community child care centers. Parents in Sweden are granted family leave as an entitlement by the government and places of employment. Each parent can take up to 9 months; in two-parent households, a combined 18-month leave is possible. Many parents (more mothers, though, than fathers) take advantage of this entitlement, so most centers tend to care for infants near their first birthday. Older children are also included in child care programs. Those who have gone on to school return to their preschool centers for after-school care. To accommodate this age range, some centers are set up as family groups, with each group reflecting the entire age range. Rather than having all toddlers together or all school-age children together, the Swedes find that their model simulates life at home and is a more natural and welcoming place for youngsters of all ages.

Finland   Finnish children are required to study a minimum of three languages before they complete their compulsory education. When asked why languages were so important in the Finnish course of study, one teacher replied, "Because nowhere else in the world do they speak Finnish!" Children can attend a school in which Finnish is the dominant language, or they can select the Swedish-language schools. In either case, all children are required to learn Finnish and Swedish and choose an elective language of English, German, Russian, French, or Spanish. English is the most popular choice, but many Finnish children speak several other languages. There is a 5% minority of Swedish-Finns for whom Swedish is their "mother tongue." The state supports both the Finnish and Swedish schools. Finns in Sweden have asked for reciprocal schooling, but, to date, the debate continues. In addition to state schools with national curriculum demands and standards of achievement, an array of private schools exists in Finland, with an emphasis on linguistic preferences, religious affiliations, or philosophical pedagogies.

Child care in Finland is a national model. In January 1996, Finland extended to every child under school age a "subjective right to municipal day care" (Estola, 1997). Finland can boast that "it is the first country in the world where every child has the right to enter day care" (Estola). However, as in Sweden, not all families in Finland choose to send their children to child care facilities. Some families take advantage of the Maternity and Child Health Care Program and the parental leave, whereby parents are "granted job protection" (Estola). Some families place children in private playschools and with family day care providers. When a child is placed in any of the child care choices, one parent can reduce the workday by two hours (Estola). Along with family leaves, sliding-scale tuition, central locations, and university-trained child care professionals are some of the support systems for parents of young children in Finland.

The most striking feature of Finnish centers is the physical plant itself. Most facilities are designed and built for the purpose of child care. Although Finnish architects are experimenting with innovative designs, most state centers share a similar layout of a central airy room with smaller facilities leading off from it. All the facilities consist of one story at ground level for comfortable access. Infants and toddlers are generally separated from the other children in a wing sufficient in size to accommodate their special

Education takes place with investigations of creatures that crawled into the pail.

equipment. A unique feature of the infant/toddler space is the outdoor porticoes, facing to the south and built for naptime. Finnish babies, as a rule, take naps outside all year long (Swiniarski, 1984). Centers are a part of the local community plan and strategically located near other facilities servicing children and family needs. In Helsinki, one child care facility is under one roof: it includes the school, youth center, medical and dental offices, library, community auditorium, and senior citizen drop-in center. This combined facility, known as a service center, resembles a shopping mall. The service center was a Swedish concept adapted by Finnish architects for an urban neighborhood (Swiniarski, 1984).

Architects often collaborate with educators on the interior design of the centers. Perhaps this joint effort accounts for the successful working of the centers. Ample space facilitates the implementation of daily activities. "Beds pull out from walls, cooking areas are customized with appliances built into child-sized work areas, ample shelving and storage ensure that everything has a place and everything is in place. The abundance of equipment and materials is critically arranged for accessibility and use" (Swiniarski, 1984, p. 186).

Furnishings reflect a beauty, color, and composition characteristic of Finnish craftsmanship and artistic interior decoration. An aesthetically pleasing environment is typical of centers dotted across the entire nation. Classrooms are color coded for easy identification, staff lounges are inviting and relaxing, and parents' rooms are welcoming to all members of the family to meet for a conference, to smooth a morning farewell, or to catch a moment for a coffee break at the end of the day before the journey home.

The Finnish centers create an ambience of home away from home. "The center is the second home and the staff, the surrogate family" (Swiniarski, 1984, p. 186). Teachers, staff members, nurses, and aides alike can be found making presents for the children. Symbols representing each child are lovingly stitched or hand stenciled on all the children's belongings.

Children are taught the native arts and crafts of Finnish designs. Prominently placed for all to enjoy are exhibits of numerous art forms and the unique Finnish folk craft, produced by the staff as well as the children. These displays are promoted as community endeavors that speak to the best of Finnish effort. Pride in the center and in being a member of its extended family are immediately evident to the visitor.

The Community as a Learning Environment

Playgrounds, Parks, and Recreational Areas

The much quoted African proverb "It takes a whole community to raise a child" speaks to the theme of this exemplar of early education, the community play and recreation areas. People too often discount the value of play as the open and free expression of childhood. Where and how children play, as well as their games, toys, and playmates, collectively contribute to the children's well-being and energize their creative and cognitive development. Play-based curriculum models are the ultimate inclusion model of education; all children, when left to their own devices, play. The format and structure of that play are shaped by culture, politics, social class, and place.

Ideal play environments should permit solitary as well as cooperative play, offer a safe and welcoming haven for children and their families, be accessible to children with disabilities, and encourage experiences that enhance the total development of the whole child. Open-ended activities, choice, and creativity should be evident in the play situations. Playgrounds can be community efforts attached to a school or center, part of a public park, or stand-alone facilities.

Denmark is credited with the development of an innovative approach to playgrounds. During World War II, the Danes used recycled materials along with the conventional playground equipment to build what has been known as the "adventure playground." The adventure playground offers an array of play activity in tree houses, boats, and cars and with building, construction, and art materials. The replication of this type of inclusionary play, with its open-ended structures and its appeal to and access for all children, led to a worldwide movement. Adaptation of this model can be seen throughout Europe in particular.

Other playground models are evident throughout Europe as well. German playgrounds are typically placed in parks for all ages to enjoy. Hamburg offers a jewel of a playground that invites all children to enjoy an array of options, including slides built at various levels on fabricated mountainsides, playhouses with sliding walls that can be converted into whatever the creative minds design, water troughs and pumps for engineering and water management schemes, large circular community sandboxes, and inviting benches for parents to sit on while they chat and watch the children.

A playground can be a single structure, as this one in Halifax, Nova Scotia.

Throughout the park are brick paths for easy access for the physically challenged child and infants and toddlers in strollers.

Not all German playgrounds are in public parks. Creative efforts are being made to use natural settings for creative play, be it in a yard or an open area (Hohenauer, 1995). Tree stumps, uprooted trees, rocks, and natural enclosures, along with formal designs such as the "labyrinth" playground, complement the purposely built play areas (Hohenauer).

Great Britain has a strong commitment to using the natural environment in its "outdoor educational centres," which are usually connected to a metropolitan school district. Often, a converted village school houses a meeting place, catering services, and overnight facilities. Children and their teachers can use the outdoor centers for a day visit or a longer, more involved, field trip. Each center has a specialty, be it nature study, animal care, or gardening. All provide playing fields for open-ended games, imaginary adventures, and moments for reflection.

A playground can be a single structure. Built in the heart of Halifax, Nova Scotia, is a boat-design playground. Because of its central location, this facility is frequented by children with their family members or child care minders. It is an aesthetically pleasant spot, as the structure fits with the buildings around it, and its maritime theme reflects the personality of the city.

Children have wonderful imaginations for turning anything into a play object. This phenomenon is noted wherever art sculpture is accessible. "The Little Mermaid" in Copenhagen harbor captivates children as they cluster around her. Recognizing

Hamburg, Germany, offers a jewel of a playground.

children's curiosity about sculpture, the Finns provide in their city parks wooden sculptures of imaginary animals intended specifically for children to climb.

Tending the parks in Helsinki are supervisors who are available year-round to mind children of all ages. They engage children in the outdoor activities and introduce play equipment and toys that are stored on-site. These supervisors are known to monitor napping infants and toddlers should a parent have a quick errand to do.

The Community Itself

While many municipalities have valuable resources such as museums, art galleries, a zoo or an aquarium, it is important to recognize that the community, itself, is a learning environment, that "third teacher" mentioned in the Reggio model. All aspects of community life provide teaching and learning opportunities, be it at the marketplace, the post office, municipal agencies, governmental centers, commerce and financial districts, the farm, the neighborhood, the beach, or the woods. All of these places make up the global village and should be mined for teaching children about themselves and others.

Distance Education for Outreach to Homes and Families

Distance education programs via television or the Internet offer a potentially powerful outreach for connecting families with one another for sharing mutual concerns, interests, insights, and understandings. Through this technology, governmental and nongovernmental agencies can provide courses and information for people living in remote areas with limited access to educational opportunity.

A successful model of the value of these technologies is the work of the Massachusetts Corporation for Educational Technology (Mass Interaction), which produced for families of preschoolers and primary school children two television series for broadcast throughout the United States. The programs in both series have a global dimension. Topics of family heritage and culture are considered in context of the global village. Many of the images telecasted, activities and materials demonstrated, resources used, guests invited, communities viewed, and children's work samples shown are international representations chosen to demonstrate the universal nature of childhood. Major themes of both series are respect for likeness and difference in the celebration of family culture and the appreciation of the world in one's community as well as the community's place in the world (Breitborde & Swiniarski, 2001). See Chapter 9 for further discussion of these programs as models for distance learning.

International Schools Bring the World Together

The International School movement is a global endeavor with schools situated in all corners of the world. The prototype for this model was established in the 1920s in Geneva, Switzerland, for the children of the delegates of the League of Nations. Despite the collapse of the league, the school continued with the intention of being a multinational school open to children from all nations of the world from preschool through secondary level. The curriculum was to be flexible enough to accommodate the diversity of such a student body. The overriding purpose of the school was to promote world peace by having children of the world learn together and respect each other. One goal was to have the students maintain their national identity for reentry to their own country while seeing themselves as citizens of the world. The faculty was to have a multinational composition as well, and the curriculum was offered in two languages, English and French. The original school, the International School of Geneva, still functions as one of the Foundation of International Schools serving the area of Geneva.

Adaptations and replications of this model are seen in such major cities as Brussels, Santiago, Tokyo, and New York. The United Nations School of New York has a worldwide reputation, although it is not the only international school in the United States. Interesting approaches to this model have been established throughout the country, some within the sphere of public schooling and others for children from other nations living temporarily in the United States. The Saudi Embassy in Washington supports its own Islamic academy for prekindergarten to grade 12, enrolling students from its own country as well as other Arab and non-Arab countries. The school is bilingual (English and Arabic), with Arabic being the first language of most students (Robinson, 1996). The curriculum follows an American scheme, which requires reading and writing in both languages, with more time in the school day spent perfecting English reading and writing skills (Robinson).

Although the international schools have open enrollment, tuition tends to be expensive, and schools can be exclusive where application numbers are high. Thus, their impact is restricted to a privileged group of children. On the other hand, the ambience of any international school produces a wonderful mosaic of merging cultures that simultaneously respects individual differences. The movement represents a legacy of commitment to global education and provides a foundation for all schools striving for a more inclusive global model.

International Programs for Special Education

The United Nations' Convention on the Rights of the Child (CRC) includes the right of all children to be "free from discrimination" and the right of all children to an education. As discussed in Chapter 3, Article 23 of the CRC specifically defines and protects children with disabilities, physical and mental (Castelle, 1990). The impact of culture, family values, and ethnic and national heritages on the acceptance of special needs children is discussed in Chapter 2. In this chapter, we will look at some of the common practices that are in place and reflect the spirit of the CRC.

In 1990 the largest North American organization for special education, the Council of Exceptional Children (CEC), established a division on international education. Its primary goal has been to share promising practices, research, and technologies and to disseminate information on the education and care of persons with special needs. It was timely and important to understand that special education was a "global phenomenon" (Barcham & Upton, 1993). Around the world, countries began to enact their own special education laws. Several of these will now be highlighted. They include a diverse approach to special education. Some nations favor inclusion models, others recommend separate schools or classes, and countries such as Canada and Ireland try to bridge the two approaches with eclectic special needs services (Mazurek & Winzer, 1994; White Paper on Education, 1995).

United States

In 1975, P.L. 94-142, the Education for All Handicapped Children Act (EAHCA), was passed. This law ensured that all children with disabilities were granted a free and appropriate public education, including special education and related services. Its concern for the very young child was limited, but it did provide service to children three years of age and above (Cook, Tessier, & Klein, 1996). The first amendment to this law came in 1986, when P.L. 99-457 was passed. Many feel that this amendment set the tone for early childhood special education (Bricker, 1988). Part of this law has enabled each state to design and implement early intervention programs for children from birth to age three if these children have delays in the areas of physical development, cognitive development, language/speech development, or psychosocial and self-help skills (Cook et al.). A 1990 federal law replaced the term "handicapped children" with "individuals with disabilities" (Cook et al.). Also in 1990, the Americans with Disabilities Act (ADA) provided civil rights protection to all citizens with respect to public accommodations, including transportation, day care centers, and family day care homes. In 1991, P.L. 102-119, the Individuals with Disabilities Education Act (IDEA) allowed states to include parents in program development and services for children from birth to age three and extended the notion of "free and appropriate education" (FAPE) to include three-to-five-year-old children (Cook et al.).

Great Britain

The Warnock Report of 1978 established policies and practices for special needs pupils in a school setting, policies incorporated into the 1981 Education Act (Davies & Landman, 1994). This law helped to define the concept of special education needs, included services for children from birth to age five, redefined and abolished disability categories, established assessment policies, and included parents in assessment and programming. It asked local educational authorities to provide necessary resources (Davies & Landman, 1994). Great Britain's 1988 Education Act provided all children, including those with special needs, a broad and balanced curriculum. It has been suggested that this law has helped foster integration for children with special educational needs, a philosophy that has existed in early childhood education in Great Britain for many years (Curtis, 1992).

The European Union

The establishment of the European Union (EU) enabled member nations to share and cooperate in education programming, while ensuring autonomy for each country's educational system. The Maastrict Treaty of 1991 allowed each country to maintain the precepts of their respective educational system "built on tradition, history, culture, national aims and aspirations," while committing the nations of the union to implementing laws requiring the education of special needs populations (O'Hanlon, 1993).

New Zealand

New Zealand's Education Act of 1989 entitled all students from age 5 to 19 to free enrollment and education in any state schools. The law includes provisions for special education pupils and support for their inclusion in regular classrooms. Although the philosophy of New Zealand's early childhood community promotes inclusion and early intervention (Mitchell, 1993), the law does not mandate the integration of special needs children under six years old. Furthermore, the law provides an exception that allows a school to exclude a child with special needs when overcrowding exists, thus compromising the spirit of inclusion.

China

It has been estimated that China has over 817 million children with disabilities (Yun, 1994). The education of children with disabilities is part of the basic education system according to the law of compulsory education of the People's Republic of China (Yun). The education of these students in many cases, however, is accomplished in special schools. Children in China are taught in groups rather than individually. In early childhood settings, even in play, teachers determine topics, themes, and activities. In schools where teachers speak and children listen, children with special learning needs may have difficulty.

Japan

Special education in Japan carries a narrower definition than in other industrialized countries. Special schools and special classes educate children who need special care because of physical and/or mental disabilities (Misawa, 1994). For young children, special schools are set up for the blind, the deaf, the physically challenged, and the mentally challenged. Each school has its own course of study. The School Education Law specifies criteria for entrance (Noguchi, Ogawa, Yoshihawa, & Hashimoto, 1992).

The Nordic Nations

The Nordic countries of Finland, Norway, Sweden, and Denmark are models for inclusion. They share information and research through transnational organizations such as the Nordic Council, the Advisory Committee for the Welfare of the Disabled, and the Nordic Council of Ministers (Tuunainen, 1994). Inclusion ideally takes place in the child's local neighborhood school, but even countries that have been leaders in the philosophy of inclusion are having problems implementing the approach. The Nordic countries struggle with the equitable provision of services to the remote northern areas of their countries (Tuunainen, 1994).

Russia

Russia's ultimate goal for special students is integration into mainstream society, but their means of achieving this goal is via a system of special schools. Laws and regulations mandate their education in many residential schools for special disabilities. Children are diagnosed by the medical community at birth and/or in their early childhood years, before they begin formal schooling, but these assessments do not include psychological diagnoses or psychological services (Lubovsky & Marlsinovskaja, 1992). Assignments to special placements are made by a psycho-medical educational commission or consultation. Parents can agree with the decisions or can veto these placements in favor of regular state schools.

Summary

In looking at a kaleidoscope of comparative models of early education, including special education, it becomes clear that no one nation has all the answers to what 21st-century schools need to teach in the global village. Many countries are striving to improve the education of their young citizens. As nations set agendas for school reform and restructuring, it becomes increasingly evident that many similar concerns must be addressed. To ensure the implementation of effective changes, the voices of the children, their families, and their teachers must be reflected in the process. When defining world-class standards, educators worldwide can profit from opportunities for exchanges of successful ideas in sharing sessions and studies of exemplars in early education. These exemplars can come from the public and private sectors of early childhood education, can include community learning environments beyond the school, and can represent national as well as international endeavors. The goals of comparative studies of education are to improve the existing educational practices and to charter new directions for the challenges of the future.

New technologies help to extend the global village in outreach to children and families, to forge home/school partnerships, and to infuse global education principles in instructional design and implementation.

Reflection Questions

1. How can teachers of young children join in a worldwide network of early childhood education professionals?
2. What values are there in studying educational practices of other countries?

References

Barcham, L., & Upton, G. (1993). Toward the comparative study of special education. *The Viewfinder: Expanding Boundaries and Perspectives in Special Education, 2*, 50–54.

Breitborde, M., & Swiniarski, L. (2001, September). *Family education and community power: New structure for new visions in the educational village.* Unpublished paper presented at the UKFIET "Oxford" Conference on Education and Development 2001, Oxford University, UK.

Brewer, J. (2001). *Introduction to early childhood education: Preschool through primary grades.* Boston, MA: Allyn & Bacon.

Bricker, D. (1988). Commentary: The future of early childhood/special education. *Journal of the Division of Early Childhood, 12*, 276–278.

Castelle, K. (1990). *In the child's best interest* (4th ed.). East Greenwich, RI: Plan International.

Checkley, K. (1996a, Winter). Immersed in Japanese. *ASCD Curriculum Update.*

Checkley, K. (1996b, Winter). Making a case for foreign language study. *ASCD Curriculum Update.*

Cook, R., Tessier, A., & Klein, M. (1996). *Adapting early childhood curricula for children in inclusive settings* (4th ed.). Upper Saddle River, NJ: Merrill/Prentice Hall.

Curtis, A. (1992). Early childhood education in Great Britain. In G. Woodill, J. Bernhard, & L. Prochner (Eds.), *International handbook of early childhood education* (pp. 231–250). New York: Garland Publications.

Davies, J., & Landman, M. (1994). England and Wales. In K. Mazure & M. Winzer (Eds.), *Comparative studies in special education* (pp. 452–468), Washington, DC: Gallaudet University Press.

Diem, R., Levy, T., & Van Sickle, R. (1997). Korean education: Focusing on the future. *Social Education 61*(2), pp. 83-87.

Estola, E. (1997, April). *Educational programs in Finland from early childhood through middle school: The changes and challenges.* Unpublished paper presented at the 1997 Association for Childhood Education International Conference and Exhibition, Portland, OR.

Hohenauer, P. (1995). *Speilplatz gestaltung.* Wiesbaden: Bauverlag Gmblt.

Jalongo, M. (2000). *Early childhood language arts.* Boston, MA: Allyn & Bacon.

Kalbus, J. (2000, February). In Israel building a future on ancient roots, *Educational Leadership, 57*, 5 78–80.

The kangaroo club parents handbook. (n.d.). Ilkley, UK: The Kangaroo Club Children's Day Nursery.

Lewis, C. (1995). *Educating hearts and minds: Reflections on Japanese preschool and elementary education.* Cambridge, U.K.: Cambridge University Press.

Lubovsky, V., & Marlsinovskaja, E. (1992). Russia. In G. Woodill, J. Bernhard, & L. Prochner (Eds.), *International handbook of early childhood education* (pp. 260–273). New York: Garland Press.

Martin, J. R. (1992). *The schoolhome: Rethinking schools for changing families.* Cambridge, MA: Harvard University Press.

Mazurek, K., & Winzer, M. (Eds). (1994). *Comparative studies in special education.* Washington, DC: Gallaudet University Press.

Misawa, G. (1994). Japan. In K. Mazurek & M. Winzer (Eds.), *Comparative studies in special education* (pp. 221–237). Washington, DC: Gallaudet University Press.

Mitchell, D. (1993). Special education down under. *The Viewfinder: Expanding Boundaries and Perspectives in Special Education, 2*, 22–25.

Moss, P. (1999). International standards or one of many possibilities. In World Organization for Early Childhood Education and the Association for Childhood Education International: *Early childhood education and care in the 21st century.*

Olney, MD: Association for Childhood Education International. (pp. 19–29).

Noguchi, I., Ogawa, S., Yoshihawa, T., & Hashimoto, S. (1992). Early education in Japan from ancient times to present. In G. Woodill, J. Bernhard, & L. Prochner (Eds.), *International handbook of early childhood education.* New York: Garland Press.

O'Hanlon, C. (1993). Inclusion and integration in Europe: A human rights issue. *The Viewfinder: Expanding Boundaries and Perspectives in Special Education, 2*, 47–49.

Peak, L. (1991). *Learning to go to school in Japan: The transfer from home to preschool life.* Berkeley: University of California Press.

Robinson, J. M. (1996, February). The effects of direct instruction on the reading achievement of bilingual students. Unpublished paper presented at the Eastern Educational Research Association's 19th annual conference, Cambridge, MA.

Swiniarski, L. (1984). Day care in Finland: A national commitment. *Childhood Education, 60*(3), 185–188.

Swiniarski, L. (1994a). Parent and teacher expectations for the kindergarten: An international perspective. *Global Connection, 3*(2), 4–5.

Swiniarski, L. (1994b, Summer). Head teachers speak out on British school reform: Implications for America in a transnational age. *Wisdom in Practice*, 10–13.

Swiniarski, L. Interview with International Students, Salem State College, MA.

Tiley, J., with Goldstein, C. (2000). *Understanding curriculum 2005: An introduction to outcomes-based education for foundation phase teachers.* Sandton, SA: Heinemann Publishers.

Tuunainen, K. (1994). Finland, Norway and Sweden. In K. Mazurek & M. White Paper on Education. (1995). *Charting our education future.* Dublin: Stationary Office, Government Publications.

Winzer (Eds.), *Comparative studies in special education* (pp. 389–402). Washington, DC: Gallaudet University Press.

Wright, A. (1994). Implementation of global education in the classroom: A comparison of Swedish and American educators. In Jean L. Easterly (Ed.), *Promoting global teacher education: Seven reports.* Reston, VA: Association of Teacher Education.

Yun, X. (1994). China. In K. Mazurek & M. Winzer (Eds.), *Comparative studies in special education* (pp. 163–178). Washington, DC: Gallaudet University Press.

Further Readings for Research

Chalker, D., & Haynes, R. (1994). *World class schools: New standards for education.* Lancaster, PA: Technomic.

Fulbright Teacher Program. (1996–1997). *Fulbright Teacher Exchange.* Washington, DC: U.S. Information Agency.

Heynemann, S. (1995, May). International education cooperation in the next century. *CIES Newsletter, 109,* 1, 8–9. Washington, DC: Comparative and International Education Society.

Kamerman, S. B., & Kahn, A. J. (1991). *Child care, parental leave, and the under 3's policy innovation in Europe.* New York: Auburn House.

McAdams, R. (1993). *Lessons from abroad: How other countries educate their children.* Lancaster, PA: Technomic.

Swiniarski, L. (1992). Voices from down under: Impressions of New Zealand schooling. *Childhood Education, 69*(4), 225–228.

Woodill, G. (Ed.). (1992). *International handbook of early childhood education.* New York: Garland Publishing.

Websites

Association for Childhood Education International: *http://www.acei.org*

Convention on the Rights of the Child: *http://www.unicef.org/crc*

International School of Brussels: *www.isb.be*

Sabis (International Charter Schools): *http://www.sabis.net*

UN System: *http://www.unsystem.org*

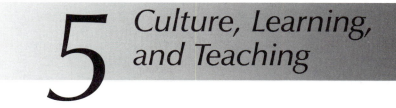

In a bilingual second-grade classroom, Ms. Chavez is conducting a math lesson on patterns. A felt board at the front of the room displays examples. She is giving directions to the children, who are already beginning to work together to create patterns with plastic shapes. The room is noisy: children are talking as she speaks to them, conferring with one another in Spanish and English about their designs, dragging desks together into small groups, seemingly bursting with energy.

Across the hall, Ms. Kim is describing the parts of a plant to her class of bilingual Cambodian third-graders. The children sit in rows, quietly attentive to the lecture. When Ms. Kim finishes her demonstration, she calls on a few students to identify the several parts of the plant in English and Khmer, and then explains the labeling task she wants them to do. She distributes plants among the children, and each begins a drawing.

Introduction: The Importance of Culture

B eyond their universal developmental characteristics, the world's children represent a plethora of diverse nationalities, cultures, ethnicities, family styles, religions, and socioeconomic classes. In our own country, our children are an increasingly complex patchwork of diverse backgrounds, due in part to America's participation in a worldwide dramatic increase in immigration. According to the United Nations High Commissioner on Refugees, more than 22 million people have sought refuge in new countries; another 30 million are displaced within their own country (Yingling, 1999). The result of this international movement is that the children in our classrooms bring with them multiple perspectives, experiences, and orientations, all of which must be considered if we are to educate them effectively. Every major educational organization today demands that teachers consider the cultural diversity of their students as they make decisions about curricula, materials, teaching strategies, and social interaction. In this chapter, we explore the impact that children's diverse cultures have on their learning, the ways culture influences us as teachers, and the need for multicultural understanding and competence.

By *culture* we mean the social backgrounds that imbue children with particular forms of knowledge, values, and expectations for behavior. Arvizu, Snyder, and Espinosa (1980) provide a definition of *culture* that conveys how wide and broad its effect is on what we know, what we value, and how we behave. In their words, culture is "a dynamic, creative, and continuous process including behaviors, values, and substance learned and shared by people that guides them in their struggle for survival and gives meaning to their lives" (p. 5).

In addition, Hernandez (1989) observes that

[Every culture is] an intertwined system of values, attitudes, beliefs, and norms that give meaning and significance to both individual and collective identity. To varying degrees, all persons are culturally bound and conditioned. Within a particular culture, they derive a sense of identity and belonging, a guide for behavior. (pp. 21–22)

Our culture defines for us what is normal, what is expected, what is the ideal way of living, and how the world works. It explains to us why the rain falls or doesn't fall; how and why people are born, grow ill, and die; and what happens to us after death. Culture explains why some people succeed and others fail. To some of us, success is a measure of our own abilities; to others, it is a matter of luck; to a third group, it is the outcome of complex factors in social and political environments; and to still others, success is the result of plain hard work. Culture guides parents in raising their children, and it guides children in learning appropriate ways to behave toward adults. Culture prescribes to adolescents how to decorate their bodies and dress themselves to be "beautiful." It leads adults to their decisions about what work and lifestyle is "worthwhile."

In the name of beauty, girls (and now boys) in America pierce their ears, noses, and more with jeweled studs or hoops. Their counterparts in some African tribes extend their lips with bones or metal. North Americans turn to aspirin and aspirin substitutes to relieve pain and fever, while Cambodian parents rub their children's ill bodies with coins to make resuscitative blood flow faster to the injured area. Christian Scientists use concentrated prayer to restore health to the sick, and traditional Native Americans rely in part on shamans for healing rituals. What we "know" about health and beauty and the "right way to live" depends on our culture, and these beliefs are so strong and firm that we do not easily give them up.

Culture, then, defines what we know, how we behave, and what we believe. It gives people within particular groups a feeling of identity and belonging and a sense that life is predictable and logical. Our culture may be associated with our ethnic group or nationality, but such a broad definition also applies to people within particular geographic areas, genders, age groups, or life situations. For example, one of the authors of this book is Jewish. This means that she grew up valuing education and a strong family, as well as having a sense of being "different" (especially at Christmas). Two of the authors grew up in New England, where people tend to value history and tradition, where a warm home environment is important (especially in winter), and where speech is faster paced and more direct than in other areas of the country. All three of us are women and mothers, which means that for many years what we "knew" were things such as how to get home in time to get the kids to soccer practice. We had the ability in those days to distinguish among the various antibiotics available to treat ear and throat infections and to tell the difference between the stances of various Red Sox pitchers. Finally, as teachers and now professors, we belong to the culture associated with an academic life and know things such as how to distinguish an "A" paper from a "B" paper.

One of us tells a story of buying lingerie at a fine department store early in her teaching career and being asked by the salesperson, for no apparent reason, "You're a teacher, aren't you?" Somehow, belonging to a culture gives us a way of behaving that identifies us as a member of that group, even if we don't realize it ourselves. Traveling abroad, an American can often recognize another American, though they may be from

The importance of culture.

very different parts of the country. Meeting someone for the first time, we draw conclusions about who that person is based on speech, dress, demeanor, and behavior. We decide whether that person is like us or not, whether we will like the person or not, whether we will have something to talk about.

Cultural groups change their boundaries and their members. We divide ourselves into large groups and smaller subgroups, depending on the situation and the historical, sociological, or political context. For example, the world is a continually changing, continually expanding and shrinking collection of identified nationalities, cultures, and ethnicities. What is for a while one country with one national identity becomes a few years later a seething mass of diverse and conflicting ethnic and religious groups. The unified Yugoslavia of 1980 became a decade later a nation with tragic competition among Bosnians, Serbs, and Muslims. But what the outside world may perceive as one nation with a particular character and culture—for example, India—becomes with deeper knowledge a collection of many states, each with its official language and religion. In the southern section of the United States, people categorize themselves as white or black, and the religious among them consider themselves members of distinct Protestant sects, while in Massachusetts, white people identify themselves as Italian, Irish, Polish, or French-Canadian. These historically Catholic groups often attend separate churches in the same city; St. Joseph's might be the "French" church and St. Ann's, the "Irish." We struggle to describe a group of children whose first language is Spanish, using labels such as "Hispanic," "Latino," "Latin American," and "Caribbean culture." But although Puerto Ricans and Dominicans, for example, share historical and cultural traditions, great differences exist between them, including the fact that Puerto Ricans are American citizens with rights appertaining, and the Dominican Republic has for some time been an independent nation. Haitians, though Caribbean, do not speak Spanish; Colombians include native Indians and people of African and Spanish descent, all of whom come in many skin colors; Cuban and Mexican immigrants come to the United States for very different reasons with very different results. It is, in fact, inaccurate to think of these groups as one monolithic entity.

Cultural Identity and Behavior

Political and historical events affect how people identify themselves by cultural group and what defines the experience of those groups. Cultural characteristics associated with ethnic origin, family style, religion, gender, age, occupation, social class, geographic region, and historical time interrelate to define the perceptions, behaviors, and beliefs of members of those groups. For example, many young African American boys live in East Coast cities in families headed by single mothers or grandmothers. These women may work at low-paying part-time jobs or receive public assistance. Because they want to keep their children safe from harm out on the streets, they may confine

A Kenyan quilt symbolizes cultural values.

the boys to their apartments, where they watch a lot of television. The commercial programs they watch are often full of sensationalist reports of "news" events and media advertising that promotes the acquisition of expensive material objects. This lifestyle influences their valuing particular notions of what is real and good and their behaving in ways that conform to popular culture. Education for the sake of greater knowledge and fulfillment has little place in such a world.

Everyone needs a sense of belonging, a feeling of being part of a community. Many African American families are deeply religious and look to the church for spiritual and social support. Children in these families spend Sundays in church, watched over not only by their own parents but by the church community as a whole. Jonathan Kozol describes the importance of a church in one New York City Bronx neighborhood in the lives of children for whom the church functions as a haven in an otherwise difficult world (Kozol, 2000, 1995). Without this kind of support, children locked away from a traditional family life and neighborhood may come to define *family* as "gang." Sometime in adolescence, African American boys may come to believe that their ethnic group or social class is "marginalized" in America, that the white middle-class dominant group will not allow them, as it did not allow their ancestors, entrance into mainstream American culture. As adolescents in search of identity and group membership, they may respond by creating an "oppositional" culture, consisting of everything that whites *don't* value, *don't* know and *don't* do. The anthropologist John Ogbu considers this effort to maintain an alternative cultural identity a positive response of human adaptation, even while in practice it is damaging to the wider society as well as to the health and welfare of the individuals within the oppositional group (Ogbu, 1993).

As a second example, young European American girls who live in two-parent nuclear families in eastern seaboard suburbs in relative wealth and whose parents work at professional jobs to pay for private schooling, health care, recreational facilities, and domestic help learn a version of reality different from that of the young urban blacks mentioned in the first example. To these children, education is a direct means to high-paying careers and material objects. Families are defined as comprising two heterosexual parents and their children; grandparents and other old people care for themselves until that is no longer possible, at which point they move to retirement facilities or nursing homes. These children may come to believe that any individual's success in life is limited by his or her own discipline and direction, and that anything other than a nice house (and hired help to maintain it), professional jobs, and pretty clothes is unfortunate, weird, and to be avoided.

A third group of children may live on the Navajo reservation in Arizona or in the Australian bush far from the world of urban affairs, taught by tribal elders who weave stories and fashion objects in patterns that represent many generations of spiritual knowledge. Their daily lives involve making and growing things, repairing shelters and vehicles, and finding ways to keep warm and dry. They learn very different lessons about the way the world works and about the place of human beings in it. Their knowledge and appreciation of the physical world is acute, and education to them must have practical value. They learn that physical, social, and spiritual realities are of one piece and that individuals are limited by natural events in their ability to make things happen. They learn that one must observe carefully and for long periods of time before trying out a new skill, for failure may have fatal consequences.

Cultural beliefs and practices change as life conditions change. As technology advances, new knowledge about the way the world works and about the characteristics of its peoples increases and is communicated to more people. As cultural groups move from place to place and interact with other groups, traditional culture bends to accommodate new conditions and new information. Jewish immigrants to America at the turn of the 20th century acceded to the American work week and its Christian basis by working on their traditional Saturday Sabbath. With difficulty, they went to work on their holy day when they should have been resting and studying the Torah. Immigrant Cambodian parents struggle with the alien "American" notion of "dating," inimical to the Cambodian tradition of arranging marriages. Caribbean islanders come to America bewildered by the faster pace, the driving ambition of urban professional life, and the loss of intimate and familiar relationships of village life. In all these cases, the children take on "American" ways and values at the cost of family conflict and their own cultural confusion. Nieto's book of case studies (1996) is filled with examples of students who remember feeling torn between loyalty to their families and the need to fit in with friends. Their voices speak of the variety of responses children can have to this dilemma as they grow away from parents into the world of school and their peers. Some become prideful of their background and value its uniqueness; others are quick to assimilate and say they are "just American."

Cristina Igoa (1995) tells a poignant story of a young Chinese immigrant boy who called himself "Dennis." He came into her language resource room having spent the previous year without speaking to anyone. He arrived at her door "small, serious, and visibly frightened" (p. 13). When she asked him to write his name in Chinese, he yelled "No!" She read stories to him about heroic animals overcoming great odds and worked with him on developing filmstrips and stories. During the course of his two years with her, he spoke more and more, describing the plots of his stories. At the end of the two years, he signed his name, Qui Liang, to his last filmstrip, in Chinese characters.

The fundamental values of new immigrant groups may puzzle and disturb the teachers of their children. For example, Puerto Ricans and Dominicans place a higher priority on family and religious obligations than on formal education. This means that if a Dominican family needs the help of an older child to care for siblings during the mother's illness or to contribute to the household income, that child will stay out of school to help at home or leave high school before graduating. When celebrating the birth of Christ means traveling "home" to be with family members for the holiday season, Puerto Rican children may be absent for three or four weeks during December and January.

Placing family before school is not peculiar to these new immigrant groups. At the turn of the 20th century, southern Italian families pulled their children out of school for similar reasons. In 1910, if an Italian immigrant family needed a child's help at home, that child would leave school temporarily or permanently as the situation demanded. In other groups, such as the Vietnamese immigrants of today or the Russian Jewish families of yesterday, families "sacrificed" their own needs in order to school their children. Teachers of Southeast Asian children report that most of these children come to school faithfully, with homework "done," despite any troubles at home, sometimes even if they did not really understand the homework.

Obviously, it is easier for teachers if children come to school with homework in hand; on the other hand, the Southeast Asian families' clear separation of home and school and their concern for privacy can be as problematical as the extended absences of Caribbean children. Teachers of Vietnamese and Cambodian children sometimes report that it is difficult to communicate with parents and to get them to come to school for programs and conferences. Southeast Asian parents have been raised to believe that teachers have complete authority over the education of children. For many of these parents, coming to school for discussion would imply that they were questioning or criticizing teachers. In Southeast Asian culture, one does not question people in positions of authority. Parents assume that they have no part to play in school other than to make sure their children come every day and do what they are asked to do. For American teachers who value parent-teacher interaction and parent participation in classrooms, this noninvolvement may be frustrating.

Different cultures respond differently to the notion of "special needs" and learning exceptionalities (see Chapter 7). In some cultures—for example, Mexican and Japanese—to need special classes or teachers means one is *loco* or not living up to one's responsibilities for study. Traditional values and orientations to learning may affect decisions about what degree and type of special needs programming a culture will support and whether parents will allow their children to make use of these services. In our own country, cultures differ with respect to their willingness to avail their children of bilingual education. Latino parents generally support bilingual education and call for curricula that preserve their cultures in public schools, while Southeast Asian immigrants expect their children to struggle along in mainstream English-speaking classrooms until they learn English on their own.

The trick for educators is to understand how culture works on the beliefs and behavior of children and their families. We believe that to respond sensitively and effectively to children from various cultures, teachers must respect their diversity while working toward a goal of social unity in the classroom and the community. If we ignore the impact of culture on differences in perception, values, language, cognition, and behavior in young children, we may find ourselves making "top-down" decisions about curriculum and instruction for children who may listen but not hear or understand what we're trying to teach them.

Culture and Language

We know now that children's culture affects not only what they know and what they value but also what they understand and how they express themselves. A child's culture, passed along primarily through her family, conveys messages about what to expect from life, what to pay attention to, and how to respond. The most powerful medium for conveying culture is language. Words and patterns of speech give us labels for identifying concepts and for communicating with each other. Anyone who listens to parent–child oral interactions or to the informal speech of children at play realizes that what is being learned is far more than words.

How we speak and what we say bonds us to others who communicate as we do. We may change our dialect and our vocabulary to show our identification with different groups in our lives. For example, it is important for Japanese American (Nisei) youths in Hawaii to speak pidgin with each other to distinguish themselves from native Japanese tourists and from other ethnic groups. The ability to speak pidgin identifies Nisei Hawaiians as "local guys." One Nisei student who learned to speak Japanese at home from her mother but never learned to speak pidgin told one of the authors that she is called "white" by her peers (Breitborde, personal conversation). "Local Japanese" watch Japanese cartoons and videos and can understand their Japanese-speaking parents, but they do not communicate among themselves in Japanese (Kondo, 1996).

Language is so powerful that it can structure what we see and hear. It is said that the Inuits have many more words than, for example, Americans to describe snow. While some of us in colder climates know the difference between "sleet" and "powder," we hardly come close to the precise distinctions of the Inuit, who have different words for snow of different textures, water content, formations, and locations. Their ability to distinguish so many different kinds of snow does not come from greater visual acuity but from the meaningfulness of these kinds of snow in how they live their daily lives. To give another example closer to the authors' own experience, our children make distinctions between "rap," "heavy metal," and other kinds of popular music, all of which might sound the same to their parents. In other words, our very perception—what we pay attention to and how we see or hear things—is structured by our culture.

Basil Bernstein's (1975) research in England on the interaction of social class, authority relations in the family, and local speech patterns demonstrates how culture constructs a child's perceptions and behavior and is conveyed through language. He researched differences in patterns of discipline within working-class and middle-class families and found that authority for working-class parents rested in their very positions as parents ("You may not do this because I am your father and I say so"), whereas authority for middle-class parents rested in the objective merit of their argument or their expertise ("You may not do this because I know from my experience that you may get hurt"). In the second case, the pattern of discipline requires a lengthier explanation (i.e., more words).

In one study, Bernstein presented a series of pictures depicting a group of boys playing ball, a broken window, and a man leaning out of the window shaking his fist at the group. Bernstein asked two groups of boys—one working class, the other middle class—to tell the story illustrated by the pictures. The working-class children's version of the story went something like this: "They were playing ball. It went through the window. He yelled at them." In the middle-class version, the children used more words and more precise words: "The boys were playing ball. One of them accidentally hit the ball through a neighbor's window. The man leaned out the window and shook his fist at them, shouting at them for breaking it."

Bernstein described the speech patterns of the first group as "restricted," noting the limited number of words they used, the generalized nouns and imprecise pronouns, and the shorter sentences. He concluded that restricted speech codes were the logical result of the boys' limited life experiences, their daily face-to-face interactions with the same friends and neighbors, and the restricted explanations given them by their parents on disciplinary issues. The "elaborated" speech code of the second, middle-class, group involved the use of precise vocabulary, longer sentences, and more descriptive words, such as adjectives and adverbs. Bernstein's surmise was that the middle-class boys did not assume that the listener shared their experiences, and therefore they knew that they must choose their words carefully. He felt that elaborated speech codes resulted from middle-class children's wider experience with more and diverse events and people: for instance, visits to businesses, museums, and libraries and rides on trains. Working-class boys assumed a similarity between speaker and listener. Their sense of neighborhood, belonging, and acceptance was strong, and this security allowed them to make false assumptions about what the listener knew. The second group assumed no such connection or sense of belonging but exhibited a greater ability to interact effectively with a wider range of people. Thus, Bernstein concluded that there were positive and negative aspects to different speech patterns associated with social class and family patterns. With respect to schooling, however, traditional classrooms based on verbalizing abstract, objective concepts would be easier to understand for children with wider experiences and elaborated speech codes. The "cultural fit" between middle-class children and traditional schooling made it more likely that they would succeed in school.

A child who lives in a neighborhood that is tightly knit and stable and whose experience is relatively restricted to the people of that neighborhood will take on the speech patterns and the cultural perceptions and assumptions associated with that neighborhood. Heath (1982) studied the speech patterns of black and white families living in the Appalachians. She described in great detail the differences between the linguistic patterns of these two groups, particularly the way parents asked questions and gave information. She found that the middle-income white parents used a question-and-answer pattern with children, which prepared them well for the typical question-and-answer format of traditional classrooms. Parents would test children's knowledge by their questions rather than ask them for information (e.g., "What color is the ball? Yes, red, very good!") The lower-income black parents would tell stories, relate information, and give commands rather than ask questions to which they already knew the answers. These black children, entering classrooms where teachers constantly asked questions, were confused; why should they respond to questions when the teacher obviously already knew the answers? The children's language was colorful and descriptive but did not fit the linguistic requirements of the classroom.

The language patterns of Native American groups, in contrast to those of white Anglo Americans, provide an interesting example of great difference and potential for misunderstanding. Phillips (1983) found clear differences in the language use of the Indians of Warm Springs Reservation in the Pacific Northwest and local whites. Observing the language and behavior of adults in community meetings, she discovered that the amount of speech, the interaction among participants, and the process of conveying information and coming to a group decision were very different for these two groups. White Americans in a community meeting typically varied in how much and how long each member spoke. Speakers would often refer to what had just been said and attempt to connect their point to the one made by the previous speaker. Body language for this group included head, hand, and whole-body movement and the use of the face to convey expression. As a rule, the group continued the discussion until some resolution or decision was reached, whether it was by vote, general consensus, or a plan for action.

In the Native American group meeting, the amount and length of speech was fairly equal, with all members having a turn to speak their minds. There was no expectation that a speaker would connect a point to what the speaker just before had said; members made their own points, without referring to the speaker before. There was little in the way of facial movement or gestures. When all who wanted to speak had spoken, everyone went home. The assumption was that people needed time to reflect on all that had been said. Many weeks might go by before the group came together for another meeting, at which time they might reach a general conclusion.

From these two examples we can learn that there were significant differences not only in how each group spoke but also in what each group believed to be the function of language and in the time required to think and come to a decision. The white group assumed that people were not equal in terms of the information they had, the worth of their ideas, and their ability to articulate and argue their points. This group assumed that articulate language included not just speech but persuasive gestures and movements. It sought efficiency by working toward resolution at the end of each discussion. The Indians accorded respect to each person there, apart from what he or she had to say. Points were made without embellishment or the need to respond. There was little arguing but much listening. And this group wanted much more time for individuals to "process" the information.

Problems will occur when native children who exhibit this kind of language behavior are taught by white teachers raised in their own linguistic culture. White teachers may assume that Indian children who are quieter, speak less and show much less facial expression, and are accustomed to having more time to reflect before answering or coming to conclusions may not know the answer or may not be interested in the subject matter at hand. Indian children may not be able to process information as quickly as their white teachers convey it. Just imagine a slow-talking Texan talking to a fast-talking New Yorker (or, in one author's case, a parent trying to keep up with the speech of a fast-talking, mumbling, teenager). One is not stupid and the other smart; the problem lies in the differences between linguistic styles.

Culture dictates who may talk to whom and how. Iranian men argue long and loudly with each other, interrupting and gesticulating. If we were to look in on an Italian American or Jewish American family dinner, we might hear (and see) the same sort of vociferous dialogue, although in the Jewish household the role of father is less authoritarian, and the degree to which a child is allowed to argue with him may be greater.

Language differences also follow gender lines. In many cultures, women talk a lot and argue with each other but speak differently, and less, with men. In America, where men and women are supposed to be equally entitled to speak, differences still exist in what is considered appropriate speech for each. What is considered appropriately assertive speech in men may be deemed inappropriate, unfeminine, and aggressive

Rebekah covers her eyes in the traditional manner as she blesses the Sabbath candles.

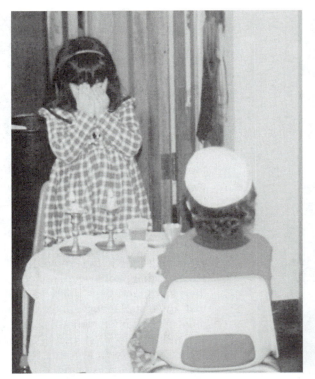

speech in women. Classroom research from kindergarten through college settings still shows differences in the frequency with which boys and girls respond to teacher questions or initiate speaking (see, for example, Krupnick, 1985; Wellesley College Center for Research on Women, 1992).

Apart from the issue of amount and perceived appropriateness of speech, differences exist in the way men and women use language. These differences can lead to disturbing miscommunication. A recent popular book, which is actually based on the scholarly work of its anthropologist author, Deborah Tannen, is entitled *You Just Don't Understand: Women and Men in Conversation* (1990). According to Tannen, male discourse often focuses on one here-and-now behavior or issue and is directed toward taking action (e.g., "I want to go to a movie tonight. What's playing?"). His female partner, on the other hand, may want to discuss all the available options, their different feelings about these choices, potential conflicts of interest with the other couple with whom they are going out, whether they should eat first or later, how they will meet the needs of the one friend who is vegetarian, and the fact that, because the man will have to get up early in the morning to go to work, time is at issue. All this may be mind-boggling to the fellow, who may balk at bringing all these variables into the discussion. He might say, "Can't we just keep this simple? Why do you have to complicate things?"

To which she may answer, "You are so insensitive. Can't you for once consider someone's feelings other than your own?" Tannen later wrote an article for the *Chronicle of Higher Education,* applying her findings to the world of the classroom (1991) and asking teachers to recognize and respect differences in the way male and female students use language. Her findings move male and female teachers to look at the way they use language themselves as well as their interactions with boys and girls in their classrooms. Perhaps male students tend to dominate classroom discussions that are subject focussed, while female students are more concerned with social and emotional issues. These studies imply that girls may be more sensitive to the social context of the classroom itself, including who is talking and how they are perceived; perhaps this very sensitivity limits their speaking out as much.

Gilligan's observations of moral reasoning in adolescent girls (1982) imply that girls often consider the feelings of others in making decisions and that they will say "It depends" when asked to make a judgment. "It depends" means girls have in mind much more than the situation that the researcher describes; they want to consider all the "what ifs," will not commit to a moral judgment without knowing all the ramifications and effects on everyone involved in the situation, and will probably want to discuss their thoughts with others. Gilligan gave girls Lawrence Kohlberg's classic "Heinz" dilemma (Kohlberg, 1984), in which a husband who needs to get his wife life-saving medicine at 2:00 A.M. calls the pharmacist at home to ask him to open the store. When the pharmacist refuses to serve him, he must decide whether to break in and steal the drug that will save her life. Typically, boys would hear the description of the moral dilemma and come to a conclusion based on their own analysis and interpretation of what they considered to be the right thing to do. Gilligan's girls asked a lot of questions first, such as, "How much does Herr Heinz love his wife?" and "What will his sentence be if he is caught and convicted?" They were sometimes unwilling to answer without more information covering all possible personal contingencies.

Another factor in culture-based communication is the degree to which a culture is historically "oral" or "literate" (Ong, 1982). In some cultures, education is carried from generation to generation through strong oral traditions. Among Native Americans, for example, stories and myths are told and retold to convey great truths to children. African Americans are also the recipients of a long history of orality, conveyed not only through stories but through chanting, music, and the participatory call-and-response of strong religious traditions (Goss & Barnes, 1989). "Testifying" out loud in church, complete with gestures and movements conveying strong feeling, demonstrates to God and congregation one's strong faith. The brilliant poetic rhetoric of a Reverend Martin Luther King or a Jesse Jackson and the lyrical messages of blues and rap are part of the tradition of teaching and learning through oral language. On the other hand, Asian Buddhism, European Judaism, and Christianity are literacy-based cultures. Knowledge is contained in important religious texts—Buddhist sutras, the Torah, the New Testament—that one masters through careful study. The printed word conveys sacred truths, although these cultures differ in the degree to which interpretation of, and even arguing about, those truths is allowed (Abramson, 2001). Traditionally, schools used these texts as material for learning to read, the justification for reading being to understand the word of God or the "right path."

Whether children come from a culture that values orality or literacy as a way to knowledge will affect how well they are prepared for traditional American book-based schooling, as well as how much meaning that schooling will have for them. Children who are raised to respect the authority of good books, whose family life reinforces the importance of reading and study, will have few problems adjusting to the world of American schools. Those who are accustomed to receiving and exchanging information through elaborate stories, whose traditional way of learning is through listening and telling and observing, may have problems spending so much time in school reading. Teachers who understand and respect this oral tradition will find ways to link oral traditions with the teaching of literacy (e.g., using children's own stories as reading materials or teaching history through journals and first-person accounts).

Culture, Cognition, and Learning Style

While some children seem to easily master information that is ordered and abstract, others understand information better if it is connected to real-world examples. Some learn better by themselves; others need to exchange ideas with their peers. Some of you may have been successful at learning multiplication by memorizing tables of mathematical patterns ($3 \times 4=12$, $3 \times 5=15$, and so on); others learned to multiply by manipulating calibrated objects. For some of you, the best environment for study is a quiet room with no distractions and no other people. Others need the support of a study group before an exam. Some would prefer to hear a good lecture on Australia; others, to read a good book on the same subject. Still others need the direct experience of a trip down under. Some of you can read a road map to find your way to your friend's new home out of town; others prefer verbal directions. Many of you need to follow another car to make the trip the first time; afterward you'll be able to find your own way.

Evidence shows that culture affects how people receive, process, and organize information and, in general, how they learn. Judith Hankes, a Native American, has given us a poignant account of her difficulties with school math and her resultant belief that she couldn't "do" math (1993). Meanwhile, she and her brother had spent many childhood years tracking in the woods, estimating distances, seeing and using the mathematical patterns in nature. Finding that the higher up in mathematics she went, the more her "intuitive" skills seemed to apply, she resolved as an adult to "master" mathematics so that she could become an educator and teach children differently. What we know about native cultures makes it obvious that for native children, learning must be connected to the physical world. Successful education for Indian peoples involved learning that bore results, learning that allowed one to survive on the land.

A clear example of the wisdom of basing teaching strategies in cultural tradition lies in the experience of the Kamehameha schools of Hawaii (Au & Jordan, 1981). Like other children of native cultures, Hawaiian children were typically not successful in "mainstream" schools. Dropout and absentee rates were high and test scores low until culturally sensitive educators began to use Hawaiian traditions to inform school curricula. For example, math was taught through fabric design and manipulation. For children of this oral culture, reading was taught through "talk-stories." Rather than being required to do "independent work," children learned in cooperative groups. Families (for Hawaiians, this could include extended relatives, friends, and neighbors) participated in school projects. Preschool teachers traveled to children's homes and playgrounds. Children were active and involved, and test scores rose. Unfortunately, a change in school leadership and economic decline resulted in the discontinuation of this successful program, but its elements have been incorporated to some degree into the new, more traditional, curriculum.

Another example of how an emphasis on "family" may impact school learning can be found among Hispanic or Latino/a Americans. Central to the cultural mores of many Latino groups is the notion of *familia* and the extent to which individual achievement is contexted in the achievement of the referent group. Griggs & Dunn (1996), Trueba (1998), and Abu-Nader (1993) detail the centrality of the group in Latino children's thinking, and describe strategies by which teachers can foster learning by incorporating *familia* in instructional organization and activities: for example, by using cooperative learning structures and relating to students in personal, parental ways.

Janice Hale-Benson, an African American, wrote a somewhat controversial book (1986) entitled *Black Children: Their Roots, Culture, and Learning Styles*. She described

Children are entranced by stories in a family daycare setting in Boston, Massachusetts.

the learning style of African Americans as "relational," in contrast to the "analytical" style of white Americans. She characterized a relational style as emphasizing social interactions, specificity and the here-and-now, physical movement, connection and continuity, variation, divergent thinking, and inductive reasoning. The analytical style dominating white, middle-class culture and traditional school classrooms, she said, was characterized by a focus on objects and ideas, generalized rules and standards, physical restrictions, decontextualized information, conformity, convergent thinking, and deductive reasoning. Interestingly, she attributed the relational style of black children to their roots in Africa, whose cultures valued spirituality, harmony with nature, expressive movement, creative thinking, interconnectedness, and person-to-person contact. Hale-Benson and others (Irvine, 1991) call for teachers of black children to use their culture to build meaningful curricula, much in the way the Kamehameha schools did for native Hawaiians, by using music, movement, storytelling, and each other as vehicles for learning.

Hale-Benson's work has been criticized as supporting stereotypes and overgeneralizations. Some argue that many white Americans have learning styles that appear to be relational and black Americans are often abstract learners. In fact, research on gender differences for whites and blacks in ways of thinking and learning (Belenky, Clinchy, Boldberger, & Tarule, 1986; Maher, 1987) seems to overlap these categorical definitions, with women displaying a more relational style and men a more abstract one. Any attempt at categorizing and generalizing comes dangerously close to unfair stereotyping, particularly for groups who have been as "mixed" as and whose experiences have been as multivariate as those of African Americans. Blacks live in urban, suburban, and rural environments and in northern cities and southern towns; they have a variety of lifestyles; and they are certainly not culturally or racially "pure." Yet Hale-Benson's linking of learning style to cultural and historical roots is interesting and valuable if it helps us understand and accept that the way people live influences how they learn. To the extent that a cultural community feels itself to be a community and shares similar experiences and a common history, tradition, language, and identity, there may indeed be typical patterns of responding to and expressing information in that community. Moreover, the fact that African American children have as a group had significantly lower success in schools, as measured by test scores and retention/dropout rates, raises serious questions about whether and how their schools are meeting their needs. Gloria Ladson-Billings (1994), Beverly Daniel Tatum (1997), and Lisa Delpit (1994) address these questions in seminal works that note the importance of black children's cultural identity in their educational experience. These authors describe teachers who have been successful in relating well to black students and in designing instruction that is meaningful and effective.

Schools in Japan and Cambodia, among those in other Asian nations, consist of large classes of 40 or more students where children learn through reading, listening, and rote memory. They are often expected to work by themselves and to put in long hours of study on their own. The larger culture assumes that all people are responsible for their own actions during their lifetime and should learn and follow "the right way." One's "locus of control" is within oneself—people make their own success and are responsible for their own failure. Students, therefore, are responsible for their own learning.

In Asian classrooms, teachers present information in carefully sequenced lessons while students listen attentively and remember. There are no individual excuses for not doing the work or mastering the information other than insufficient study. Japanese and Cambodian children grow up expecting to receive information in ordered ways, to process it in ordered ways, and to be asked to recall it in ordered ways. The emphasis on order, form, and balance appears in learning as it does in life. This may help explain why American teachers so often see Asian children trying to memorize information they do not really understand.

Finally, we would be remiss if we did not connect the groundbreaking work of Howard Gardner to the matter of culture-based cognition and learning. Gardner's theory of "multiple intelligences" exploded the idea that people were either intelligent or not (1983). His observations led him to refuse to accept the traditional notion that intelligence means only being linguistically or mathematically able, the talents typically measured by standard IQ tests. Gardner expanded the concept of intelligence to include eight varieties, including linguistic and mathematical/logical but also spatial, kinesthetic, musical, interpersonal, intrapersonal, and naturalistic. He essentially gave equal respect to abilities in each of these categories (e.g., an ability to execute a complicated gymnastic move; to reproduce a tune without effort; to recognize, manipulate, and design visual patterns; to empathize with another's feelings; and to know oneself thoroughly). He suspects that we have multiple intelligences in varying degrees.

It is interesting to speculate on the cultural bases for some of these intelligences. One might call the ability of the native Hawaiian to navigate by the stars "spatial intelligence," a talent that is reflected in much of Hawaiian culture today. Elements of traditional African life, including the need for speed and athleticism and the salience of music and rhythm as communication modes, may appear as kinesthetic and musical intelligence. The close family and village life of Caribbean peoples may be reflected in an interpersonal and linguistic intelligence that attracts children to group activities and lots of talk. The emphasis on order, balance, form, and hierarchies may inform a logical-mathematical intelligence among many Southeast Asians.

Again, we must be careful not to stereotype and overgeneralize. In any group of Puerto Rican, Japanese, or native Hawaiian children we will find a variety of cognitive and learning styles and talents. The important thing to remember is that we must not expect children to learn the same way. Understanding and valuing cultural differences may help us change our teaching strategies to respond more effectively when children are having trouble learning. We have known for a long time that children are not blank slates whose empty heads can be filled with the information we intend them to have. What we say to them will never be exactly what they hear. What they understand depends on what they already know and on how well the new information fits in with the old. As Piaget told us, children come to us with ideas and mental pathways already constructed, albeit perhaps half formed or misinformed. Learning is interactive; it requires a learner as much as a teacher.

Much of what children come to us with is based on their culture, which helps define what they know, what they value, and what they think is normal. If they are to understand, we educators had better know something about "where they're coming from." In classrooms that are increasingly multicultural, we cannot expect that the culture that has informed us is the culture that informs them. In attempting to provide at least basic education to all the children of the world, educators probably need to take account of the plethora of cultural contexts in which the world's children find themselves. Efforts to export someone else's version of education without reference to or respect for children's particular cultural experiences are bound to fail.

Culture and Teaching

Finally, teachers' own cultures affect our assumptions about learning and teaching and our decisions about what and how we teach. Our expectations for children, our hopes and dreams for them, are influenced by our cultural background. Perhaps we grew up in a culture with a long tradition of study and scholarship, where being a teacher was a mark of honor and high intelligence, where learning was considered to be its own reward. In such a culture, teachers were never to be defied or argued with. Conversely, we may have grown up in a culture where an "honest day's work" meant physical labor and a physical product created by one's own skilled hands. Learning in this culture would have value only in demonstrable practical outcomes, and books might be only short-term tools for instruction, of lesser worth than direct, hands-on experience. School would be worthwhile only to the extent that it was useful; working and contributing to the family economy would be far more important. Perhaps we grew up with serious and lively debates around the dinner table, with points given for logic and loud articulation. Perhaps we grew up with clear understandings of our subservience to the authority of our parents and those in higher positions or of greater age. If we were schooled in Japan, we might assume that teaching is directed to groups; teachers in America, on the other hand, tend to teach to individuals, even when they are organized into groups (Hamilton, Blumenfeld, Hiroshi, & Miura, 1991).

We teachers might look to our own backgrounds to understand "where we are coming from" in our teaching and our expectations for student behavior and performance. The children in our charge may have arrived in our classrooms with assumptions and understandings far different from our own. Lisa Delpit (1994) makes a strong case for teachers' self-reflection on the matter of recognizing our own cultural assumptions. While America's public schools are increasingly populated by children of color, their teachers are mainly white, a situation likely to continue and grow given the disproportionate failure rates of candidates of color on high-stakes state teacher-credentialing tests (Fowler, 2001). Delpit is concerned about white teachers' ability to relate to and understand the needs of "other people's children," that is, children of color. She asks us, for example, to reexamine what our profession considers "best practices" in literacy education and be flexible enough to change and adapt these practices to particular populations. "Whole language," she says, does not serve the needs of many African American children, for whom "fluency" is not as important as the acquisition of the conventions of standard English in the context of respect for their "first language," the language of home and neighborhood. But Peggy McIntosh and others (McIntosh,

1989; Tatum, 1997; Gannon, 2001) ask white teachers to begin the process of understanding "other people's children" by acknowledging their "white privilege" and the pervasive effects of racism on the behavior and attitudes of students of color.

> As a White educator, it is imperative that I inform myself about who is in my classroom and consider the implications of these diverse racial identities and my own for the learning environment. In order to do this, I need to engage in self-discovery, owning my whiteness and acknowledging my White skin privilege. (Gannon, 2001)

Gary Howard, a white man of English origins, has written extensively about how his exploration into his own background has helped him appreciate the rich and interesting cultural roots we all bring to this diverse world. The "luxury of ignorance" that had characterized the first part of his life gave way to his constructing an authentic white identity for himself, an identity that then allowed him to enter into a "dance of diversity" as a person of a culture interacting respectfully and equally with people of other cultures (2001). As teachers, we play important roles in the lives of our students, as decision makers, information disseminators, instructors, and role models. To do this work effectively, it is important to be culturally competent and to include ourselves in the process of teaching and learning.

Summary

This chapter defines *culture* broadly as the sum of knowledge, behaviors, and attitudes that help us communicate with each other and negotiate through life. It argues that culture is an important part of one's identity, an identity that may be problematical or confusing to ethnic-minority and immigrant children. We have reviewed differences among cultures in values and norms, linguistic patterns, and styles of learning and teaching, all of which may affect the expectations or performance of children and their teachers. We concluded by advocating that teachers must know and respect the cultural backgrounds of their students as well as their own and expect that cultural differences will call for culturally sensitive teaching responses.

Reflection Questions

1. What resources can teachers use to learn about the backgrounds of children in their classes whose cultures are unfamiliar to them?
2. How can a teacher both support children's pride in their first languages and strengthen their ability to achieve literacy in standard English?
3. How has your culture influenced your conceptions of "good teaching" and "good learning"?

References

Abramson, H. (2001, Summer). Studying the Talmud: 400 repetitions of the divine voice. *Thought and Action: The NEA Journal. XVII*(1), 9–18.

Abu-Nader, J. (1993). Meeting the needs of multicultural classrooms: Family values and the motivation of minority students. In M. J. O'Hair, & S. J. Odell (Eds.). *Diversity and Teaching: Teacher Education Yearbook I.* Orlando, FL: Harcourt Brace.

Arvizu, S. F., Snyder, W. A., & Espinosa, P. T. (1980). *Demystifying the concept of culture: Theoretical and conceptual tools. Bilingual Education Paper Series, 3*(11). Los Angeles: Evaluation, Dissemination and Assessment Center, California State University.

Au, K., & and Jordan, C. (1981). Teaching reading to Hawaiian children: Finding a culturally appropriate solution. In H. Trueba, G. Guthrie, & K. Au (Eds.), *Culture and the bilingual classroom: Studies in classroom ethnography.* Rowley, MA: Newbury House.

Belenky, M., Clinchy, B., Goldberger, N., & Tarule, J. M. (1986). *Women's ways of knowing: The development of self, voice and mind.* New York: Basic Books.

Bernstein, B. (1975). *Class, codes and control* (vol. 3: *Towards a theory of educational transmissions*). London: Routledge & Kegan Paul.

Breitborde, M. L. (1996). Personal conversation, Honolulu, HI.

Delpit, L. (1994). *Other people's children: Cultural conflict in the classroom.* New York: New Press.

Fowler, R. C. (2001). What do the Massachusetts Teacher Tests say about American education? *Phi Delta Kappan 82*(1), 773–780.

Gannon, M. M. (2001). What could a white girl from South Boston possibly know about racism? Reflections of a social justice educator. In C. Clark & J. O'Donnell (Eds.), *Becoming and unbecoming white: Owning and disowning a racial identity.* Westport, CT: Bergin & Garvey.

Gardner, H. (1983). *Frames of mind: The theory of multiple intelligences.* New York: Basic Books.

Gilligan, C. (1982). *In a different voice: Psychological theory and women's development.* Cambridge, MA: Harvard University.

Goss, L., & Barnes, M. E. (1989). *Talk that talk: An anthology of African-American storytelling.* New York: Simon & Schuster.

Griggs, S., & Dunn, R. (1996). *Hispanic American students and learning style* (ERIC Digest). Urbana, IL: ERIC Clearinghouse on Elementary and Early Childhood Education. (ERIC Document Reproduction Service No. ED393 607)

Hale-Benson, J. E. (1986). *Black children: Their roots, culture, and learning styles.* Baltimore: Johns Hopkins University.

Hamilton, V. L., Blumenfeld, P. C., Hiroshi, A., & Miura, K. (1991). Group and gender in Japanese and American elementary classrooms. *Journal of Cross-Cultural Psychology, 22*(3), 317–346.

Hankes, J. (1993). *A call for collaborative research to investigate the "Indian Math" problem.* (ERIC Document Reproduction Service No. ED364 387)

Heath, S. B. (1982). Questioning at school and at home: A comparative study. In G. D. Spindler (Ed.), *Doing the ethnology of schooling: Educational anthropology in action* (pp. 102–131). New York: Holt, Rinehart & Winston.

Hernandez, H. (1989). *Multicultural education: A teacher's guide to content and process.* Columbus, OH: Merrill.

Howard, G. R. (2001). White man dancing: A Story of personal transformation. In C. Clark & J. O'Donnell (Eds.), *Becoming and unbecoming white: Owning and disowning a racial identity.* Westport, CT: Bergin & Garvey.

Igoa, C. (1995). *The inner world of the immigrant child.* New York: St. Martin's Press.

Irvine, J. J. (1991). *Black students and school failure.* New York: Praeger.

Kohlberg, L. (1984). *Essays on moral development: The psychology of moral development.* New York: Harper & Row.

Kondo, K. (1996). Language and needs for affiliation and achievement: A comparative study of English and Japanese bilingual and English monolingual Nisei students in today's Hawaii. Paper delivered at the Western Conference of the Comparative and International Education Society, Honolulu, HI.

Kozol, J. (1995). *Amazing grace.* New York: Crown Publishers.

Kozol, J. (2000). *Ordinary resurrections.* New York: Crown Publishers.

Krupnick, C. (1985). Women and men in the classroom: Inequality and its remedies. In *On teaching and learning* (Journal of the Derek Bok Center for Teaching and Learning) (pp. 18–25). Cambridge, MA: Harvard University.

Ladson-Billings, G. (1994). *The Dreamkeepers: Successful teachers of African American Children.* San Francisco: Jossey Bass.

Maher, F. (1987). Toward a richer theory of feminist pedagogy. *Journal of Education*, 169(3), 91–99.

Nieto, S. (1996). *Affirming diversity: The sociopolitical context of multicultural education.* New York: Longman.

Ogbu, J. U. (1993). Variability in minority school performance: A problem in search of an explanation. In *Anthropology and Education Quarterly 18*(4), 312–334.

Ong, W. (1982). *Orality and literacy: The terminologizing of the word.* London: Methuen.

Phillips, S. U. (1983). *The invisible culture: Communication in classroom and community on the Warm Springs Indian Reservation.* New York: Longman.

Tannen, D. (1990). *You just don't understand: Women and men in conversation.* New York: Morrow.

Tannen, D. (1991, June 19). Teachers' classroom strategies should recognize that men and women use language differently. *Chronicle of Higher Education,* p. B2.

Tatum, B. D. (1997). *Why are all the black kids sitting together in the cafeteria? and other conversations about race.* New York: Basic Books.

Trueba, H. T. (1998). The Education of Mexican immigrant children. In M. M. Suarez-Orozco (Ed.), *Crossings.* Cambridge: Harvard University Press.

Wellesley College Center for Research on Women. (1992). *How schools shortchange girls: The AAUW report.* Washington, DC: American Association of University Women Foundation.

Yingling, P. (1999). Chair's report (introduction to special issue on refugees). *Peace and Freedom: Magazine of the Women's International League for Peace and Freedom.* 49(4), 3.

Websites:

AskERIC (Q & A for teachers on educational research topics): *www.askeric.org*

Center for Research on Educational Diversity and Excellence, University of California Santa Cruz: *www.crede.ucsc.edu*

ERIC Digests (research reports): *www.ed/gov/databases/ERIC_Digests*

National Association for Multicultural Education: *www.nameorg.org*

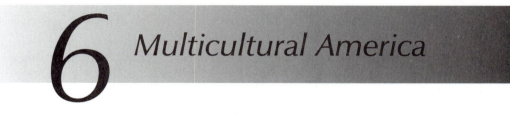

6 Multicultural America

"We didn't all come over in the same ship, but we're all in the same boat."
(Bernard Baruch)

"I miss being someplace where everybody knows what you're talking about."
(immigrant child, in Fassler & Danforth, 1993)

It is "Family Math Night" at a large urban elementary school in Lynn, Massachusetts. Three hundred people of all ages are spread throughout the first-floor classrooms, engaged in games and experimenting with manipulative materials. In one room, a family of Somalian immigrants, a mother, father, aunt, and six children, is playing a math game aided by a student from the local college. The women wear long skirts and headdresses. The adults speak no English, and the children are trying to translate. The children, eager and energetic, are having trouble taking turns. The college student is unsure about whether the game's rules are being followed, but everyone is smiling and having fun.

Introduction: America's Changing Portrait

The cultural diversity of the world's population is coming home to the United States. Twenty-five years ago, when many of our readers were born, America was largely a white, middle-class nation. Yet, pockets of real poverty existed, "discovered" 10 years earlier by Michael Harrington. His book *The Other America* (1962) woke up the general public and its political leaders to the fact that many people living in this self-named "greatest nation on earth" were abjectly poor. Others told us about the disenfranchised and the undereducated, about racism and inequity (see, e.g., Jonathan Kozol's *Death at an Early Age* [1967]). The Civil Rights movement of the 1960s helped people of color to understand their entitlements as Americans and supported their battle for equal employment opportunities, equal education, equal justice, and equal respect. Suddenly, Americans saw this country as more varied and more colorful than before. It took a few more years for women to realize that they, too, suffered inequities in legal, economic, educational, and social treatment.

The 1960s awakened Americans to the fact that this country is made up of many peoples with many different experiences of living in America. In the years following, world events precipitated the arrival of new populations of immigrants to our shores, creating an even more complex picture of American demographics. From 1970 to 1990, the foreign-born population in the United States grew from 9,619,000 to 19,767,000 (Bouvier, 1993, p. 14). The U.S. Census Bureau reports that the number of immigrants has risen beyond expectations; the 281 million people in the U.S. in 2000 was 7 million more than what had been projected. Most of that 7 million entered the country illegally in the 1990s (Rodriguez, 2001).

The aftermath of the Vietnam War brought to our shores new peoples whose backgrounds were very different from that of the dominant Anglicized European Americans. The "first wave" of these immigrants consisted of an educated elite who had escaped the communist takeover of Vietnam, bringing with them their high expectations and their money. Their children were model students in our schools, availing themselves of the free public education here that guided them toward business and professional lives like their parents'. They learned English with breathtaking speed and soared to the top of high school honor rolls in record time.

Ten years later, in the mid-1980s, a second wave of Southeast Asian immigrants arrived, less advantaged and longer traumatized by political and economic upheaval than the first group. These were the Vietnamese villagers ruined by the war and/or driven from their country slowly and painfully by poverty and politics, allowed to immigrate by America's feelings of guilt, shame, and humanitarian sympathy. In a family of eight children, two or three would be selected to make the perilous journey, usually including a teenager old enough to take care of a younger sibling but too young to marry. The travelers might be a 16-year-old and his 9-year-old brother or sister. Their family would have spent its resources to provide them with the bribes and passage money necessary for the trip. The first two or three attempts to leave might fail, possibly ending in capture and escape or the theft of the passage money. The fourth or fifth attempt would succeed. After a months-long trip by foot, truck, boat, and plane, the pair would arrive in their adopted land, knowing no English, dependent on a sponsoring parish, organization, or family for the means to survive, and knowing they would probably never see their parents again.

This group also included great numbers of Cambodian refugees fleeing the oppressive regime of Pol Pot, which had massacred millions of their people and scarred their land. In the name of "democratization," the Khmer Rouge had systematically decimated Cambodian culture, killing as many "intellectuals" as they could find, including teachers, and forbidding the expression of traditional arts, literature, and religion. Much as our southern states, fearing insurrection by an educated slave population, enacted laws forbidding teaching slaves to read, so did the Kampuchean regime seek out and kill teachers. One woman remembers hiding her glasses so as not to be marked as educated (Breitborde, personal interview, 1990).

Escaping on foot to the safety of relocation camps in Thailand, these Cambodians endured unspeakable tragedies. Many had witnessed the kidnapping of their own children, on-the-spot executions of their spouses, and slower, painful deaths brought on by untreated disease and infection. One woman lost her three young children when they were taken from her in the fields where they worked alongside her, presumably to be raised and "reeducated" in state-run residential schools (M. Breitborde, personal interview, 1990). (Lest we assume that the United States is exempt from the apparent barbarism of wresting children from their own parents, we should remember that the U.S. Bureau of Indian Affairs, until the 1950s, did much the same thing to Native American children, convincing or bribing their parents or otherwise stealing the children away from their tribal homes to be educated in special boarding schools [Wax, Wax, & Dumont, 1989].)

After years in the Thai camps, Cambodian refugees were finally allowed to emigrate to America, often with Thai-born children in tow. In the interest of distributing state and regional burdens, the U.S. Immigration Service settled them in various geographic areas nationwide. Soon, however, they found significant numbers of their countrymen in other parts of the country and found ways to join them. Cities like Lowell and Revere, Massachusetts, experienced huge influxes, to the point at which whole neighborhoods and local school populations changed. To save money, several families rented one apartment, bought one car, and put each other through school.

It is important to note that the average age of the Southeast Asian immigrant is low (National Coalition of Advocates for Students, 1991, p. 5). Those who immigrate are adolescents or young adults at or near child-bearing age and school-age children. This low age of immigration has great implications for local and state services. The resources of local school systems may be strained, as, following the 1974 *Lau v. Nichols* Supreme Court case, they must by law provide bilingual education for these children. Health services and employment training programs are affected. There may well be short-term welfare costs, although the adults find work as quickly as possible. Southeast Asian immigrant communities take care of their own, relying less on public authorities and programs than many whose families have been in this country for many generations. In part because of their deep suspicion of government officials, they often allow themselves to be victimized by crime, discrimination, and mental health problems, loath to call on even the local police for help.

Asians, including Southeast Asians from Vietnam, Cambodia, Thailand, and Laos (and the Hmong group indigenous to those areas), as well as Chinese and Japanese who continue to immigrate to the West and East coast, have constituted approximately 42% of immigrants to the United States in the 1980s and 1990s. Another 42% of immigrants come from Latin America, the greatest number from our neighbor to the south, Mexico (National Coalition of Advocates for Students, 1991, p. 4). The border between Mexico and the southwestern states of California, Arizona, New Mexico, and Texas has always been busy with northbound travelers. Conditions of poverty and unemployment have driven Mexicans into the border states either to better themselves and their families in the long term or to secure temporary work in the short term. In the first case, whole families arrive to make a new life. In the second case, men may slip into the country illegally to obtain seasonal farmwork, sending money back to Mexican villages until they can return.

Similar back-and-forth patterns exist for some Puerto Rican travelers to New York and New England. Families seeking economic and educational gain experiment with life in the United States, where, although the money is far better, the way of life is so different it proves sometimes impossible to sustain. For Puerto Ricans, who have American citizenship, the passage is easy, inexpensive, and without commitment. Should they find that the pace and quality of life (and the weather) in eastern-seaboard cities are too different and too difficult, they can easily return to the island, and many do. Immigrants from the Dominican Republic similarly come to America for economic and educational opportunities, but they find the cultural differences so great that many, especially the elders of the family, return. After a difficult year in the Boston area, the grandmother of one of our students went back home to her Dominican village; she was driven away by the harshness of the New England weather, the competition and driving ambition of her neighbors, the impersonality of her interactions with local businesspeople, the disrespect accorded to the elderly, and the general lack of community and *familia*. Schooling for some Dominican children is compromised by their families' assumption that they will not be in this country for long (Breitborde, personal interview, 2001).

The Special Case of Refugees

> When the sun began to shine, we began the shooting. My brother, who was 19, was the first who got hit. I heard him crying for help and I ran to see him. His body was covered with blood. I held him in my arms.... He said to me, "You must not fight any more. Try to get yourself to Thailand and then go to America." (Xiong, a Hmong student, in National Coalition of Advocates for Students, 1991, p. 37)

For some immigrant groups, the trip to America is a one-way escape from political oppression and grinding poverty. They must "make it" in the States because to return home may mean imprisonment or worse. Somalians, Vietnamese, Cambodians, Cubans, Haitians, Rwandans, Central Americans, and victims of the post-Soviet internecine wars in Eastern Europe are examples of immigrants who have sought refuge from intolerable conditions in their homelands. As defined by the 1967 Protocol of the United Nations Convention Relating to the Status of Refugees, a refugee is

> any person who, owing to a well-founded fear of being persecuted for reasons of race, religion, nationality, membership in a particular social group or political opinion, is outside the country of his nationality and is unable or, owing to such fear, is unwilling to return to it. (in Martorella, 1993, p. 158)

This definition is problematical because it favors those in high political or social circumstances who may have been personally targeted by oppressive regimes. Poorer people who anticipate persecution but cannot prove that they have been personally persecuted may be perceived by the asylum nation as fleeing from economic rather than political or ethnic hardship. This country has turned away poor Haitians floating in the Caribbean on overloaded homemade rafts because they were unable to meet the evidentiary criteria. Many critics of America's refugee policies have questioned the fairness of our Haitian policy, as we have applied much less stringent rules to Cubans seeking asylum from communism. Religious and community groups have sheltered illegal Central Americans under the roofs of churches and homes sympathetic to their need to escape political and economic repression.

From 1980 to 1990, the United States admitted about 1 million refugees from Southeast Asia, Eastern Europe and the former Soviet Union, Iran, China, Central America, Cuba, Africa, Haiti, and other areas of political upheaval (in Martorella, 1993, p. 159). Although these people share many of the same needs as other immigrants to our shores, the special circumstances attendant to their leaving their homelands add a psychological and practical dimension to their situation. Refugees have left their country under traumatic conditions and probably for good. Most have witnessed the bloody results of conflict, including the death or disappearance of close relatives, kidnapping and rape, the destruction of their homes, discrimination based on race and ethnicity, and the persistent fear of the military, police, or vigilante groups. Saddled with mixed emotions—grief for the loss of a known and beloved homeland, relief at having escaped, worry for those left behind, and sadness at the possibility of never returning—refugees may suffer long-term emotional distress such as depression and anxiety. They may be understandably loath to let their children out of their sight and may avoid contact with public authorities even when it would help them. Because they do not expect to return home, they may work very hard to achieve economic independence here.

Often, refugee groups push their children to achieve in school, recognizing that economic success in America is linked to school success. In the words of a student of one of the authors, "You Americans don't realize what an amazing thing it is for people coming to this country that they can send their children to school, that there's a way to get them there, and that it's all free" (Breitborde, personal interview, 2001). But their children may be indelibly scarred and unable to concentrate or perform. Teachers have told stories about young children recently arrived from El Salvador or Haiti, for example, unable to speak. What emerges from a look into their histories are their experiences of having watched their parents shot dead before their eyes or having seen babies washed away in rivers—too many stories like Xiong's above. In the words of the National Coalition of Advocates for Students, they have had an "abbreviated childhood" (1991, p. 36).

Political Issues

The dramatic increase in immigration in the past 20 years, the young average age of immigrants, and the higher birth rate of several of these groups relative to that of white Americans are changing the face of America's people. This rapid demographic change has been called "the browning of America." Whereas in 1990, white people accounted for 74% of this nation, the Population Reference Bureau (O'Hare, 1992) estimates that by the year 2050, the number will have fallen to 52% of the population. Blacks, who were 12% of the population in 1970, will grow to 14% by 2050; Hispanics, from 10% to 20%; and Asians, from 3% to 10%. These percentages show that the greatest growth is occurring in the numbers of Asians and Hispanics relative to that of whites and blacks, which is understandable, given that these groups make up most of our immigrants. In 1994, of the 300,000 legal immigrants to the United States, 85% were from Latin American and Asian countries (National Coalition, 1991, p. 4). (In contrast, Germany was the source of the greatest number of immigrants in 1950.) Thirty-three percent of today's immigrants live in California, with New York, Florida, Texas, New Jersey, and Illinois having significant numbers as well (O'Hare).

Reports on the changing composition of the nation are reflected in the changes in student populations in our public schools. According to the Harvard Civil Rights Project (Orfield, 2001), the number of Latino students in American public schools grew 245% in the 30 years between 1968 and 1998. In the Pacific coast and Rocky Mountain states and in the American South and Southwest, public school populations are 52%–55% white (Orfield). The College Board's *Road to College: Educational Progress by Race and Ethnicity* estimates that the percentage of students of color in our schools will have grown from 23% in 1976 to 70% by the year 2026. The relative proportions

The need for multicultural education.

of white students and students of color will have been reversed in the years between 1990 (when white students constituted 70% of the entire school population) and 2026 (cited in Garcia, 1994, pp. 11–12).

That America has always been a land of immigrants seems to have been forgotten by those who resent the newcomers. In "Beating Up on Immigrants," Robert Kuttner (1995) decries the immigration bills passed by Congress and several states that would severely limit the social services available to immigrants and/or hold their sponsors financially liable for these services. Deportation penalties are proposed for immigrants who accept more than one year's worth of services, including job training, English classes, prenatal care, public health services, and college loans. A congressional majority would deny public schooling to the children of illegal immigrants, effectively leaving them on the streets of California cities during the day. Sadly and ironically, says Kuttner, no one in public office targets the employers who hire the cheap illegal immigrant labor, often crossing the Mexican border to recruit them. In Kuttner's words, "Politically, immigrant families make a much easier target than American employers. But kicking kids out of classrooms and clinics is merely punitive and not likely to deter immigration as long as migrant parents can find jobs."

The easy assumption behind these bills is that immigrants come to America to take advantage of public welfare, social services, and free public education. A darker fear is the xenophobia that affects an insecure majority population unprepared to deal with people of new and different backgrounds. Neither feeling is new to the 1990s. Here are voices from earlier times (from Glenn, 1988):

> There are great masses coming in upon us who are not educated, except to vice and crime; the creatures or the victims of the oppression, or the overpopulation of the old world.... Immigration is constantly countervailing the Puritan leaven of our people, and reducing the scale of public morality and public intelligence. (p. 65)

> It is almost too much for the children of the Puritans to bear. Out from the heart of our beloved Commonwealth are now to be graduated Jesuit priests—the O'Briens, the O'Flahertys, and the McNamaras. Ireland and Rome together make a combination of a not very attractive character to the sons of New England sires. (p. 71)

These statements were made by members of the Boston School Committee, writing in 1846 about the "problem" of mushrooming Irish immigration into Boston. From 1820 to 1850, the number of poverty-stricken Irish refugees from the potato famine grew from 2,000 to 30,000.

The following quotation is taken from Boston's Unitarian newspaper, reacting to the ultimate insult of the founding of Holy Cross College:

> The dominant race must regularize the incoming class ... to dispel from popular use every foreign language ... to print all public documents in the English tongue alone ... to ordain that all schools aided by the State shall use the same language ... to develop a high and vivid patriotism ... to return the Bible in our common schools ... to nationalize before we naturalize, and to educate before either. (in Glenn, 1988, pp. 72–73)

Writing in 1909, the prominent educational historian Elwood Cubberley reflected the general public concern over the millions of "first wave" European immigrants at the turn of the 20th century: "Largely illiterate, often lacking in initiative, and almost wholly without the Anglo-Saxon conceptions of righteousness, liberty, law, order, public decency, and government ... Their coming has served to dilute tremendously our national stock and to weaken and corrupt our political life" (1909, 1965, pp. 485–486). Cubberley's words are all too familiar to those of us who have read and heard the words of some political figures of the 1990s and 2000s.

The reality is that immigrants come for work, education, and the chance for a better life, and it takes a while for them to reach their goals. They come speaking little or no English and need time and ways to learn it. Many come from rural, undeveloped areas and have knowledge and skills very different from those needed to get along in America's industrialized and sophisticated urban society. It takes time to learn how to survive, how to get a job and get to it every day, how to deal with our many social institutions. A look at welfare rolls would reveal that most recipients are not in fact immigrants but people whose families have been in this country for generations. While no one is happy with the social or economic cost of illegal immigration (including jobs lost to legal workers), the alternative of leaving hundreds of thousands of children un-schooled, unhoused, and unhealthy is far worse.

The Immigrant Experience: Children's Voices

The developmental limitations of young children can be a boon to their adjustment to a new land. Children are remarkably flexible and somewhat protected from the full range of traumatic experiences by their cognitive simplicity. Their impressions about coming to America may rest on simple details: "I like when it snows." "There are lots of movies." "It's too hot." "It's too cold." "Everything costs a lot of money." "There's lots of food in the store and no long lines" (Fassler & Danforth, 1993, pp. 92, 121, 125). Or immigrant children's impressions may reflect the apparent influ-ence of their parents: "Everything costs a lot of money." "In America you can say what you want" (Fassler & Danforth). On the other hand, they do worry, and their worries reflect their own histories as well as their incomplete conception of their new land: "Are we safe in our new house?" "What if I get all used to living here and have to go somewhere else?" "What if everyone has lots and lots of money?" "What if I'm no good at baseball?" They have been torn away from their homes and their cultures, and the decision has not been theirs: "I miss the mountains." "I miss my grand-mother. I hope I get to see her again." "It makes me sad to see pictures of El Salvador on TV." "I miss being someplace where everybody knows what you're talking about" (Fassler & Danforth).

Immigration is a lonely and confusing experience, at least for a while. According to the Harvard Immigration Project, almost half of all immigrant children have been sep-arated from one or both parents during their move to America, including a disturbing 80% of Central American children (Suarez-Orozco, Todorova, & Louie, 2001). Even if children arrive with both parents, the stress of finding a home and a means of support in a new land can overwhelm a family. Rosario came to America at the age of six from the Philippines. Her parents, both working long hours, were too tired to spend much time with her at the end of their work days. Like many immigrant children, she was moved from school to school, five times in her case, as teachers and administrators made different decisions about appropriate grade placement and the availability of bilingual and ESL classes. She spent some time each week in a literacy development center for immigrant children created by Cristina Igoa, also a Filipino immigrant, in Hayward, California. During her time in the center, Rosario created a filmstory called "The Lonely Bear," about a bear who had no friends until he offered help to a squirrel who had been hurt and needed care. "Like the hurt squirrel, Rosario had needed care both night and day; warmth and caring at home; warm, caring friends outside the house; and support in school" (Igoa, 1995, p. 92).

Young children whose families have immigrated to the United States bear special family burdens not shared by those whose parents were born here. They are often asked to take on responsibilities beyond what is appropriate or understandable given their ages and developmental levels. Seong Yang remembers negotiating rent payments with the landlord, bearing the burden of the family's financial welfare. "I was always on the brink of a nervous breakdown," he says (Alvarez, 1995, p. 29).

In families where parents have not yet learned English, English-speaking children have to accompany their mom or dad to the employment office, the social service department, the bank, the insurance agency, the doctor, or the hospital. Quite often, these children miss school to serve their parents and grandparents as translators. They may be asked to convey information that has serious consequences. The accuracy of their understanding and speaking English may affect whether the doctor learns the full range of their mother's symptoms and whether she takes the right dosage of medicine. There may in fact be no terms available in the native language for the English counterpart. Often, these young children do not have a good conceptual basis for what is being told to them. Given children's lack of perspective on the seriousness of different illnesses, for example, the young translator may emerge from the doctor's office worried that a parent will soon die who in fact is only suffering from an ear infection.

This heady responsibility forces the adults to be dependent and the children to take charge. Seong Yang remembers having to memorize the family's phone number and address, "drilling the syllables into his head" to keep his family from getting lost in their new home, New York City (Alvarez, 1995). Another young child writes, "I helped my dad fill out some forms for work" (Fassler & Danforth, 1993). Elizabeth Tejada accompanied her mother to factories from the age of nine, embarrassed at having to ask for a job on her behalf (Alvarez, p. 29). Sometimes parents know some English but are uncomfortable with their vocabulary and accents: "I help my mom in the store. She doesn't like to speak English" (Alvarez).

The upended parent–child relationship can lead to conflicts when parents try to discipline children who have a greater command of the language at hand. English-speaking children soon come to recognize the power they have in the family. Some will manipulate information to their own advantage, "misinterpreting" report cards or notes home, for example. Parents whose experiences in their native lands make them afraid of losing their children, or whose culture limits the independence of children more than mainstream American culture does, tend to want to keep their children at home. Cambodian parents, for example, typically will not allow their children to leave the house or the immediate neighborhood after school, even to the point of forbidding telephone calls to "American" friends (M. Breitborde, personal interview, 2001). This is especially true for the girls in the family. Ultimately, immigrant children want to "Americanize." When they reach the age of 10 or 11, the age when children generally seek identities independent of their parents and when the peer group becomes the more important reference for what is "appropriate," these children begin to clash with the older, more traditional, generation. It is important for teachers to know that immigrant children's development is complicated by cultural dissonance between the world of their parents and the world of their new society. It may be advisable for teachers to work with younger children and their parents to smooth the way as much as possible by inviting families into school to share their traditions, instilling pride in cultural heritage, and gently exposing parents to the positive aspects of "American ways."

Assimilation, Amalgamation, and Cultural Pluralism

> Before I started school in America I was Edite. Maria Edite dos Anjos Cunha. Maria, in honor of the Virgin Mary. In Portugal it was customary to use Maria as a religious and legal prefix to every girl's name.... Edite came from my godmother, Dona Edite Baetas Ruivo.... The dos Anjos was for my mother's side of the family. Like her mother before her, she had been named Maria dos Anjos. And Cunha was for my father's side. Carlos dos Santos Cunha, son of Abilio dos Santos Cunha, the tailor from Sail. I loved my name.... It was melodious and beautiful. And through it I knew exactly who I was. (Pedrosa, 1990, p. 34)

Edite goes on to describe her immigration to Peabody, Massachusetts, in 1961, where she encountered a well-meaning second-grade teacher by the name of Mrs. Donahue. Portuguese by birth, Mrs. Donahue had married an Irishman and changed her name. She changed Edite's name, too, on the first day of school:

> "Your name will be Mary Edith Cunha," she declared. "In America you only need two or three names. Mary Edith is a lovely name. And it will be easier to pronounce." My name was Edite. Maria Edite dos Anjos Cunha. I had no trouble pronouncing it. "Mary Edith, Edithhh, Mary Edithhh." Mrs. Donahue ... wrinkled up her nose and raised her upper lip to show me the proper positioning of the tongue for the "th" sound. She looked hideous. There was a big pain in my head. I wanted to scream out my name. But you could never argue with a teacher.... Day after day Mrs. Donahue made me practice pronouncing that name that wasn't mine.... Later my other teachers shortened it to Mary. And I never knew quite who I was. (Pedrosa, p. 36)

Mrs. Donahue's intentions were good. She hoped to ease Maria Edite's transition to American life by finding ways to help her "fit in." She thought that having a name that the English-speaking children could pronounce would be important. She probably believed that the fastest way to social comfort was by quick Americanization. This approach to the role of schools and social agencies with respect to cultural differences is called assimilation. In this view, it is the responsibility of social institutions to help those who are culturally different to "become American," by speaking, acting, dressing, and believing in "the American way." *American* was in Mrs. Donahue's time still defined as "Anglo-Saxon." For this reason, millions of people were encouraged to take new "American" names, ignore the religious holidays of their own traditions, give up their native foods, work on their Sabbath, get rid of their accents, and dress "appropriately." The immigration officials at Ellis Island in the early 1900s at times changed people's names to conform to typical American spellings. Many schools until the 1960s forbade the speaking of a "foreign" language in classrooms and on the playground. In the name of helping newcomers and the culturally different to fit in, assimilators helped destroy in children an appreciation of their ethnic heritage.

The social revolution of the 1960s brought with it a new understanding of difference and the idea that the many different cultures of America contributed to a general amalgam. The new definition of *American* was not Anglo-Saxon–based but was the result of our "melting pot." Schools and social institutions accepted that children came from different backgrounds; however, they assumed that these different backgrounds would somehow meld with each other, creating a single new cultural ideal out of the mix. The ultimate goal for the culturally diverse was amalgamation.

Those who could not achieve the new cultural ideal were deemed "culturally deprived." To bring the culturally deprived up to the desired level of mainstream cultural knowledge and behavior, federal and state governments and private groups implemented a myriad of "compensatory education" programs. Examples of such programs are Project Head Start (for "underprivileged" preschoolers), Title I of the Elementary and Secondary Education Act (providing remedial reading and math for low-income children), and A Better Chance, whereby black urban youth moved to white suburban communities to live together and attend the local high school. What was lost, however, was a sense that different cultures are unique and worthy of respect. A melting pot, after all, destroys the individual integrity of each ingredient. A newer metaphor, developed in the 1980s, is the "salad bowl," where each vegetable contributes to the whole while preserving its separate identity. This approach to cultural diversity is called pluralism.

Rather than see poor Mexican American children as "culturally deprived," for example, pluralists respect the rich culture that is Mexican American. Rather than insist that only English be spoken in schools, pluralists not only invite Mexican American children to speak Spanish but may even create two-way bilingual programs in which native English-speaking children learn Spanish as a second language. Pluralists build school curricula from the best of all cultures, showcasing the contributions of each culture to the multivariate picture that is America. Pluralists ask teachers to consider the cultural roots of the knowledge, skills, and attitudes that different children have and to modify their instructional strategies to respect these differences.

Culture and Achievement

Cultural pluralism in America, however, is not a rosy picture of unity and diversity. Great disparities exist in the welfare and status of our many cultural groups. Huge gaps exist between blacks and whites, for example, in employment, criminal justice, and access to health services. With regard to education, African American children leave school sooner and succeed less often than do whites. They are disproportionately represented in "low-ability" groups and tracks, are referred more often for special education, and are more likely to be disciplined or suspended (Irvine, 1991; Oakes, 1985). Latinos, African Americans, native Hawaiians, and Native Americans are similarly behind most white children on standardized tests and on school completion (Belkin, 2001; Bennett, 1995; Johnston & Viadero, 2000). In an age when a college degree is a necessary credential for entry into business and professional life, the discrepancies in college entrance and graduation rates among blacks, whites, Latinos, and Asians are important.

Asians (the "model majority") as a group score as well as or better than white students and have higher college admissions and graduation rates (Berliner & Biddle, 1995). However, the overall figures break down when the group is divided by national origin. Many of the "second wave" Vietnamese children, those whose parents lived through the war or were poor, uneducated villagers, do poorly in school. Cambodian children have typically missed years of schooling in their homeland and have spent much time in Thai refugee camps, where education was nonexistent or inconsistent, making the transition to American schools difficult. Among California's large Filipino student population, 46% drop out before high school graduation. Samoan immigrants drop out at the rate of 60%. The achievement of Hmong immigrant children is similarly problematical (National Coalition, 1991).

Several theories attempt to explain these discrepancies. Some attribute the difference to biology. The controversial book *The Bell Curve* (Herrnstein & Murray, 1994) argues that genetic differences in intelligence passed along from generation to generation explain one genetic pool's greater aptitude for education over another's. This argument is decried by those like Howard Gardner, who believe there is not one intelligence but are many distinct intelligences (1993). Many believe intelligence can be learned or at least modified by experience and education. After all, say these critics, why bother with education if intelligence is biologically determined?

Other explanations of differential achievement point to the influence of political and social inequities in the larger society. Whether because of residential patterns or because of "white flight" from integrated city schools, racial segregation in American schooling has actually increased in the past decade (Orfield, 2001). The Harvard Civil Rights Project found that in the 1998–99 school year, 70% of black students attended predominantly minority schools, as compared with 66% in 1991–92. Latino students are even more likely to be schooled separately; 76% of them attended majority-minority schools in 1998–99. According to the author of the study, the problem with majority-minority schools is that they are almost always inferior to those with predominantly white populations. As a result, high schools in our largest cities, which are overwhelmingly minority, graduate less than half of their students, while successful minority college students tend to have been graduated from integrated high schools. (Orfield).

Pervasive racism may account for the fact that many black students are mislabeled as learning disabled and that disproportionate numbers of students of color are "tracked" into "low-ability" groups. Racism may account for disparities in the physical and educational resources, such as computers and artists-in-residence, provided to schools with predominately minority populations, and for lower teacher expectations for children of poverty and/or color. Jean Anyon's work describing differences in the resources afforded to schools of children of different social classes, differences in the degree of creativity and choice offered in the curriculum of each, and differences in the attitudes of teachers toward their students is an important example of research grounding this explanation of achievement differences (1981, 1997).

Schools, these theorists and researchers say, are not exempt from the racial and ethnic discrimination that persists in American social life. Too many poor black and Latino children have been written off by teachers and administrators who don't expect that they'll amount to much. In a famous study, Ray Rist observed that early childhood teachers developed academic expectations for children in the first week of school from observations that had nothing to do with their actual performance (1973). Rist's teacher subjects formed impressions based on whether children spoke often, with confidence, and in Standard English; whether they dressed well; how dark the color of their skin was; and whether their families received public assistance. Twenty years after this study, former president George Bush, addressing the Mexican American student body of Garfield High School in East Los Angeles (made famous in book and film by teacher Jaime Escalante's success in teaching mathematics there), told the students that a college education was not necessary for everyone: "We need people to build our buildings … people who do the hard physical work of our society" (in Nieto, 1996, p. 45). Studies done by the American Association of University Women, some in cooperation with the Center for Research on Women at Wellesley College, attest to the continuing problem of differential expectations for boys and girls, problematic for girls studying math and science but affecting academic and behavioral expectations for boys as well (Wellesley College Center for Research on Women, 1992; American Association of University Women, 2001).

Another factor in the disparity between the academic achievement of majority and minority students may be the appropriateness of the curriculum. Lisa Delpit, an African American educator, has argued for years that inadequate attention is paid to the particular strengths and needs of black children. Too often, she says, "white" assumptions about what skills children already have and what they need to learn are inappropriate for many blacks (Delpit, 1994). School curricula are reflections of the pervading culture, traditionally determined by local political and educational leaders, increasingly now by state-level policy makers concerned with standardizing the information and skills children are exposed to in schools. The trouble is, the twin goals of equalizing access to education and providing substantive learning experiences for all children must be sensitive and responsive to the diverse experiences and backgrounds of our multicultural school population. "A valid school curriculum includes both cultural knowledge and knowledge about culture," says Etta Hollins; that is, it is both an extension of children's "home-culture" and a conscious building upon that culture toward new knowledge and new skills (Hollins, 1996). Central to the task is the involvement of children's families and their community, not only as supports for children's learning but also as resources for constructing a curriculum that validates and prizes the rich and diverse experiences of the human experience.

Within the problematic and pervasive picture of racial and cultural achievement disparities, there are examples of successful efforts at "closing the gap". Schools in Fort Wayne, Indiana, Charlotte-Mecklenburg, North Carolina (Sadowski, 2001), Harlem, New York (Meier, 1995), and elsewhere are examining the extent and nature of racial/cultural and socioeconomic differences in the school experience and performance of their student populations, and engaging in targeted efforts to correct them.

The Need for Multicultural Education

The increasing cultural diversity of America's children requires changes in what we must teach them and how. The degree and speed of demographic change in our communities and our schools require that we address issues of differences and social relations to maximize educational opportunity for all children and to prevent the possibility of intergroup conflict. As traditionally white monocultural communities undergo sudden demographic change, and especially during periods of economic hardship and demographic change, it is essential that educators take on the responsibility of teaching children to welcome diversity, eliminate prejudice, and increase tolerance and communication skills. A student in one of our classes shared with us the written account of her friend, Quan, who fled Vietnam for America at the age of 8: "When our family moved to Medford, I had to learn new things. The first thing I learned was the word 'gook.' I was called this by someone in church my first day living in Massachusetts" (M. Breitborde, personal correspondence, 1991). Quan spent much of his time confused and in trouble because of miscommunication and the insensitivity of principals and teachers:

> I once took seven cans of Mighty Dog to school for the Thanksgiving Drive. I spent twenty minutes being scolded by the principal. On another occasion I had to stand in the corner for calling a girl in my class a hooker. She had been absent for over a week and I was speculating that maybe she was playing hookie.… I assumed one who plays hookie was a hooker; after all, one who bakes is a baker. (Breitborde, personal correspondence, 1991) Despite the insults he endured, and although "words can hurt more than fists," Quan says he has grown to love his adopted country.

Ethnocentrism, the belief that one's own culture is not only valid and superior to those of others but is also universally applicable in evaluating and judging human behavior (Hernandez, 1989, p. 25), occurs early in childhood. After all, young children are egocentric. One five-year-old, when asked to give his whole name, kept answering "Robert." When the interviewer prodded him with, "Isn't your last name 'Galardi'?" he replied, "Oh, but *everyone's* last name is Galardi!" (Nitka, 1977). As children grow in their powers of observation, conception, and classification, they become aware of similarities and differences. It is important from the beginning to recognize that without guidance, egocentric children will ethnocentrically assume that their way is the only way and that other ways are weird and wrong. The valuing that accompanies children's awareness of differences will be either positive or negative, depending on what they have learned from listening to and observing the adults in their lives. Sometimes, despite the best efforts of teachers, other influences prevail:

> A first grade teacher invites one of her students, a six-year-old Vietnamese American girl, to share with the class how her family celebrates the Vietnamese New Year. At the back of the room, three boys giggle among themselves, pushing at their eyes to show each other how to look "Chinese." The teacher, whose year-long curriculum presents information about many cultures and who has made "respect" a fundamental classroom rule, is frustrated. She asks herself, Where have I failed? (Breitborde, 1996)

Multicultural education has many definitions. To some educators, it means exposing children to information about many cultures through special lessons, units, performances, and field trips. To others, it means revamping traditional curricula to include the voices and points of view of more than the mainstream. To still others, it means teaching children to get along with each other. To a few (including these authors), it means including the world in the spectrum of education that is provided to children. As the case above shows, a definition of *multicultural education* limited to conveying information as though it were separate from values is inadequate to the task of changing the prejudicial attitudes that govern hurtful behavior.

James Banks, author of the National Council for the Social Studies' *Curriculum Guidelines for Multicultural Education* (Banks, Cortes, Gay, Garcia, & Ochoa, 1991) and a noted expert in the field, presents a developmental scheme to portray incremental change from a traditional to a multicultural curriculum (Banks, 2001). His four stages of change begin with the "Mainstream Perspectives" stage, where the curriculum follows from the perspectives of mainstream (white Anglo-American) historians, writers, and artists. In this curriculum, Columbus "discovers" America and everyone celebrates Thanksgiving and Christmas. In the second stage of curriculum reform, the "Cultural Additive" stage, ethnic content is added to the existing mainstream curriculum. Children learn about Native Americans, Chanukah, Martin Luther King, and Chinese New Year. This approach has been nicknamed "Holidays and Heroes" and represents too much of what passes for multicultural education in our schools and child care centers.

Not until educators realize that the mainstream perspective is only one of many and that the entire curriculum needs to be evaluated for bias are they ready to make education truly multicultural. Here, in the "Multicultural Model," the curriculum is transformed to include the history, art, literature, concepts, and points of view of several cultures. Columbus has no longer "discovered" America, because the Arowaks were a thriving people already here, with their own perspective upon his arrival (Fritz, Peterson, McKissack, McKissack, Mahy, & Highwater, 1992). Children learn that people have different versions of harvest holidays, different religions, different ideas about what is beautiful, and different interests, which sometimes conflict with others.

Finally, Banks believes, a fully developed multicultural curriculum includes the world in its focus. The "Ethnonational Model" links events and phenomena in America

An American "global village" classroom in Lynn, Massachusetts

to events, issues, and concepts from cultural groups around the world. An issue such as respect for the natural environment, for example, can include the perspective of the local community, exposure to Native American attitudes toward nature, and the ways that different peoples of the earth use and preserve their land.

As the scenario in the first-grade classroom described earlier shows, multicultural education must involve more than curriculum reform. Teachers must decide whether their goal is merely to convey a great deal of information about different cultures and points of view or to ensure that children will accept and be able to deal with those differences in their peers. Many decry multicultural education as focusing too much on differences among people and thus creating a society made up of separate "balkanized" groups in conflict with one another. They are afraid that multicultural-ism will lead to ethnic conflicts such as those in Balkan Bosnia and the former Soviet Union. To an extent, their fear is justified. If we only convey information without at-tending to the matter of values and attitudes and without teaching children how to communicate respectfully and effectively with one another, we in fact leave the door open to competition, conflict, and discrimination. We must go further and include as multicultural education what has been called "anti-bias" or "prejudice-reduction" education, as well as the teaching and reinforcing of social and communication skills.

Anti-bias education is social and moral education—that is, education that includes acceptance of the responsibility to instill in children values of equality, fairness, and tol-erance. Proponents argue that these values are fundamental to American ideology and are supported by our constitutional principles. They would agree with John Dewey that education is never value-neutral. To anti-bias educators, multicultural education is an approach that teaches children how to communicate, how to esteem themselves and others, how to resolve conflicts peacefully, and how to advocate for their own rights and the rights of others. (Chapter 7 further explores the importance of teaching social skills and values.)

Summary

This chapter attempts to describe the complex and diverse backgrounds of American schoolchildren and the impact that the diversity of their lives may have on their expe-rience of school. While our nation has always been a land of immigrants, we are expe-riencing at the end of the 20th century tremendous demographic change, as another wave of immigrants and refugees comes here for work, shelter, education, and the op-portunity to escape the past and create new lives. The experience of moving to a new land is difficult, if not traumatic, especially if the conditions left behind have scarred those who are leaving.

The arrival of new immigrants, primarily from Latin and Asian countries, and the growth of ethnic minorities whose ancestors have lived here for generations are liter-ally changing the face of this country. Serious differences exist in how easily their chil-dren fit into the culture of our public schools and begin to achieve (see, e.g., Jonathan Kozol's *Savage Inequalities,* 1991). The chapter details theories and research that help

Manna paints a picture.

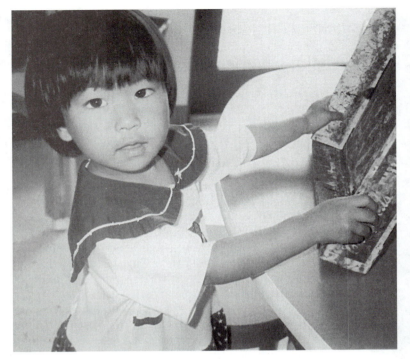

to explain these differences in adaptation and success and offers suggestions for addressing them. We believe schools and child care agencies can provide for an increasingly diverse student population by offering a comprehensive multicultural curriculum, involving a multicultural and global perspective on subject matter, plenty of time for strategies that promote cultural pride and acceptance, and direct teaching and support of positive social interaction.

Reflection Questions

1. "My grandfather came over on the boat in 1915 and had to learn English to get along here like everyone else. Sure he suffered, but he worked hard and he made it. Why can't these people do the same?" This is an often-heard argument against bilingual education, special programs for immigrants and refugees, and social welfare programs for immigrants in general. Do you agree? How would you respond to the speaker?

2. Which of the theories that seek to explain differences among ethnic groups in terms of school success (achievement, attendance, graduation rates, college entrance, etc.) seem most valid to you given your readings and your experience?

3. Given the special problems of refugee children, the possibility that they may not articulate their feelings about their past, and the need to respect families' privacy, how would you help a young refugee child whose past was problematical and who was withdrawn from your classroom?

4. Immigration continues to change the face of America. How can American public schools ensure that children "become American" without losing their own cultural histories?

References

Alvarez, L. (1995, October 1). Interpreting new worlds for parents. *New York Times*, pp. 29, 36.

American Association of University Women (2001). *Beyond the gender wars: A conversation about girls, boys and education*. Washington, DC: Author.

Anyon, J. (1981). Social class and school knowledge. *Curriculum Inquiry, 11*(1), 3–41.

Anyon, J. (1997). Social class, race, and educational reform at the Marcy School. In Anyon (Ed.), *Ghetto schooling: A political economy of urban educational reform* (pp. 14–38). New York: Teachers College Press.

Banks, J. A. (2001). *Cultural diversity and education*. Boston: Allyn & Bacon.

Banks, J. A., Cortes, C. E., Gay, G., Garcia, R. L., & Ochoa, A. (1991). *Curriculum guidelines for multicultural education*. Washington, DC: National Council for the Social Studies.

Belkin, D. (2001, April 7). Growing divide noted on best, worst readers. *The Boston Globe*, p. A3.

Bennett, C. I. (1995). *Comprehensive multicultural education: Theory and practice*. Boston: Allyn & Bacon.

Berliner, D. C., & Biddle, B. J. (1995). *Manufactured crisis: Myths, fraud, and the attack on America's public schools*. White Plains, NY: Longman.

Bouvier, L. (1993, Summer). The newest immigrants. *Center for Immigrant Studies, 15*, 12–15.

Breitborde, M. (1991). Personal correspondence.

Breitborde, M. (1996). Creating community in the classroom: Modeling "new basic skills" in teacher education. *Journal of Teacher Education, 47*(5), 367–374.

Breitborde, M. (2001). Personal interview, Salem, MA.

Cubberley, E. P. (1965). Changing conceptions of education [originally published 1909]. In R. L. Vassar (Ed.), *Social history of American education: Vol. 2. 1860 to the present* (pp. 149–156). Chicago: Rand McNally.

Delpit, L. (1994) *Other people's children: Cultural conflict in the classroom*. New York: New Press.

Fassler, D., & Danforth, K. (1993). *Coming to America: The kids' book about immigration*. Burlington, VT: Waterfront Books.

Fritz, J., Peterson, K., McKissack, P., McKissack, F., Mahy, M., & Highwater, J. (1992). *The world in 1492*. New York: Henry Holt.

Garcia, E. (1994). *Understanding and meeting the challenge of student cultural diversity*. Boston: Houghton Mifflin.

Gardner, H. (1993). *Multiple intelligences: The theory in practice*. New York: Basic Books.

Glenn, C. L., Jr. (1988). *The myth of the Common School*. Amherst, MA: University of Massachusetts Press.

Harrington, M. (1962). *The other America: Poverty in the United States*. New York: Macmillan.

Hernandez, H. (1989). *Multicultural education: A teacher's guide to content and process*. Upper Saddle River, NJ: Merrill/Prentice Hall.

Herrnstein, R. J., & Murray, C. (1994). *The bell curve: Intelligence and class structure in American life*. New York: Free Press.

Hollins, E. R. (1996). *Culture in school learning: Revealing the deep meaning*. Mahwah, NJ: Lawrence Erlbaum Associates.

Igoa, C. (1995). *The inner world of the immigrant child*. New York: St. Martin's Press.

Irvine, J. J. (1991). *Black students and school failures*. New York: Praeger.

Johnston, R. C., & Viadero, D. (2000, March 15). Unmet promise: Raising minority achievement. *Education Week*, 1, 18-19.

Kozol, J. (1967). *Death at an early age: The destruction of the hearts and minds of Negro children in the Boston public school*. New York: Houghton Mifflin.

Kozol, J. (1991). *Savage inequalities: Children in America's schools*. New York: Crown.

Kuttner, R. (1995, June 3). Beating up on immigrants. *The Boston Globe*, p. 11.

Martorella, P. (1993, Spring). Refugee issues in a globally interdependent world. *Educational Horizons, 71*(3), 157–160.

Meier, D. (1995). *The Power of their ideas*. Boston: Beacon Press.

National Coalition of Advocates for Students. (1991). *New voices: Immigrant students in U.S. public schools*. Boston: Author.

Nieto, S. (1996). *Affirming diversity: The sociopolitical context of multicultural education*. White Plains, NY: Longman.

Nitka, M. (1977, October 6). The class of 1990. *Burlington News*, p. 9.

Oakes, J. (1985). *Keeping track: How schools structure inequality*. New Haven, CT: Yale University Press.

O'Hare, W. P. (1992). *America's minorities: The demographics of diversity*. Washington, DC: Population Reference Bureau.

Orfield, G. (2001). *Schools more separated: Consequences of a decade of resegregation*. Cambridge, MA: The Civil Rights Project at Harvard University [www.law.harvard.edu/groups/civilrights/].

Pedrosa, E. C. (1990, August). Talking in the new land. *New England Monthly, 34–81*.

Rist, R. (1973). *The urban school: A factory for failure*. Cambridge, MA: MIT Press.

Rodriguez, C. (2001, February 6). Impact of the undocumented. *The Boston Globe*, pp. A1, A6.

Sadowski, M. (2001). Closing the gap one school at a time. *Harvard Educational Letter, 17*(3), 1–3, 5.

Suarez-Orozco, C., Todorova, I., & Louie, J. (2001). *The transnationalization of families: Immigrant separation and reunification*. Cambridge, MA: Harvard Graduate School of Education, Harvard Immigration Project.

Wax, M. L., Wax, R. H., & Dumont, R. V., Jr. (1989). *Formal education in an American Indian community*. Prospect Heights, IL: Waveland Press.

Wellesley College Center for Research on Women. (1992). *How schools shortchange girls: The AAUW report*. Washington, DC: American Association of University Women Foundation.

Websites

American Association of University Women (research on gender and education): *www.aauw.org/2000/research.html*

Annie E. Casey Foundation: *www.aecf.org*

Harvard Civil Rights Project: *www.law.harvard.edu/groups/civilrights/*

Harvard Immigration Project: *www.gse.harvard.edu/~hip/*

National Children's Advocacy Center (for physically and sexually abused children): *www.ncac-hsv.org/*

Part III

Implementing a Global Education Curriculum

7 Creating Community

Introduction: The Medium Is the Message

Teachers can create or buy beautiful materials to use in their classrooms for global education. They can design lessons with substantive global themes and convey important global concepts to the children in their charge. But the most important opportunities for teaching children the knowledge, values, and behaviors required for global citizenship probably lie not so much in what is designated as formal learning as they do in everything else that the child experiences in the classroom. The most powerful learning in schools and child care centers occurs informally, accidentally, unintentionally, through the "messages" we send to them about who they are as people and where they fit in the world. It occurs in the way we design their environment and organize their learning experiences, in the way we interact with them and guide their interactions with each another.

Think back to your earliest school experience—your preschool and early childhood days. Chances are what comes to mind is not what the teacher was trying to teach you but how. What we remember from those days is how we felt about the teacher, how welcomed we felt in the classroom, whether we felt accepted and part of the group or whether we felt like an outsider. How were children treated in that classroom? Were we happy?

Betsy hid her first-grade papers in her desk. For months, she kept them wadded up, away from the eyes of her mom and dad and from her high-achieving older brother and sister. They were full of black and red marks, shameful examples of her failure to complete her schoolwork with ease, her failure to learn. She told her mother there were no papers to bring home. She endured her placement in the "low reading group." She kept as quiet as she could in front of the teacher, this lively creative child who at home staged plays and carnivals, made up inventive stories and songs, and was the social leader of the neighborhood. When her mother came for the teacher conference, Mrs. Foley told her that her daughter would never learn to read and, worse, that she was a liar. Because teachers were not to be argued with, Betsy's parents agonized at home but said nothing. Betsy spent the rest of her childhood believing that she was stupid and that she was a very bad person. It took her 10 years and three schools to get through college. It took her longer to understand that she was brilliantly creative, that she had a tremendous ability to contribute to the world of people and ideas, and that she was a lovable, good person. In the world of her first-grade classroom, Betsy learned some terrible and wrong lessons that stayed with her for the next 30 years. Only through her own resilience and the support of her family did she overcome what could have been a personal disaster.

Teachers have unmatched power to affect the lives of children and what they "know" about themselves and the world. Sometimes this power is overt; that is, a teacher is supposed to make sure that children learn appropriate values and behaviors along with concepts and skills. For example, in traditional schooling in Asia, teachers educated children in "the way," the Confucian right path for living. In the early history of our own country, Puritan teachers in Massachusetts used biblical verses to teach reading, linking school to religion and knowledge to virtue in unambiguous ways. Early readers exhorted, "In Adam's fall, we sinned all." In today's multicultural America,

where there is no clear agreement on "the right way" and where our national constitution guarantees separation of church and state as a principle of freedom, a teacher's
effort to instill values in children may be more difficult to defend, or more "covert."
She may run her classroom based on a set of beliefs that are never really discussed. We
contend that teaching is never value-neutral. Teachers always operate according to assumptions about, for example, what is valid information to learn, what is a "good student," how children should conduct themselves in school or child care centers, and
how much choice children should have in classroom activities. This chapter explores
the matter of the values and attitudes teachers convey to children, the informal but
pervasive lessons children learn behind the stated curriculum, the nature of a teacher's
influence, and the nature of teaching/learning experiences that are much more important in the long run than the materials and lesson plans we put before them.

Recognizing the Hidden Curriculum

School is made up of the actual printed curriculum—lesson plans and materials, concepts and skills—but also what has been called the "hidden curriculum," meaning all
that we learn incidentally. Is it okay to make noise in this classroom? Are children encouraged to experiment? What are the rules, and what are the consequences of mis-
behavior? Are the rules applied fairly and consistently? Do girls and boys play together?
Can children maintain friendships in the classroom? Are they guided to work on tasks
with other children? Are they protected from bullying and kept from bullying others?
Are they given open access to, and responsibility for, learning materials, or must they
ask the teacher, or wait until "it's time" for her to give them out? What happens when
a child decides to paint a tree purple?

Educators differ on the issue of "character education." Some advocate for a conscious, step-by-step approach, which includes listing the attributes of "good character"
that we would like to see children develop (for example, sharing, taking turns, speaking kindly), and teaching or rewarding children for exhibiting those behaviors (see for
example, Lickona, 1999). Others eschew teaching values, wary of treading on families'
rights and responsibilities to instill in their children a set of values particular to families'
belief systems and/or religions. Some ask teachers to recognize the spirituality that is
part of being human. Aoestre Johnson (1999) and Parker Palmer (1998), for example,
treat the "spirits of children" and of teachers as welcome and unavoidable aspects of
experience. Distinct from religious beliefs, our spirituality, they say, is what makes us
fully human. It is what gives our lives purpose and direction, and we should help children ask and answer the "big questions" about what is right or wrong, why we are here
on earth, what part we humans play in the ecology of the world, and what values are
important to us. Jonathan Kozol (1995, 2000) goes so far as to say that spirituality is an
essential element in helping children and their families resist the sometimes overwhelmingly difficult conditions of their lives.

Alfie Kohn (1997) has written and spoken extensively against the kind of formal
teaching of values that Lickona and others promote and the practice of rewarding
children for good behavior. Character, he says, develops from sustained exposure to

a climate where positive social behavior, kindness, sharing, and the like are expected and are consistently modeled. Children should not learn that prosocial behavior results in external rewards such as class pizza parties or gold stickers at the end of each day. The rewards for good behavior should be intrinsic; it should seem logical and important to the smooth and happy functioning of a classroom or center. While Kohn may underestimate the need to teach prosocial behaviors to children who have not learned them at home and in their neighborhoods, his ideas that we should focus on creating an ethos in the classroom which expects and supports positive interaction and that children's potential to act with kindness can be compromised by external rewards for good behavior are worth serious consideration.

The first and most important rule for teachers wishing to educate for global citizenship is to create a climate in the classroom and the school that represents the knowledge, behaviors, and values they're trying to teach. Children must *live* things to learn them. After all, we know they learn from direct, concrete experiences. If we provide them with formal learning experiences according to global themes, espousing the values of cooperation, equality, tolerance, and social responsibility and conveying knowledge about global issues, and then arrange our learning environments in ways that deny those values and possibilities, we will be guilty of hypocrisy, and our teaching will be empty and ineffective. What children observe in and experience in people's actions and how they feel in reaction to those observations and experiences is much more powerful than the formal tasks they are asked to accomplish. The teacher who talks about pollution and world hunger and then uses Styrofoam plates and cups for snacks and throws extra food away sends a message that is muddled, academic, and shallow. The teacher who preaches about participatory democracy around the world but makes all the classroom rules sabotages the lesson.

Creating a climate that embodies global citizenship takes time and careful attention. Teachers need to look at all aspects of the learning environment—its physical contents and the organization of space, materials, and "traffic"; behavior expectations, the formal rules that guide them, and the way these rules are implemented; how and when children are encouraged to work or play alone or separately; the question of ownership of materials, children's work, and the classroom in general; and the quality and quantity of teachers' interactions with the children, as individuals and in groups. Besides making careful decisions about all these aspects of classroom life, teachers have to conduct direct lessons related to positive social behavior and "community life." The amount of time a teacher spends constructing that climate of community is time well spent and should include team-building activities, review and practice of positive social behaviors, and regular conferences and classroom meetings where children share problems, issues, and questions that come up. Plenty of time should be used to involve children in classroom decisions, even about what should go up on the display walls. This chapter includes some suggestions for community-building activities (see also Chapter 10).

Several authors have written about the disjuncture between the world of the child at home and the world in the classroom. Sara Lawrence Lightfoot called this "worlds apart" (1978). The sociologist Robert Dreeben (1968) wrote that, while the family provided foundational emotional security, the school was children's introduction to

*Exploring globes helps children
see the world as a whole
community.*

what norms of behavior they would have to learn to function in our larger, more formal, society.

Phillip Jackson wrote a seminal book in 1968 entitled *Life in Classrooms*, in which he explained that because of the way schools are peopled and organized and because of the nature of the goals and tasks of schooling, all classroom environments are characterized by crowds, praise, and power. As children move from the intimacy of home and family, with relatively few children and low adult–child ratios and what sociologists call "primary social relations," to the larger world of the classroom, they learn that schools are crowded places where they have to wait their turn (sometimes for a long time) to get the teacher's attention, that there are many children vying for the same space or the same toy or the same friend, and that they will not be the center of attention very often, if ever. Crowds mean that children cannot use the bathroom whenever they want, or always play with the favorite puzzle, or decide they want to spend all afternoon in the play yard. Teachers manage these "crowded" conditions in different ways: by having children "line up," establishing procedures for distributing materials, organizing quiet times and noisy times (because crowds tend to make noise), and structuring how often and under what conditions they make themselves available to individual children.

In crowded classrooms, it is difficult for teachers to have personal contact with every child every day. But we know how important that immediate contact is, even in high school, which is a far less personal environment than early childhood settings. Theodore Sizer, an advocate of small middle and high schools, says that it is essential that all students in every school have someone they feel they can talk to, someone who they trust who knows them (1984). Because the authors of this book believe that the foundation for global citizenship is children's strong sense of themselves as secure, worthy, capable human beings, we feel it is important that life in classrooms include attention to the child as a growing person. Children must have ready access to adults when they need help; they need readily accessible materials that they are trusted to be responsible for; they need predictable and reasonable rules for sharing space, things, and people.

A second aspect of Jackson's view of the hidden curriculum in classrooms is praise. Children at home may be asked to help with chores and praised for doing them, but for the most part they are just accepted as whole people rather than as a sum of skills, talents, and responsibilities. In school, on the other hand, they are judged almost all the time. Only a part of them is invited into the classroom—the part that reads and does mathematics well or not, the part that communicates effectively or not, the part that can kick a ball far or not, the part that can find the right puzzle piece or draw a recognizable person. Even when children are invited to play, to create, to share experiences, there are limits present in schools that are not present at home. Their behavior is always observed; their privacy, compromised. In the most "open" of school environments, children are expected to behave in ways acceptable to that environment. Through praise, conveyed through verbal responses and on written evaluations, children learn whether they are adequate to the tasks of school. Do they know enough? Do they behave appropriately? Does the teacher think well of them? Do their peers like them? Will they be rewarded or punished? A child who is only criticized comes to feel like a failure. A child who is ignored comes to feel like a nonentity. In a comprehensive study of teacher–student relationships, Jere Brophy and Thomas Good have described the effects of differential teacher interaction, the results of unfairly distributed attention and rewards, and the devastating effects of a teacher's "indifference" (1974).

Praise should be authentic and specific, say Brophy and Good. Just as we hurt children by withholding praise, we do them no good by praise that is unmerited or confusing. If we accept wrong answers or tell them their work is wonderful without telling them why, children lose faith in their own ability to judge. On the other hand, if our praise is specific and directed at the behavior rather than at the person, they hear about what was good and bad, about what should be repeated and what should not. It is essential that teachers face the fact that their opinions are important and influential. It is also essential that they understand how to communicate to children that they are fully accepted and welcomed as unique people, with differing strengths, talents, weaknesses, and limitations, and that specific performances, though important, are only part of the whole. They are not awful people if they have trouble learning to read; they only have trouble learning to read.

If praise comes only from sources external to children, they will be more sensitive to teachers' and others' opinions and perhaps come to depend on these opinions to judge their performance and their worth in general. We recommend using multiple and alternative means of evaluation, including self-evaluation and portfolio assessment, which emphasize the interesting process of learning and draw children into monitoring their own work. By helping them to assess how much they have learned and grown, we can help them to depend more on themselves for praise, which will ultimately be more immediately available and more generously given.

Because school is characterized by limited access to people, things, and rewards—in other words, because of its characteristic crowding and dispensation of praise—the world of the classroom is a world of power. Teachers exercise power as the primary decision makers in the classroom. They dispense power in determining where children sit, what they can and cannot do, what things they are allowed to have. They decide who can pass out snack napkins and who must stay after school. In their choices about which children to speak to, in their choice of words, and in their tone of voice, they exert powerful messages about children's very abilities and worth.

Teachers can abuse their power. Some use intimidation and fear to "control" the classroom. They can, like Betsy's teacher, destroy a child's good feeling about herself. Or they can use their power sensitively with children to make them feel safe and welcome, raise deflated egos, give them choices and chances to make decisions, allow them to make mistakes, and ensure that they do not abuse each other.

Children also exercise power in the classroom. Those with powerful personalities and strong talents and interests can influence a teacher's decisions about the content, pace, and organization of the curriculum and classroom. Some students are central figures among their peers. Because of their forceful personalities or their attractiveness, other children want to be with them or be like them. They have the power to lead. They can lead their peers into negative antisocial behavior, or they can help to establish a norm of positive, prosocial interaction. Think of the power of the ringleader of a group of eight-year-olds who singles out a classmate to make fun of or ostracize. Think of the first-grader who sneers at a classmate, "How can you wear those kind of pants?" Then think of the kindergartner whose imaginative stories are fodder for friends' dramatic play and who suggests, "You be the queen.... You be the wild beast." Or the four-year-old who "translates" for a best friend, whose speech is difficult for everyone else to understand. These last two scenarios are examples of power exercised positively and constructively.

It is important that teachers keep in mind the inevitable factors in classroom life—crowds, praise, and power—and use them to enhance rather than deny the values and goals of global education. The relative difficulty of getting attention and having access to materials and space and the lack of privacy inherent in classroom life should lead teachers to construct opportunities to further global educational goals. Sharing, for example, is necessary in classroom life but also necessary in the larger world. The need to establish fair procedures for sharing time, space, and materials provides an opportunity for participatory decision making and peaceful conflict resolution. Even the criteria for judging whether students' work is excellent, good, fair, or poor—part of the dispensation of praise—can be determined through discussion involving the children.

Children will not shrink from the inevitably unequal praise and criticism of classroom life if a teacher separates their performance from their personal worth. Teachers who reinforce again and again the idea that everyone does some things well and other things not so well are teaching children to accept differences. Teachers who facilitate the sharing of talents through cooperative learning projects are demonstrating to children the need for interdependent collaboration and the value of differences among the individuals who contribute to the product of the group. Teachers who share power with children and who facilitate the sharing of power among children are using their influence to teach children about the responsible and prosocial exercise of power. They are also providing children with the experience of having and using power in the service of the classroom community. Children who have been the victims of the misuse of power, especially through abuse or intimidation, need a guided experience of using power in positive ways (Gootman, 1993). We can often turn our worst offenders into positive members of the classroom community by entrusting them with responsibilities they have never before been allowed. Philip comes to mind: a boy with a reputation for stealing and disrupting his third-grade class, whose mathematical ability was the one academic skill he was sure of. Amid his classmates' audible gasps of dismay, his teacher asked him to take responsibility for collecting and recording the money they would bring in to school that week to buy books. At the end of the week, Philip proudly presented his records and his cash box, with every penny accounted for, having gained in self-respect and the respect of his peers.

The hidden curriculum of schools has a powerful effect on children's learning what is appropriate and acceptable behavior. In addition, it has the potential to turn into children's internalized judgments about their own worth as students and as people. Particularly for children without strong alternative support from their families or their communities, school provides clear expectations about correct behaviors, important knowledge, and valuable skills necessary to succeed in life. To the extent that their own behaviors, knowledge, and talents fit in with what is expected of them in school, they will come away feeling successful and worthwhile. If, however, the fit isn't good, they may never understand what is required or may feel that the effort is impossible. What further complicates the situation is that very often teachers convey different expectations for different children, surmising sometimes on the basis of limited information that some children will succeed and others are bound to fail. The next section of this chapter describes research that corroborates these differential expectations on the part of teachers and their effects on the children who experience them.

Recognizing Teacher Expectations

In a now classic study, Rosenthal and Jacobson (1968) found that teachers had different expectations for different children and that somehow these expectations translated into actual differences in achievement for these children. Randomly selecting a group of children in each class of the study, Rosenthal and Jacobson told their teachers that, based on the results of intelligence tests (which were actually fake), this group of children were "late-bloomers" whose high intelligence would make itself known by the end of the year. When the researchers tested the classes at the year's end using real achievement tests, the "late-bloomers" did, in fact, score significantly better than their classmates. Rosenthal and Jacobson speculated that the teachers' higher expectations for this group, which had been "manufactured" by the experiment, somehow caused the teachers to teach them more effectively and behave more positively toward them, resulting in their higher achievement.

Later studies have replicated and extended those findings. One such study was Ray Rist's (1973) observation/participation in a kindergarten class outside Chicago. The teacher in that class had formed expectations about whether children would achieve by the eighth day of school, having little real information to base her expectations on except for their family background and income, the quality and quantity of their verbal interaction (including whether they spoke Standard or Black English), how well they dressed, and, most disturbingly, the relative darkness of their brown skin. Children who were not comfortably verbal, whose parents were not educated, who were on welfare, and whose skin was very dark were assumed to be her "slow learners." Rist documented the very different ways that that teacher interacted with her "bright" children and her "slow learners," including more attention and privileges extended to the first group, more and longer verbal interaction, more support for their schoolwork, and more interesting academic tasks. By the end of the year, the achievement gap between the two groups was great. The higher-achieving children were beginning to read and were well prepared for first grade; the "slow learners" had learned very little and were destined to continue on in the "low group" in first grade.

It seems that we teachers may form unfounded and unjust expectations of children depending on our surface impressions of them. We may use bright, quiet children as models for others, putting pressure on them to continue to be "good" and perhaps alienating them from their peers. We may "write off" others, assuming that "they'll never get it." We may show quick exasperation to some children, while working patiently with others to help them understand. We may look to one group of children to help us with putting up decorations or taking messages to the office and convey to another group that they have nothing to offer in the way of help or that they are not trusted.

Forming expectations is natural and cannot be avoided. After all, if we've had four children from the same family, all of whom were underprepared for academic tasks, had difficulty learning, and acted defiantly and aggressively, it is natural to think the fifth sibling might well exhibit the same problematical behaviors. But, Brophy and Good say (1974), we can be "proactive" teachers. We can observe behavior carefully, laying aside our assumptions, and work with the actual behaviors children arrive in our classrooms with, giving them whatever help they need to grow and achieve. Again, the message to children should be, "You all have talents and abilities. None of you is perfect nor has to be; we will work together to see that you succeed."

Making the Curriculum Confluent

The point made by this chapter is that what children learn in schools and child care centers is not just information but also attitudes and habits. We cannot separate "facts" from feelings and behaviors. Learning always involves three domains: the cognitive domain of the mind, the affective domain of the heart or spirit, and the behavioral domain of action. To recognize and plan for the interrelationship of all three domains of learning is to support what we might call "confluent education" (Breitborde, 1987).

The stated and the hidden curriculum in classrooms should be confluent. One should not preach equality and then establish "ability groups" that allow some children to write and perform a play and restrict others to "basic" skills-and-drill tasks. One should not teach about democracy and cooperation and then not allow children to have a voice in what happens in the classroom. One should not talk about cultural diversity and then not address the ethnic jokes that children (and teachers!) tell. Every experience within the walls of a school is a learning experience, what John Dewey called "a teachable moment" (1979), and is fodder for the curriculum. The ethnic heritage of cafeteria workers, the food served at lunch, the books selected for story time, the limits put on "show and share" objects, the way children are grouped for learning tasks, all are part of the school's curriculum.

To teach about the world is to offer children a set of information, a set of values, and a set of skills they can use. Teaching about immigration, for example, involves conveying knowledge about who comes from where and for what reasons, how immigrants' feelings are affected by the change, and how difficult it is to change old habits and behaviors to survive in new cultures. Teaching confluently, we inform children of the conditions and experiences of immigration, help them to understand how immigrants feel about leaving their homelands, and teach them ways of behaving and communicating that help bridge different life experiences and cultures. A teaching unit on immigration ought to involve learning about the experiences of immigrants in history and the role that immigrants have played in their own communities (see, for example, Breitborde & Amaria, 1998). It ought to be broad enough to address, for instance, the concept of migration in general, as applied to the animal world, as well as in terms of the experience of a child moving across town to a new neighborhood and a new school. It ought to include role play and practice in ways of making newcomers feel welcome, activities that sensitize children to the problems inherent in not speaking the dominant language, and direct experiences in sampling the richness and variety of different cultures, especially those found in the school.

Teachers committed to global education need to look at the school day in its entirety through the eyes of the children. It may be that children are getting "mixed messages" that obviate the goals of global education. It may also be that teachers committed to global education are missing important opportunities to teach values and behaviors that would strengthen the impact of the knowledge they intend to convey about the world. Congruent education makes learning an integral part of children's experience by moving beyond conveying information to changing attitudes and instilling new behaviors. True learning, said Pestalozzi (1954), Dewey (1979), and many others, involves the head, heart, and hand and results in new habits of mind, new beliefs and assumptions, and the skills to carry out these beliefs in practical, everyday ways. In studying world food distribution and the problems of hunger, for example, children might inquire about where the cafeteria food comes from and how it gets to school, its nutritional value, the way prices are determined, and the extent to which food is wasted. They may determine that they can take certain actions to influence changes in the cafeteria service or to help distribute extra food to those in need. What they learn may impel them to contribute to local food banks or initiatives to bring food to hungry children in other places in the world.

Using Multiple Modalities

Previous chapters have discussed the diversity of children's learning styles, cultures, language patterns, intelligences, exceptionalities, and life conditions and the ways these differences affect their processing of information. A basic tenet of this book is that teachers need to attend to and respect these learning differences and respond to them with different teaching strategies. Students should have opportunities to learn through many modalities, by using visual images such as art forms and graphics, by manipulating objects and artifacts, by listening to stories and accounts, by reading and being read to, by creating drama and play, and by being wholly involved in direct experiences (see, e.g., Gardner, 1983; Guild & Garger, 1985).

Children should be allowed to learn from each other in cooperative groups or with partners, alone through independent work, and in close conference with a teacher or another adult. As the Johnson brothers, authors of several books on cooperative learning (1999, 1994, 1991), tell us, teachers should consider seriously the characteristics of their students and the nature of the task at hand as they determine how to organize children for learning. For some children and some tasks, independent work is best. For other children and other purposes, group work is more effective. Still other options involve learning partners, triads, teacher–student conferencing, and peer teaching. Children should have experiences with all these social forms. For example, children need to experience learning from another child as well as teaching a peer, so that each is sometimes the one who knows and other times the one who doesn't. In creative writing, a period of group brainstorming works to generate ideas, followed by a period of quiet independence for personal reflection and persistence.

Adapting instruction to children's different learning needs does not mean designing instruction differently for each of the 25 children in one classroom. It merely means providing a wealth of ways by which children can get information and experience new concepts and skills so that every child has a chance to "get it." More than making sure that children's primary learning strategies correspond to teaching strategies, teachers should expose children to all teaching/learning modes. If you are an "auditory learner," who receives information best by listening, you still need to practice your visual and kinesthetic capabilities. If you are more kinesthetically or spatially intelligent than linguistically intelligent (Gardner, 1983), you still need to be able to learn information through printed material. Even if you like working with others to understand new materials or complete a task, you still need to develop your ability to work independently.

As children differ in the ways they process information, so too do they differ in the ways they best express what they have learned. Paper-and-pencil tests work well for some, but others will not reveal their knowledge best that way. Perhaps they express what they know better by means of artwork, or by telling you what they've learned, or by showing you through focussed activities. Keeping in mind that we believe global education should be confluent, involving the head, the heart, and the hand, teachers' assessment of children's learning should include opportunities to demonstrate values, attitudes, and behaviors.

Has your unit on unity and diversity changed one child's habit of criticizing another's different dialect? Has it resulted in a change in the way the class responds to the Jehovah's Witness child who doesn't celebrate Halloween? Do children demonstrate tolerance, acceptance, respectful curiosity? Do they offer questions and examples that relate to nations and cultures around the world? Are their recommendations for changes in cafeteria service well founded and realistic? Are their plans for smoothing the way for immigrant children in the school sensitive and responsive to actual needs?

Good teachers design assessment strategies that demonstrate learning in creative and involving ways. Children can compile portfolios with samples of their best work throughout a teaching unit. They can produce murals, interpretive dances and plays, class logs, poetry and fiction, songs and sagas, reports and speeches, and board and computer games. They can teach each other, teach their families, and make presentations to school committees. And they can take tests, as well. Quite often, assessment strategies become ways for children to share what they know with others; that is, these strategies become additional educational tools. Even a well-designed test can be educational, stimulating children to think about and apply what they've learned.

The global education activities suggested in this book are meant to include a variety of instructional and assessment strategies. We urge teachers to consider all the ways children learn and demonstrate their learning as they use and adapt these activities or design their own curricula. We hope that teachers will address all learning modalities and intelligences at some time in their curriculum.

Teaching Constructively

Children arrive in the world curious and open to experience, ready to take risks and driven by a need to experiment, to learn. Even when left in a crib with no external stimulation—no colorful mobiles to bat, no pictures to look at, no cuddly toys to hold—infants will play with their interesting body parts. In so doing, they learn that toes are small round things, legs bend, hands sometimes grab feet and sometimes miss, and so on. Piaget told us (1962) that children learn by constructing meaning from their experiences. First by experiencing directly the objects in their world and later by abstracting general principles from their experiences with similar and different objects,

Figure 7.1   For Martin Luther King Day, January 1996, first grade children composed a group poem about what peace meant to them.

Source: Mary Ann Grassia, teacher, Salem, Massachusetts.

Peace is . . .

love,
a big circle of children,
a butterfly,
people helping each other,
Martin Luther King, Jr.,
friends,
animals,
caring,
sharing with a friend,
the world,
the beach,
the stars,
your heart,
playing,
helping the animals,
the moon,
children sledding,
children playing in a playground,
green grass,
fishing, and
taking a nap.

the end

Grade 1 Room 9
Witchcraft Heights School
Salem, Massachusetts
Teacher: Mary Ann Grassia

children learn about the world and how it works. Any teacher of young children can tell a story about having carefully explained some phenomenon to a child, perhaps about what caused the latest hurricane, and then learning that what her listener heard was that the sign over the local bakery nearly fell down, leading him to conclude that hurricanes are dangerous for bakeries.

The authors believe that learning is not a "top-down" process, whereby the teacher teaches and the student learns exactly what is taught. In fact, we all may "hear" or attend to different aspects of an experience, and the way we make sense of that experience probably differs for each of us. For example, those who live near the Atlantic Ocean will read a story about a hurricane and take away meanings that are different from someone who has only seen pictures on the national news. Learning is, in fact, interactive, relying as much on the "bottom-up" perceptions and understandings of the learner as it does on a teacher's effectiveness at presenting information.

If we understand how much learning depends on a learner's meaning making, then we will design instruction that allows children to construct and express their own meanings. We can turn children's attention to particular experiences and guide them in understanding what they are experiencing, but we must leave room for their own interpretations. Authentic learning is the expression of children's understanding. Anything else may be learned only "for the moment." Think of the typical weekly spelling test, where children memorize lists of words out of context and perhaps without understanding what they mean or how they are used. Though some children may achieve a grade of 100% by Friday, we might question how well, or for how long, they have learned the new words.

The activities described in this book are designed to build on children's experiences and to encourage personal and creative expression. For teachers to teach constructively, however, they must let go of the idea that they control all the learning in the classroom. A teacher who understands the cognitive basis of constructivism (Fosnot, 1996) will allow children, for example, to teach each other, to work and create together, to design their own versions of what they have experienced, and to formulate generalizations and test them out, using journals, group stories, retelling of experiences, creative drama, drawing, and hands-on discovery.

We must give children plenty of time to ask questions rather than ask them always to respond to our questions. *Inquiry* and *discovery* learning techniques are based on the fact that children naturally ask questions about the world. We must allow them to voice their curiosity and give them the tools to explore their own answers. The 21st-century classroom corrals children's natural curiosity and provides them with whatever tools are necessary to help them be independent information seekers and information presenters. Those tools can be books, paper and pencils, computers, the Internet, works of art, science equipment, cameras, field trips, community resources, stage props, or each other. By respecting children's role in their own learning and giving them the tools and resources for undertaking and expressing it, we provide a confidence-building "hidden curriculum" to support meaningful and confluent subject matter.

Essential to constructivist teaching is time to observe, to question, to explore, to think, to talk, to hypothesize, to try things out (Duckworth, 1987). Young children especially need time to play, for play is the primary vehicle for children's learning. Play is where they act out their hypotheses and their emotional reactions. It is also where they learn to plan and carry out ideas and to cooperate. Piaget (1962) distinguished four types of play with regard to children's constructing of meanings: practice play, symbolic play, games with rules, and construction. He assumed a hierarchy of cognitive functioning as engaged in each type, with practice play requiring little thinking or understanding and construction engaging the child in decision-making and cause-and-effect paradigms. Chaille and Silvern (1996) part with Piaget in arguing that all forms of play involve children in developing understandings, whether they be understandings about their own abilities to jump farther and farther with practice or to build a tower that doesn't fall down. These authors further tell us that we can distinguish different types of knowledge that children gain through play, including knowledge of the physical world, logico-mathematical knowledge (e.g., in replacing one big block with two half-sized ones), knowledge of oral and written language, and knowledge of social and moral behavior. "Play," they say, "offers the child the opportunity to make sense out of the world by using available tools." Children create meaning "by doing [and] by doing with others, and by being completely involved in that doing" (Chaille & Silvern, p. 277). Clearly, then, we need to provide children with uninterrupted time and environments rich in "available tools," other children to share ideas with, and adults who support them as they engage in communities of learning.

At the beginning of the 21st century we see too many children in our classrooms who have not had sufficient opportunity to play or research their own questions and who have not learned how to cooperate. The next section of this chapter addresses the inevitable and growing need for teachers to guide and sometimes to teach directly the social skills required for life in our global society.

Teaching Social Skills

A look at American classrooms and child care centers of today reveals the reasons that so many teachers are frustrated by children's behavior. It appears that too many of our children are arriving in school without having learned how to get along with others, not knowing how to get what they need without resorting to violence. Many do not know how to be patient, how to share, how to take turns, how to listen respectfully or speak politely. Many children are angry and frustrated and are unable to control or express their anger and frustration in constructive ways. While educationists exhort teachers to use cooperative learning, peer conferencing, heterogeneous grouping, and creative play, many teachers report failing in the attempt because children cannot work peacefully and productively with each other. These teachers may blame poor parenting or the loss of religion or disintegrating community life or violent images in the media. Perhaps children are too busy in some classrooms negotiating for their own safety, their "place" or their "face" in a mini-society of competing and conflictual individuals (Breitborde, 1996).

Whatever the sources of the problem, the authors believe that it falls on teachers to teach these skills that children have not learned elsewhere. If we are to take our social responsibility seriously, global education may need to begin with basic social skills such as communication, cooperation, and conflict resolution. We agree with Nel Noddings (1992, 1995) that education should produce people who are competent, caring, loving, and lovable, who contribute to the social good at home and in the world. The task of teachers is to love attentively, reduce violence, care for the world's children, and "ensure a place for every child and emerging adult in the economic and social world" (1995, p. 368). To Noddings, our ability to function effectively in the world is predicated on our ability to care: "Caring … implies competence…. It is the strong, resilient backbone of human life" (1995, p. 368). Well before Noddings, John Dewey wrote that teachers cannot avoid the responsibility for social education:

> The sum of the matter is that the times are out of joint…. Teachers cannot escape even if they would, some responsibility for a share in setting them right. They may regard it, like Hamlet, as a cursed spite, or as an opportunity. But they cannot avoid the responsibility…. As a matter of fact, they are strengthening one set of forces or the other. The question is whether they are doing so blindly, evasively, or intelligently and courageously. (1935, p. 7)

Psychologists who have studied "resilient" children—those who seem to have overcome the harsh conditions of their lives—have found common characteristics. Summarizing the results of several studies, Breitborde (1996) listed three shared sets of abilities: social skills, including empathy, communication, active participation, and general

Teaching acceptance and appreciation are important social skills in early education.

friendliness; a sense of power, self-confidence, and efficacy; and problem-solving skills and goal-directed behavior, including the ability to plan realistically. This list suggests that incorporating the teaching of social and problem-solving skills and promoting participation and self-confidence in our classrooms might benefit many individual children and the life of the community as well.

The Johnson brothers, authors of many studies and strategies for cooperative learning, tell us that the prerequisites for effective cooperation include similar abilities and skills. Children need to be able to listen actively, speak clearly, trust and be trustworthy, accept differences, participate in setting group goals, solve problems, and negotiate or mediate conflicts. The Johnsons' book *Joining Together* (1999) offers many strategies for teaching and practicing these skills for people of all ages.

William Kreidler, author of *Creative Conflict Resolution* (1984), a helpful resource for teaching strategies for peaceful and constructive problem solving, lists five ingredients necessary for effective conflict resolution. Again, these ingredients recall the skills and abilities described above and include self-awareness, tolerance, communication skills, and problem solving. His book offers many strategies for kindergarten to grade 8 (adaptable for younger and older children, as well) for teaching and practicing these skills. Among them are "Effective Rule-Making," which structures children's participation in creating the rules and consequences for classroom community life; "Time-Out," which allows children to try to work out their differences together with the teacher's support; and role play and reverse role play ideas. (Kreidler is a Quaker and a staff member of Educators for Social Responsibility, a national organization based in Cambridge, Massachusetts, whose goal is peace education and critical social awareness.)

In the opinion of the authors of this book, a central problem limiting many children's (and many adults') learning and cooperation is their inability to handle anger constructively. The media, community incidents, and, too often, life in children's own households are replete with poor models for handling anger. Children are surrounded with images of adults and older children blowing up (figuratively and literally), responding quickly to frustration and anger with fists and weapons, harsh language, and promises of revenge. Violence reigns in movies, on television, in music, and on newsstands. Peace, it seems, doesn't sell. It's no wonder that so many of our children are unpracticed at managing their anger constructively.

Children should understand that anger is not a bad feeling but that there are good and bad ways of expressing it. A simple but effective exercise for children who need to learn alternative ways of handling anger, based on an idea offered by Kreidler, is an "Anger Brainstorm" session, where the group lists all the ways people might handle anger and then, using consensus and critical thinking, categorizes these ways into "good," "it depends," and "never." Angry children might be encouraged to draw pictures or write about how they feel. Teachers might establish a private "cooling off" space. Conflicts between children and between children and teachers will be resolved only if the participants have had time and opportunity to let their anger cool. Negotiation, mediation, and timed discussions, for example, will work only when the parties are ready to think and speak clearly and listen to each other.

Other strategies for teaching social behaviors and promoting community in the classroom can be found in Chapter 11. In general, however, we would advise teachers to take seriously their responsibility to create environments where children feel safe, to monitor children's interaction with each other, and to model the kind of behavior they would like to see children exhibit. Research demonstrates that programs that are successful in promoting safety and preventing violence are those that (1) are integrated into school life, (2) focus on specific prosocial behaviors to teach children, for example, what respect "looks like" and "sounds like," (3) provide children with opportunities to practice them in workshop settings such as daily classroom meetings, and (4) offer feedback on their social performance. Even children whose families and neighborhoods do not model peaceful interaction or provide social safety can develop new behavioral repertoires and expectations by spending hours in a protected environment where "we don't allow that here" (Pirozzi, 2001).

Expanding the School's Mission: Full-Service and Community Schools

Life in the 21st century can be complex and difficult for many children and their families. While the school or child care center can be a haven for children from troubled families and communities, the problems they find at home inevitably invade their experience at school (Breitborde & Swiniarski, 2001). A child in need of eyeglasses, ill with an untreated infection, worried about how parents will pay next month's rent, concerned about violence or substance abuse at home, or hungry, will not be able to concentrate on math. As Abraham Maslow told us, basic needs for physical sustenance, safety, and security must be satisfied before individuals can be free to develop and learn (1962). Moreover, parents who speak little or no English or whose own schooling has been limited and negative, or parents who work three jobs at minimum wages to support their families, may not be available to attend conferences or to help with homework. In many communities, the stresses of immigration, under-or unemployment, single parenthood, and poverty impact life in schools and child care centers. Increasingly, schools are widening their missions and professional networks to secure basic services for families in need in order to free children to learn.

An important initiative in this regard is a movement toward full-service or community schools (Dryfoos, 1994). These schools take on the responsibility of marshaling health and social resources on behalf of families by providing services under their roofs to children and their families. One such school, the Robert L. Ford School in Lynn, Massachusetts, is a large (900-student) urban elementary school whose population is multicultural, multilingual, and poor. Ninety percent of Ford children qualify for free or reduced-price school lunches. More than half are children of immigrants. Unemployment among parents is high. Rates of domestic violence and substance abuse in the neighborhood are among the worst in the state. The school houses a health clinic, an evening school for parents seeking citizenship education, General Education Diploma (GED) and English as a Second Language classes, before- and after-school children's programs, and an information and referral network for families in need of social services. A partnership with Salem State College offers basic college courses at the school for adults seeking to further their education, workshops in life skills and parenting, intergenerational curriculum activity nights, and tutorial programs for children.

In this "Partnership for the Educational Village," parents have felt welcome in the school, have used the services to advance themselves educationally and vocationally, and are taking a more active role in their children's schooling. Rather than bemoan the lack of parent involvement typical of many urban elementary schools, the Ford has taken seriously its role as a community institution, built on family strength, and successfully sought help from city agencies, volunteer organizations, and a local college to provide a comprehensive program of services. One result is that in the ten years of the full-service programming, standardized test scores have risen significantly (Partnership for the Educational Village, http://www.salemstate.edu/education/pev).

Summary

Our instructional medium is the message that children will learn, through their direct experience interacting with us teachers, the degree of choice we allow them over the events of their classroom lives, the relative success they experience, and the relationships they forge with their peers. For young children to experience concretely the goals of global education, their teachers must provide them with a sense of belonging and acceptance and the skills for interacting in prosocial ways. Classroom communities are academically necessary for young children, especially in light of the degree of failure in their families and their larger communities. To create communities, we must first understand the powerful impact of the hidden curriculum of classrooms and the influence of a teacher's communicated expectations on children's sense of well-being and self-worth. We ought to respond to them in ways they can understand, respecting their differences in receiving information, constructing meaning, and expressing what they know. Teachers can organize the environment to provide positive peer experiences, reinforce opportunities for cooperation, and teach directly the behaviors that are necessary for responsible, productive, and caring social interaction. Finally, schools and child care centers in communities where families lack basic services and resources to support their children's learning may need to expand their missions and find ways to provide these services in collaboration with local agencies.

Reflection Questions

1. How have the expectations of the teachers you have had affected your concept of yourself as a learner?
2. Nel Noddings believes that the goal of teaching children to care should be at the center of school curricula in this period of history, more important than the teaching of academic information. Do you agree?
3. Argue for or against the proposition that schools and child care centers have a responsibility to help families secure basic health, education, and social services.

References

Breitborde (Sherr), M. (1987). Educating for peaceful and just relations: Confluence and context in teaching and learning. In T. M. Thomas, D. R. Conrad, & G. F. Langsam (Eds.), *Global images of peace and education*. Ann Arbor, MI: Prakken Publications.

Breitborde, M. (1996). Creating community in the classroom: Modeling "new basic skills" in teacher education. *Journal of Teacher Education*, 47(5), 367–374.

Breitborde, M., & Amaria, R. P. (1998). *Constructing meaning in teacher education: Building learning on local culture*. Paper presented at the Lilly Conference on College/University Teaching, Towson, MD.

Breitborde, M., & Swiniarski, L. B. (2001). *Family education and community power: new structures for new visions in the educational village*. Paper presented at the Oxford Conference on Education and Development, Oxford, England.

Brophy, J. E., & Good, T. L. (1974). *Teacher-student relationships: Causes and consequences*. New York: Holt, Rinehart & Winston.

Chaille, C., & Silvern, S. B. (1996). Understanding through play. *Childhood Education, 72*(5), 274–277.

Dewey, J. (1935). The teacher and his world. *The Social Frontier, 1*(4), 7.

Dewey, J. (1979). *Experience and education*. New York: Collier Macmillan.

Dreeben, R. L. (1968). *On what is learned in schools*. Reading, MA: Addison-Wesley.

Dryfoos, J. (1994). *Full-service schools: A revolution in health and social services for children, youth and families*. San Francisco, Jossey-Bass.

Duckworth, E. (1987). *The having of wonderful ideas and other essays on teaching and learning*. New York: Teachers College Press.

Fosnot, C. (1996). Constructivism: A psychological theory of learning. In C. Fosnot, (Ed.), *Constructivism: Theory, perspectives, and practice*. New York: Teachers College Press.

Gardner, H. (1983). *Frames of mind: The theory of multiple intelligences*. New York: Basic Books.

Gootman, J. E. (1993). Reaching and teaching abused children. *Childhood Education, 70*(1), 15–19.

Guild, P. D., & Garger, S. (1985). *Marching to different drummers*. Alexandria, VA: Association for Supervision and Curriculum Development.

Jackson, P. (1968). *Life in classrooms*. New York: Holt, Rinehart & Winston.

Johnson, A. (1999). Postmodern perspectives in education and spirituality. *Encounter, 12*(2), 41–48.

Johnson, D. W., & Johnson, F. P. (1999). *Joining together: Group theory and group skills*. Boston: Allyn & Bacon.

Johnson, D. W., & Johnson, R. T. (1994). *Leading the cooperative school* (2nd ed.). Edina, MN: Interaction Book Company.

Johnson, D. W., & Johnson, R. T. (1991). *Learning together and alone: Cooperation, competition and individual learning*. Upper Saddle River, NJ: Prentice Hall.

Kohn, A. (1997). How not to teach values: A critical look at character education. *Phi Delta Kappan, 78*(6), 428–439. http://www.alfiekohn.org/teaching/hnttv.htm.

Kozol, J. (1995). *Amazing grace*. New York: Crown Publishers.

Kozol, J. (2000). *Ordinary resurrections*. New York: Crown Publishers.

Kreidler, W. J. (1984). *Creative conflict resolution*. Glenview, IL: Scott, Foresman.

Lickona, T. (1999). Character education: The mission of every school. *Journal of Research in Education, 9*(1), 38–47.

Lightfoot, S. L. (1978). *Worlds apart: Relations between families and schools*. New York: Basic Books.

Maslow, A. (1962). *Toward a psychology of being*. Princeton, NJ: Van Nostrand.

Noddings, N. (1992). *The challenge to care in schools*. New York: Teachers College Press.

Noddings, N. (1995). A morally defensible mission for schools in the 21st century. *Phi Delta Kappan, 76*(5), 366–368.

Palmer, P. (1998, December/January). Evoking the spirit. *Educational Leadership, 55*, 6–11.

Pestalozzi, J. H. (1954). Leonard and Gertrude. In R. Ulich, (Ed.). *Three hundred years of educational wisdom*. Cambridge: Harvard University Press, 485–507.

Piaget, J. (1962). *Play, dreams and imitation in childhood*. New York: Norton.

Pirozzi, K. (2001). "We don't allow that here": Effective programs to curb violence. In D. Gordon (Ed.), *Violence prevention and conflict resolution*. Harvard Education Letter Focus Series No. 6. Cambridge, MA: Harvard Graduate School of Education.

Rist, R. E. (1973). *The urban school: A factory for failure*. Cambridge, MA: MIT Press.

Rosenthal, R. E., & Jacobson, L. P. (1968). *Pygmalion in the classroom*. New York: Holt, Rinehart & Winston.

Sizer, T. (1984). *Horace's compromise: The dilemma of the American high school*. Boston: Houghton Mifflin.

Ulich, R. (Ed.). (1954). *Three hundred years of educational wisdom*. Cambridge, MA: Harvard University Press.

Websites

Collaborative for Integrated School Services, Harvard Graduate School of Education: *www.gse.harvard.edu/~ciss/*

International Association for the Study of Cooperation in Education: *www.iasce.net/welcome.htm*

The Jigsaw Classroom: *www.jigsaw.org*

Partnership for the Educational Village: *www.salemstate.edu/education/pev*

Teaching Steps to Tolerance (Museum of Tolerance): *www.tst.wiesenthal.com/index.html*

Teaching Tolerance (Southern Poverty Law Center): *www.tolerance.org*

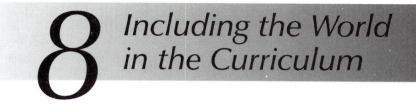

8 Including the World in the Curriculum

A Classroom Vignette

"First Mr. S. showed us maps of how Salem was over 300 years ago, Wow! I was impressed on how much land was added to Salem over the years." (Alex)

"On one image . . . I saw big red splotches. I was wondering what they were when he told us that they were golf courses. The grass on the golf courses give off a red color because the heat measures red on the infra red image." (Jacob)

"It surprised me that Logan Airport is bigger than the city of Salem. Imagine how many people can fit in Salem then double that and you have the amount of people that can fit in Logan." (Meagan)

"Mr. S. showed us a large satellite picture of the USA and he wanted us to find the state of Massachusetts. It was very easy because we could see the arm of Cape Cod sticking out." (Brandon)

Fourth-graders are learning about their world with the use of technology. A cartographer has been invited to show them how to interpret remote sensing images from satellites in space and air photo images as well as an array of maps of their locality and the world. Some teachers might think GIS, old historical maps, and air photography are beyond the grasp of 9-year-olds, but globally literate teachers have the confidence in their children to present the world from many perspectives for interpretation.

Introduction: Infusing Global Education

But now I am Six, I'm as clever as clever.

(A. A. Milne, "Now We Are Six")

The classic poem "Now We Are Six" captures the optimism and confidence of the early childhood years. Maintaining that optimism and confidence is the goal of any early childhood curriculum. In the area of global education, being secure with yourself and confident with others is crucial to facing issues and formulating a world perspective for solutions to complex problems. Global education extends the existing curricula to counter parochial tendencies that limit students' experiences or foster uncertainty about themselves when dealing with something different or new.

The first place to start is with children in their own environment. Affirming that it's OK to come from different kinds of families and homes is the initial step in exploring new homes and families in the neighborhood, community, and nation and beyond the borders. The goal of global education is to foster the growth of the confident child in accepting challenges and taking the risks required for effective citizenship in the global village.

Supporting that confidence, nurturing it when it falters, and developing it when it is missing are the tasks of the teacher. Providing a learning environment with a curriculum and assessment process that sustain the confidence of the young learner is another goal of global education. Global education should permeate the entire knowledge base of the early childhood curriculum, provide skills for competent living, and be infused in a process approach consistent with how young children learn and develop.

To help you infuse global education in your early childhood curriculum, this chapter will provide an overview of appropriate practices, reform initiatives in curriculum development, and planning strategies essential in the teaching of any content area. It is important to remember that infusing global education means looking at the early childhood curriculum and its content and presentation from a world perspective as well as providing for a spectrum of learning needs and styles.

For example, children in a primary class are learning about the houses in their neighborhood. They have discovered that many people live in different styles of houses. Some people live in a variety of multifamily dwellings, while others live in single-family homes. A broad study of those homes has the children researching the geographic origins of the designs of the houses. They find that the bungalow design, ubiquitous across the United States, was an adaptation of homes in Asia. The term *bungalow* is a derivative of the Hindu word *bangla,* which was, in turn, adapted by the British in India "to mean a seasonal house, one suitable for warm climates" (Kassabaum, 1981). The Georgian colonial style home refers back to King George III and is based on English architectural style, while some of the Federal period homes find their roots in a Greek Revival period to symbolize the fledgling new republic's efforts at expressing the democracy of ancient Greece. Victorian houses borrowed from several European sources, including France's mansard roofs, Italy's impressive Italianate grandeur, and England's romantic Gothic castle look of the Queen Anne style, while the modern contemporary design the children found in their neighborhood is evident in cities and towns internationally (Kassabaum). In the spirit of a cooperative learning project, the children have organized themselves into research groups, with each group looking for a particular style of home during the class walk around the school's neighborhood. Then, each group collects data, analyzes it, and shares its findings with the entire class. This project stretches the typical community study into history, geography, and global education.

All sound teaching requires careful planning. Infusion implies integrative teaching, using a unit or a learning center approach to curriculum organization. Themes and topics that lend themselves to global connections need to be selected. Goals and objectives must be clearly stated so that actual learning can be assessed and evaluated in authentic situations and activities. The materials used carry a message and require careful consideration of what they are and how they will be used. Where learning will take place and how it will guarantee inclusion of all children require equally careful consideration. Planning strategies are reviewed in this chapter to chart a course that ensures the teaching of global education throughout your daily instruction.

Questions arise when you are teaching and infusing any new area. This chapter will answer the following questions:

- What is developmentally appropriate practice for global education in early childhood education?
- What standards and educational reform measures address global needs?
- How do you plan for a global education curriculum?
- How do you put theory into practice?

Using Developmentally Appropriate Practices

To foster the security and confidence necessary for effective living in today's world, guidelines have been defined that promote teaching practices based on the stages of development of the child. Such guidelines have been offered by the National Association for the Education of Young Children (NAEYC) and have been adapted and supported by other organizations, like the National Association of State Boards of Education (NASBE) and the National Association of Elementary School Principals (NAESP), as resources for "thinking about, planning and implementing high quality programs for young children" (Kostelnik, 1996–1997, p. 95). These developmentally appropriate practices (DAPs) set forth by such organizations structure the methodology for the early childhood curriculum in all areas, including global education. These principles are based on a philosophy of active learning, which is child centered and respectful of the child's family values, cultural background, and individual learning styles, needs, and challenges. A DAP approach is holistic and integrative, with a focus on inquiry and mastery.

Curriculum Content Standards

The content of the DAP curriculum is in part derived from voluntary national standards set by professional subject matter organizations, state frameworks, and mandated curricula, along with local community interpretations. Global education, as indicated earlier, can be infused in all the areas of the curriculum but possibly is most specifically addressed in the guidelines set by geographers in *Geography for Life*, namely the following:

The World in Spatial Terms

Places and Regions

Physical Systems

Human Systems

Environment and Society (Bednarz et al., 1994)

For all curriculum mandates, we advocate a process approach to content, which stimulates children to want to learn how to learn about their world.

All curriculum mandates outline their areas around basic principles or guidelines, according to grade levels. Global education can expand the literal meanings of these mandates. Global education should be integrated into the guidelines as a point of view, a perspective, a way of dealing with an issue, a stance for evaluating the consequences of an action, or an involvement of peoples, laws, organizations, or natural resources generally beyond the scope of any locality.

Dealing with the Curriculum Dilemma

Many educators are rightfully concerned about the demands that standards-based education puts on the curriculum. Most mandated curricula are assessed by standardized tests. Some teachers feel compelled to "teach to the tests" and view global education as an unnecessary add-on. Other teachers limit their teaching to the narrowly defined standards or curriculum strands of the mandate. If global education is not defined, it is not "covered".

While these sentiments are understandable, it might be argued that global education as a theme or perspective connects the various curriculum areas. The twelve principles of global education lend a comprehensive and coherent context. Since children do not learn or retain knowledge when material is presented as isolated facts, as irrelevant information, or in bits and pieces, global education gives relevance and a thematic approach. Thus, it can be argued that global education enhances the mandated curriculum and provides a framework for effective teaching.

Planning in Response to Standards-Based Education

Since the first principle of global education is that global education is basic, teachers can readily address core curriculum standards in any global education project, unit, or lesson. The English class that writes a letter to Congress in support of environmental protection laws is using communication skills as well as engaging in social action. The earth science class that charts worldwide weather patterns uses math skills with a global awareness of happenings in the physical world. Many of the curriculum experiences suggested in this text are designed to implement both state frameworks and national standards. In schools with standards-based requirements, teachers plan global education projects under designated curriculum strands and document the process with specific standards as goals and objectives.

Implementing a Thematic Approach

As with any sound approach to curriculum, the thematic approach is an advisable methodology for infusion of global education. The major theme itself could be a topic central to global education, or the theme could be expanded to include global consequences. Universals such as homes, food, clothing, families, friendship, nature study, artistic expression, and toys and play are topics that relate to the child's daily life and are suitable for teaching global education in the early childhood or elementary years. In all cases, content, skills, and attitudes define the knowledge base and must be carefully charted in the planning schemes by the teacher.

Assessment and Analysis

To begin planning for global education, assessment is really the first step. The teacher should select themes/topics that are relevant to the children's needs, interests, lives, and scope of understanding, based on an inventory of needs assessment and a task analysis of what the children know, what they have to learn, and how they will learn. From these assessments, goals and objectives become defined. Caution must be taken to ensure that expectations match developmental stages of growth and that there is a spiraling of the knowledge base. Skills and content must build on the present, so the children's previous experiences should not be underestimated. Although differences exist, even young children bring an already established background to any learning situation. A careful analysis of what the child already knows helps to define what you as the teacher want to include in your teaching schemes. Knowledge of the backgrounds of your children will help you frame your approach. For example, should you want to teach about the rain forest, find out what children already know about forests and conservation of natural resources. Maybe some of your children once lived in a region of the world with a rain forest habitat.

Brainstorming and Webbing

Brainstorming with your children for topics to explore is one way to get their input. Having the curriculum emerge from the children's needs and daily experiences is defined by Bredekamp and Rosegrant as "the emergent curriculum… a strong tradition in the best early childhood programs" (1995, p. 11). Connecting what your children already know to what needs to be learned can be done by webbing all ideas around a specific theme and then selecting the best topics and desirable outcomes. Webs can be open-ended or structured around curriculum areas, skills, or mandated standards. Webbing can demonstrate that your theme is in itself a universal, world issue or that you are treating the theme in terms of its global consequences.

Goals and Objectives

Central to all curricula are the goals. They define your intention for your curriculum. They are the engine that drives the train. Goals can emerge from your assessment of your students' needs. They can be predetermined by state or local mandated curricula, built upon recommendations from the national Goals 2000 initiative, state frameworks, professional organizations, or a combination of sources. Throughout this book, the authors have referred to numerous goals of global education in the context of the topics discussed. The Association for Supervision and Curriculum Development presents a model goal in promoting people "who are citizens of a MULTICULTURAL SOCIETY living in an increasingly INTERRELATED WORLD and who LEARN, CARE, THINK, CHOOSE, and ACT to celebrate life … and to meet the global challenges confronting humankind" (Anderson, 1994, p. 9).

Goals are ends or aims, while objectives are the intermediaries that define the purposes for any learning experience. Objectives center on the learner. The purposes of the lesson should reflect the total development of the child in all three domains, namely the following:

- Cognitive development: the content, knowledge, and intellectual areas
- Psychomotor development: the physical, neurological processes that impact all learning (such as gross motor, fine motor, and attending skills)
- Affective development: the social, emotional, moral, and cultural areas of human experiences

The objectives structure the learning experiences. Some curriculum schemes design objectives in terms of outcomes, behaviors the child must demonstrate or perform.

Learning Environment, Materials, Technology Resources

Environment Careful attention must be paid to where the learning is to take place, what kinds of resources are to be utilized, and how the materials are to be implemented. Particular care should be given to safety concerns and the provision of appropriate space for easy and equal access for all children, especially the physically challenged. A good variety of media materials is necessary to address the multiple intelligences brought to any learning task, the numerous learning styles and modes of attending represented in any group of children, and the levels of difficulties learning tasks present. Artifacts, maps, globes, posters, toys, books in many languages, open-ended play equipment, videos, tape recorders, radios, computer technology, and televisions are some resources that can be easily added to the typical learning materials found in any early childhood setting.

Tone Upon entering any classroom, you immediately know the tone and climate set. The physical environment speaks to the pedagogy and the philosophy of the class. A model global education setting is rich in print, posters, friezes, artwork, and structures that invite group and cooperative play. The environment ideally is one that leads to a continuous indoor/outdoor access for young children, particularly physically challenged children. Both the indoor and outdoor environments should be center based

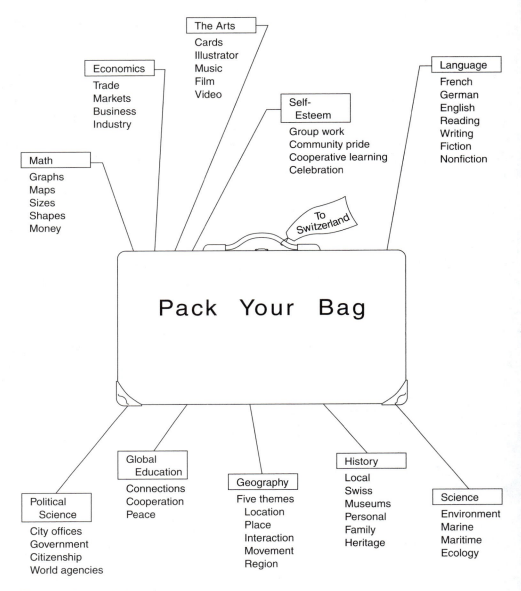

Figure 8.1   Web Sample Inserts

and inviting for young children to explore, discover, and actively engage in a variety of learning opportunities.

Materials The print materials might reflect more than one language. Books, posters, charts, labels, and such should extend the children's vocabulary so that they learn that objects and ideas can be expressed in many ways. In New Zealand, for example, you will typically find English and Maori labeling around the entire primary school.

In books, posters, charts, and other print media, illustrations of people, places, cultures, races, and nationalities should not be restricted to the exotic, the cute, or the stereotypical. For example, Hawaiian children do not typically wear grass skirts, nor do Scots wear kilts daily to school. Rather, national dress is special and often worn for festivals, family celebrations, and special occasions. However, in some instances, native dress is commonplace in a culture. An Indian girl might wear a sari because of the tradition of her family lifestyle and the appropriateness of the dress to the culture and climate of her community. Many recent picture book publications try to weave the traditional dress of a region with the daily wear of contemporary society into the story line and illustrations. Likewise, not all children and not all peoples have the same features. Depicting different races doesn't mean painting different-colored skin tones on the same face. Sensitivity to how children are presented is an important criteria in selection of print media.

Toys and Artifacts Learning centers can contain toys from different cultures that realistically represent the uniqueness of each culture. Artwork reflects the creativity of artists from around the world. Listening experiences can include songs, poems, and stories that can be read, sung, or chanted not only in different languages for multilingual children but in a variety of dialects. Music might be played on a rich array of instruments from different cultures. A variety of classical, popular, folk, and ethnic music can be routinely piped into the class or available to hear at a center.

Construction corners allow children to build multiple types of communities—urban, rural, or suburban—using a variety of materials. Different structural styles of communities, dwellings, homes, shops, or public buildings can be seriously studied in any construction corner. Three-dimensional art projects can complement the construction activities to create a center's or class's global village.

Maps Maps and globes help children find their way, but in the early childhood years they are a very abstract medium. Building map-reading skills takes time. Future cartographers start by making three-dimensional representations of familiar surroundings, moving to iconic representation before the land and water formations can be understood. Detailing comes with experience of making and using maps. Many schools paint maps on their tarmac schoolyards. One primary school in Britain has a simple neighborhood map painted in its schoolyard that clearly illustrates the school's location in relation to other places in the community.

Media for making maps can include blocks, water, clay, sand, and recycled materials, as well as writing and drawing implements. For the primary-grade child, computer cartography offers an enriching environment for charting the universe as well as the child's world. Children's imaginations allow them to map a fantasy world or chart courses for imaginary travel around the world or in space. Compasses, sextants, and telescopes can be used for motivating future explorers.

Computers Like print matter, computer software, CDs, and audio and video tapes need to be scrutinized to avoid images that diminish a culture, depict limiting gender roles, or represent unauthentic lifestyles. The Internet and email have increased opportunity for worldwide communication for children as well as the adults in their world. Designing a school exchange via the web is a great way to connect children. Each class can have its own website. With the help of technology staff and the supervision of the teacher, children update information on class happenings or share projects with students in other parts of the world. Matching "email pals" has proven to be a successful exchange with schools in Great Britain and the USA. Fourth-graders in the Horace Mann Laboratory School at Salem State College and the Brussels International School exchanged their study of their respective cities by designing class websites.

Activities

Learning activities must require active participation on the part of the young learner. These activities can be whole-class projects, individual experiences, or small-group ventures. They can take place at learning centers, inside or outside the confines of the classroom. Select activities that bolster understanding of one's place in the world and identify the consequences of one's behaviors on world events. Based on Piagetian epistemology, we know that children construct their own knowledge base through experiences. As in all good teaching, you can plan for activities that permit your children to experience choice, inquiry, creative thought, critical analysis, and synthesis of ideas.

Global education permeates all that you do, especially the incidental way you use language, set up class routines, and select experiences. If in your dress-up corner there are clothes from different regions or climates, label and call them *clothes*, not *costumes*, unless of course they are costumes for a play or special celebration. During calendar time, use a variety of calendars from other cultures (such as a Jewish calendar or a Chinese calendar) that mark time differently and denote holidays from other societies. For children who can tell time in their time zone, stretch their knowledge of time by setting up a series of clocks recording other time zones. Listen to music from other cultures and have the children play and create music from their own backgrounds. Visit museums, art galleries, and theaters that perform and/or display art forms from a variety of cultures. Have the children put on their own dramatic productions and art shows that are representative of each other's heritage.

Learning new roles for the future global village through play.

To help you plan global education activities, a plethora of guides is available. Be wary of those that oversimplify global concepts, represent only the exotic, stereotype lifestyles, or present ideas from an ethnocentric point of view. For example, some global education series of different countries treat the entire continent of Africa as if it were a country! Some intended bilingual alphabet books depict the teaching of languages by using the English alphabet only, while other texts label all languages other than English as foreign rather than world languages.

Evaluation

Techniques to evaluate your desired outcomes depend on how you define your intentions, goals, or objectives. Essentially, you want to know whether the children's intended behaviors become their actual behaviors. Questions, checklists, performances, and oral or written discourse are documentation for evaluation. Portfolios, journals of writings, email messages, drawings, audio/video tapes, and computer outputs can be tools to record achievement as well as assess it. Evaluation should be ongoing and continually defining the next learning experience. How the problems are solved, what kinds of questions the children ask, and how they answer questions posed by others are important details to note in anecdotal records for future reference and planning for subsequent lessons. Follow-up is critical to all teaching.

State-mandated tests are determined by state standards. Global issues are embedded in the core curriculum areas, such as geography, world history, literature, and political science. These tests give a partial picture of the child and need to be supplemented by a variety of evaluations and assessments.

All evaluations and assessments have to be inclusive of the needs of exceptional children, with adaptations for each student's individual educational plan (IEP). Adaptive assessments using technology can help the physically challenged child. Time restraints need to be modified for children with learning disabilities. The test-taking environment needs to be conducive to the learning styles of all children, provide assistance, and be easily assessable for equitable opportunities.

Including the Exceptional Child

In 1978, the Council for Exceptional Children initiated a world view of special education at its first world congress, held at the University of Stirling, Scotland. The mandate of this congress was not just to provide a forum for comparative study of world practices in special education; it also put forth a global call for including exceptional children in all curriculum considerations. Global education readily addresses the challenge of that call.

The divergent thinking required by the inquiry approach to world issues motivates all children to grapple with difficult problems. Instilling in children the sensitivity to differences and individuality needed to achieve harmony and unity is a goal of global education. Extensions of that goal involve including the physically challenged, acknowledging a range of possibilities and solutions, providing for the variation of learning styles and levels, and adapting to emotional and psychological stresses. All planning for global education, then, implies provision for the exceptional child. Using guidelines of the developmentally appropriate practices, you must plan for the whole child, with all her uniqueness.

Putting Theory into Practice: Making Schools Ready for Children

To put theory into practice, you start with some planning strategies. Planning can involve various strategies, including a lesson plan. The lesson plan format is a map that helps the teacher chart a course to ensure that all the unique aspects of each child are met. Lessons can be shaped by thematic units, learning centers, field trips, events, and activities in and out of school, along with the children's interests and needs. There is no one format for effective planning. Figures 8.2 and 8.3 present outline formats for consideration. The plan lends structure to your teaching and allows you to determine whether goals and objectives are being met in the activities and assessment tools. The

---

The Web: Is the integration of subject areas evident?

Introductory Information: Does it include age of children, topic or theme covered, time span, learning environments, and grouping patterns of learners and teaching teams, as well as other relevant matter?

Goals: Are they clearly stated and developmentally appropriate?

Objectives: Are they behavior specific and age appropriate? Do they address the three domains of cognitive, affective, and psychomotor development?

Activities: Do they integrate learning? Are they connected to the topic or theme? Do they take into consideration the developmental needs of young children? How are they organized and managed?

Evaluation Techniques: Are they appropriate means of assessment of young children? Is there a variety of assessments? Are they consistent with your goals, objectives, and activities? Do they address the three domains in evaluating and assessing: development of knowledge, comprehension, application, analysis, evaluation, synthesis, social/emotional growth, and psycho-motor needs?

Culminating Activities or Follow-through Experiences: Do they pull the unit together or help lead into a new topic or cycle? Do they evidence the growth evaluated and assessed?

Resources: Are there references to technology and multimedia for both children and teacher? How are the resources organized and used? Is there a complete bibliography?

Figure 8.2   Unit Format

Topic Theme or Content: What are you teaching? What curriculum goal does it address?

The Learner: Whom are you teaching? What are their ages? Are there special considerations?

Learning Environment: Where are you teaching? What is the grouping pattern?

Objectives: Are they expressed in specific behavioral terms? Do they address the three domains of development?

Procedure:

> **Materials:** Have you listed and given bibliographic credit where appropriate?

> **Activities:** Have you indicated what the learner will be doing, what the grouping patterns are, and what organization and management are needed?

Assessment and Evaluation Techniques: Do you specify a variety of techniques, including but not limited to behavioral checklists, questioning (oral or written), observation, anecdotal notes, work samples, running records, parental reports, tests, follow-up?

Teacher Reflections: Has the actual behavior/learning met your intended goals?

Figure 8.3   Lesson Plan Format

plan connects and sequences learning experiences in unit or project activities, particularly when lessons are planned around a theme.

Educational Reform Mandates Goals for World-Class Standards

Educational reform is an international happening. Goals 2000, the education reform mandate of the Clinton administration, grew out of an earlier effort, America 2000, the educational platform of the first Bush administration. Both of these efforts for reforming the American curriculum had a similar ring to their predecessor in Great Britain, the General Education Reform Bill, in which a mandatory national curriculum was set. All three endeavors initially focused on the content areas of English, mathematics, science, history, and geography. They were then expanded to include other areas of social studies, such as economics and civics, along with the arts, technology, health, physical education, and world languages. Unlike Great Britain's standards, the American national standards are voluntary and leave it to state frameworks or local mandates to decide further definition and required implementation. All the mandates are very comprehensive. Considering that the early childhood educator and elementary school teacher must address the entire spectrum of the curriculum, some critics feel that the task is overwhelming and that the curriculum reform will bury itself from the force of its own weight (Bredekamp & Rosegrant, 1995). Indeed, the British found it necessary to "slim down" their regulations and attainment targets in their 1995 revision of the national curriculum. So, as noted previously in this chapter, "adding on" is definitely not in our rationale for global education.

As in Great Britain and other nations revising school practices, in the United States reforms speak directly to teaching and learning by beginning with the education of the 5-year-old. Concern for preschool education is noted in Goal 1: "By the year 2000, all children will start school ready to learn" (Bredekamp & Rosegrant, 1995, p. 6). This concern for readiness mirrors that in New Zealand, where early childhood education was under the auspices of the department of education and its educational schemes. The readiness notion was expanded by Ernest Boyer in his book *Ready to Learn* (1992) and challenged by NAEYC when Bredekamp and Rosegrant asked, "How do we know if a child is ready?" (1995, p. 6). We as early childhood educators might want to turn the phrasing around to ask, "Are the schools ready for the child who will be the decision maker in tomorrow's global village?"

Making Schools Ready

If the goal of education is to promote world-class standards, some definition of such standards is required. Attempts have been made (Chalker & Haynes, 1994), but frustrations lie in the changing nature of world-class educational practices. The goalposts are constantly being moved, rendering the most recent declaration of standards obsolete. Add to that the competitive voice in the rhetoric of some of the items in Goals 2000, where America is named to be the first in the world for math and science achievement by the beginning of the new century (Bredekamp & Rosegrant, 1995, p. 6). Such sweeping statements, goals, and standards are not the foundation for an efficacy model for schools. They do not provide guidelines that foster a curriculum that prepares youngsters for the eventualities of the 21st century. Rather, professional associations are providing guidelines for emerging and effective curriculum reform.

Beginning in 1989, the National Council of Teachers of Mathematics produced the first of a series of curriculum standards for the implementation of mathematics. These standards are based on the ways people learn and grapple with the difficulties of changing content matter. They give students tools for problem solving, inquiry, and research. Following the mathematics teachers, educators from other curriculum areas (through professional organizations such as the National Council of Social Studies, the National Council of English Teachers, and the National Council of Geographic Educators) have shaped their standards for an effective curriculum. The task for the teacher of young children is to connect these standards in a cohesive plan. Cross-disciplinary approaches such as global education help to blend curriculum strands. But in making these connections, teachers must avoid the superficial treatment of a topic, the "Cook's tour" type of global education program, and stereotyped or unbalanced comparisons of the known with the unknown.

Schools that are ready for children base curriculum practices on standards centered on the way children learn and construct their world. A universally acceptable approach to practices in early education is a play-based curriculum, which is open ended and ready for whatever children bring to the experience of school. The following approaches exemplify approaches that start with the child to impart the curriculum.

A Play Curriculum

All curriculum considerations, reforms, and guidelines must be enacted against the backdrop of play. Traditionally, dating back to Froebel, play has been valued as the medium through which children learn. Over the years, many play curricula patterns have emerged. Play routines have been prescribed, left to the whim of the child, carefully structured and stylized, or open to a choice among purposeful options. In all times and places, play attracts children and engages them in the learning process.

For the early childhood years, play, play materials, toys, games, and open-ended and fantasy experiences are at the core of the global education curriculum and provide a myriad of opportunities for learning about the world. Role playing can result in the development of empathy for others, improved listening skills, and creative thought. In role playing for global education, situations are constructed that require problem solving and investigation about happenings around the world. Children need to act out their interpretations of events, places, peoples, and possibilities. Preparing for space travel, taking an excursion on a mighty river, or tracking an expedition into the rain forest can help produce the future geographer or astronaut. For the young child, imaginary trips to places around the globe equal in value the actual experience.

Play gives meanings. In any play experience, as children move from solitary or parallel play into cooperative modes of play such as group activities or socio-dramatic play, abstract concepts such as agreement, consensus, negotiation, and mediation begin to make sense. Games help children fathom the need for rules and regulations.

Play should be not restricted to a period of the day or presented as limited activities given for rewards but should be the foundation stone for building global concepts through hands-on experiences, in which children construct their knowledge base of the world and learn appropriate behaviors that provide a safe and just environment for all. By interacting with the children in a play-based curriculum, teachers can weave a world perspective and guide appropriate reactions in a milieu comfortable for children to respond and grow in.

Incorporating Gardner's Theory of Multiple Intelligences

Howard Gardner, a psychologist from Harvard University, formulated a theory that people learn in many different ways with varying strengths. Because the world is so diverse in its populations, people have more than one intelligence. He believes we have a multiplicity of intelligences, which he describes as ways to be smart in the world. Originally, he had defined seven intelligences, but to date, he has expanded his intelligences to include the following eight areas:

Linguistic

Logic-mathematical

Kinesthetic

Spacial

Musical

Inter-personal

Intra-personal

Naturalistic (Swiniarski, 1999)

Schools have adapted his theory into their teaching practices. These schools are labeled as multiple intelligences (MI) schools, since their teachers have structured their curriculum around his eight intelligences. Many of these schools have met the challenges of state-mandated standards and have performed well in standardized tests.

One such school in Massachusetts is the Saltonstall School, a professional development school for Salem State College. The school seeks to develop all eight areas in each child, but contends good teaching starts with teaching to the specific strengths of each child. The children are grouped in multiple-age classes, from K/1 to 4/5, and remain with the same teacher for two years. This extended time period allows teachers to know their students well, identify their strengths, and develop the eight areas.

Teachers at the school are selected on the basis of their commitment to Gardner's epistemological theory. They must be willing to develop strategies that reflect his philosophy. Likewise, parents with a commitment to his philosophy choose this school from other public schools in the community and play a role in the hiring of staff. The school has been recognized by the Massachusetts Department of Education for its successful scores on the Grade Four Massachusetts Comprehensive Assessment System, the state-mandated test for all students in grades 4, 8, and 10. The teachers claim to do little specific preparation for the test. Rather, they credit their effective teaching practices and successful test results to Gardner's work, which they believe is grounded in children's ways of knowing.

The Montessori Method: A Worldwide Model

A teaching methodology used around the world is the Montessori method. Maria Montessori developed her method in Italy over a hundred years ago, primarily for children who today would be identified as having special needs. As a physician, she based her method on her professional knowledge of children and their physical, emotional, social, moral, and cognitive development. Now her teachings are inclusive of all children. Montessori schools are worldwide for children of all ages, beginning with the early childhood years.

The foundation of her method is the rhythm of the developing child, which she believed to be innate in each child. She felt it was necessary to know the child and match the learning environment to the learner's needs. Learning begins with sensorial experiences, so she encouraged children to use all of their sense modalities to enhance the learning process. The teacher, known as the directress, directs the learning process and facilitates learning with the use of specifically designed teaching materials. These materials are called didactic, or self-teaching, materials. Central to Montessori's method is

Teachers and administrators can provide experiences for their students to develop skills in computer technology.

the prescribed use of these materials. Each was carefully designed with a purpose and is to be used only for its intended goal. The directress's role is to model how the didactic materials are to be used. Once instructed on the proper way to handle the materials, children are given freedom of choice. Children are not encouraged to experiment or explore with the materials. Order is a key component to a Montessori school. Materials are maintained, stored, and cared for so that they remain attractive and equally available to all.

Since young children are sensorial in their learning experiences, Montessori devised color-coding schemes for the teaching materials. For example, blue letters represent the consonants and red, the vowels, but numerals are green so not to be confused with letters. Color coding is used to maintain an orderly environment. It helps children decide what materials go together and where they are to be stored. Since young children are expected to be autonomous and responsible for keeping this order, the method provides them with the means.

Montessori initiated many techniques that have been replicated in educational materials and toys. While she would not permit her teaching experiences to be considered as play, sandpaper letters and numerals, seriation games, stacking cups, puzzles with knobs for ease of handling and development of fine muscles for writing have been adapted from her designs as toys produced and marketed around the world. Her materials can be purchased for use at home as well as in any school or child care center. Her method is documented in all forms of professional publications. Her own works have been translated into many languages for both family members and educators, but Montessori professionals are specifically "trained" and need to be certified to teach in an accredited Montessori school.

Summary

Extending the curriculum to include the world requires a pedagogy that allows for an integrative approach. Much has been written about curriculum reform, with new directives and national standards being developed worldwide. Global education is perspective taking. The daily routines, the curriculum, and the school's climate must be open to the world, its happenings, and the impact these events have on the lives of the children. Avoiding cute or exotic presentations of others from around the world is crucial and sometimes difficult at the early childhood levels. Some educators feel that, in making the curriculum relevant to the young child, issues must be simple or presented simply. The results are sometimes worse than having no global education at all. Our recommendations are that global education be connected to daily experiences and infused into the existing curriculum. It is not to be an "add-on" to an already full teaching/learning day.

Following sound methodology and meeting curriculum mandates, while tailoring the curriculum around topics that include the theme of unity in diversity, teachers can move the curriculum beyond the parochial to the global. The goals of global education include developing people, secure in their immediate surroundings, to be confident to take on the challenges of the world beyond. Teachers must connect the here and now with experiences that require children to identify and understand the interdependence of world events in terms of what they already know and experience.

Guidelines for global education foster the philosophy of making schools ready for children with a play-based curriculum. The universal appeal of play as a medium for learning is central to all early childhood curricula and reflects in particular the goals of global education.

Howard Gardner's epistemological theory of multiple intelligences provides a base for effective teaching practices. Using his work, skillful teachers identify, respect, and meet the strengths of each individual child. The theory is inclusive of diverse learning styles and speaks to all learners on eight ways to be smart in the world.

Maria Montessori's program was developed in Italy at the end of the 19th century. She based her approach on the rhythm of the developing child, engaged the use of all of the sense modalities in carefully orchestrated experiences, and emphasized the child's autonomy to make choices with self-teaching materials. Maria Montessori designed her first school for children whom she felt had special needs, but later her method was one of inclusion for all children. The teacher at a Montessori school is trained and certified for the role of directress. Families are expected to be involved and responsible for their children's education. The sense of respect for the child, order in the learning process, and autonomy are prevalent in all Montessori schools.

Figure 8.4   Don Quixote. A visit to Spain inspires this 8-year-old artist to interpret the cultural heritage and heroic legend of the La Mancha region.

Reflection Questions

1. Brainstorming with peers, decide how you can make daily routines take on a global perspectives. For example, how might you revise calendar time to be a global education experience, as well as a math, language arts, and social studies activity?
2. Many how-to books that teachers use for global education promote stereotypes or "Cook's tour" approaches. What would you include in your guidelines for critiques of such resources?
3. Web your next unit to include global education experiences, or take a universal theme as the topic for your next learning center. How would you web your curriculum?
4. Design a lesson plan with Gardner's theory of multiple intelligences framing your goals and objectives. Think about the kinds of activities you can include for your children. Consider how the experiences address the standards in your state's curriculum.
5. Visit a Montessori school, perhaps in your area. Note the features that are unique to its setting, the ways the directress and children interact with each other and their environment, the tone of the school, and the use of teaching materials for curriculum design.

References

Anderson, C., with Nicklas, S., & Crawford, A. (1994). *Global understandings: A framework for teaching and learning*. Alexandria, VA: Association for Supervision and Curriculum Development.

Bednarz, S., Bettis, N., Boehm, R., De Sousa, A., Downs, R., Marran, et al. (1994). *Geography for life*. Washington, DC: National Geographic Research & Exploration.

Boyer, E. (1992). *Ready to learn: A mandate for the nation*. Princeton, NJ: Carnegie Foundation.

Bredekamp, S., & Rosegrant, T. (Eds.). (1992). *Reaching potentials: Appropriate curriculum and assessment for young children: Vol. 1*. Washington, DC: National Association for the Education of Young Children.

Bredekamp, S., & Rosegrant, T. (Eds.). (1995). *Reaching potentials: Appropriate curriculum and assessment for young children: Vol. 2*. Washington, DC: National Association for the Education of Young Children.

Chalker, D., & Haynes, R. (1994). *World class schools*. Lancaster, PA: Technomic Publishing.

Kassabaum, D. (Illus.). (1981). *Good old house neighborhood*. Ann Arbor, MI: Educational Designs.

Kostelnik, M. (1996–1997). Recognizing the essentials of developmentally appropriate curriculum. In K. Paciorek & J. Munro (Eds.), *Annual editions early childhood education*. Guilford, CT: Dushkin Publisher Group.

Swiniarski, L. (1999). Home Support for Successful Schools—Video 2. In *Building bridges for excellence in the early grades: A home-school partnership*. Cambridge, MA: Massachusetts Interaction.

Further Readings

Gardner, Howard. (1983). *Frames of mind: The theory of multiple intelligences*. New York: HarperCollins.

Gardner, Howard. (January 1997). "The first seven ... and the eighth", *Educational Leadership*, *(55)*, pp. 12–15.

Lillard, Paula. (1996). *Montessori today: A comprehensive approach to education from birth to adulthood*. New York: Schoken Books.

Montessori, Maria. (1914). *Dr. Montessori's own handbook*. New York: Frederick A. Stokes.

Websites

Family Education Network: *http://www.familyeducation.com*

National Coalition for Parent Involvement in Education: *www.ncpie.org*

National Information Center for Children and Youth with Disabilities: *http://www.nichcy.org/*

National Parent Information Network: *http://www.npin.org*

National Parent Teacher Association: *http://www.ed.gov/pubs/PFIE/epkit/intro.html*

9 Teaching Global Issues and Themes

Introduction: Confronting World Concerns

Andrew, at 18 months of age, has mastered the complexities of the TV remote control. As he is surfing the channels, images of children under stress in a world of turmoil, victims of violence, hunger, and abuse, flicker on the TV screen. Andrew's parents, diligent about his welfare, have a sense of what is happening and turn off the television. Their response is one approach to dealing with such issues with a young toddler. But many questions are still left unanswered:

- What are the global issues facing today's children?
- How well can young children understand these issues?
- How does a sensitive teacher address such issues with young children?

If you were asked to list the most pressing concerns facing the world's children today, what might you include? In books, journals, and the news media, the most frequent issues addressed are war, hunger, abuse, poverty, disease, homelessness, and social, economic, and gender inequities. Many of these problems are interdependent and ubiquitous, as they are often caused by war, terrorism, environmental disasters, political unrest, and civil and economic upheaval. Children are not immune to these distresses. Sometimes, they are the innocent victims; other times, they question the causes. Globally literate teachers cannot ignore the issues or their students' concerns. Ultimately, such teachers are faced with the task of trying to find answers to the questions posed in this chapter.

Beliefs and Values

Your values and belief systems are the core of the strategies you use to face the issues of living in a global society. Likewise, as a globally literate teacher, you must concern yourself with the diverse values and beliefs of your students and their families. Race, class, gender, ethnicity, nationality, geographic region, and religion are factors that define those values and beliefs. Each family's culture defines its way of explaining the world in a way that makes sense for all of its members. For example, recent immigrant families may perceive an event differently than community members with many generations tied to a place. Urban family concerns can differ from a rural family's perspectives; some religions prohibit what others endorse; political beliefs shape the causes families endorse. These factors need to be understood and reflected in any approach a teacher takes in confronting global issues.

War and Peace

War

Children around the world play war games. Typically, 6-to 8-year-old boys draw war pictures, whether they have had any direct experience of war or not. Parents and

Andrew surfs the channels.

teachers can ban war toys and play or discourage war art, but children find modes for expressing their knowledge of war. War is pervasive. Children are affected by its presence. Unfortunately, wars are breaking out in parts of the world as much today as in generations past. In the 50th anniversary issue of UNICEF's summary of the *State of the World's Children*, the report acknowledges the organization's frustration with the inevitability of war occurring in some corner of the globe. "To an organization born among the detritus of war, it sometimes seems as if the historical wheel has come full circle" (United Nations Children's Fund, 1996, p. 12).

UNICEF is well aware of the devastation that war causes for young children. The organization has dealt with children who suffer the long-lasting traumas of war. Some of these traumas include anxiety about parent separation, loss of home and homeland, mobilization of children as soldiers, rape, abuse, injury, disease, and hunger. To counter this peril, the organization has proposed under its Convention on the Rights of the Child that children be viewed as "zones of peace" (United Nations Children's Fund, 1996, p. 5). To bolster this notion of a wartime sanctuary for children, UNICEF has set five tasks to provide "war relief for children":

1. Reunite children with their families or surrogates.
2. Demobilize child soldiers.

3. Heal mental wounds with counseling and care.

4. Restart schools.

5. Educate for peace. (United Nations Children's Fund, 1996, p. 6)

The impact of war is long lasting on both children who experience it firsthand and children who are on its periphery. Children on the perimeter of war can be as adversely affected as those in the center of the conflicts. Jane Rohrer noted in her study on children's and schools' responses to televised war that television has had an enormous impact on American children, bringing "detailed images of war into 98 percent of American homes" (1996, p. 201). She found that lacking in schools is "a cohesive, prepared plan to address children's reactions to televised war" (p. 205). Earlier studies bolster Rohrer's claim that schools avoid the issues posed by war (Law, 1973). In fact, often the opposite is true. War is frequently extolled in schools through history texts, heroic literary figures, and holidays. Schools have not had a good track record in dealing with the pain of war in children's lives (Law; Rohrer). Yet we know the scars are permanent. One of this text's authors was born during World War II. She has flashbacks to an incident that exemplifies the seminal study of Anna Freud (Law), which identified separation anxiety caused by war as being more devastating to children than the actual destruction of war itself. The author's memory recalls herself as a 3-year-old American child traumatized by a black-and-white wartime poster. Framed against the backdrop of a bombed-out city skyline is the image of a baby, alone, crying in its carriage, with its dead mother fallen onto the pavement. This image continues to haunt her today. As a child, anxious about being separated from her own mother, this author identified with that baby. Children of today must also retain such mental images, which schools cannot afford to ignore.

War takes on many faces. Acts of terrorism and violence in a community impact children as negatively as war. Children in Northern Ireland play under the shadow of fear and terror. Children in Israel, both Jews and Palestinians, have been innocent victims of violence. Children in America have been traumatized by the events of September 11, 2001. Parents and teachers need to be ever vigilant about the impact disasters have on children. Wise counsel is needed. Children should be encouraged to speak about their concerns, express them in art forms, and act on them in play situations. Many agencies offer teachers and parents suggestions in dealing with fears from terrorism, war, and disasters. The Federal Emergency Management Agency (FEMA) cautions adults to be reassuring, share information that children can understand, and restrain from giving too much detail or exposure to a situation via news coverage in the media (www.fema.gov/nwz01/nwz01_99.htm.) The agency has established a website, which offers guidelines for helping children cope with disaster and provides opportunities for schools to share children's artwork that expresses their feelings (www.fema.gov/kids).

Teach Peace

Schools cannot begin a peace education program too early in children's educational process. Teachers must deal openly and directly with war issues. Carlsson-Page and Levin (1990) realistically face the thorny issues of war play and toys. They contend that

An Israeli soldier talks on a cellular phone as he guards a playground in Hebron.

war play of today's children is caused more by violence on TV than the children's own ideas or exercises. Such war play is acted out by following a script the children see on TV rather than being created by the imaginations of children to resolve their anxieties, as in the past (p. 44). War play is appealing to children, generation after generation, because "it allows children to feel so powerful" and in control of circumstances (Carlsson-Paige & Levin, p. 34).

The group Educators for Social Responsibility provides curriculum schemes for conflict resolution that are immediately applicable to school and life experiences of today's children. Peace education begins with the resolution of daily disruptions and conflicts normal in any child's life. Young children's social skills need adult guidance. Children also need the security of an adult's confidence before they share their fears about war, terrorism, or violence in their own homes and neighborhoods.

The number of incidents of violence in homes, schools, and neighborhoods seems to be escalating. One antecedent of violence is the bullying behavior of youngsters (Roland & Munthe, 1989). Bullying is an international concern (Byrne, 1993; Roland & Munthe). Teachers need to curb such behavior by confronting it directly.

In playgrounds and schoolyards around the world, many children are reluctant to join in activities for fear of being teased, taunted, and threatened with physical abuse

(Byrne, 1993; Roland & Munthe, 1989; Ross & Ryan, 1991). Many resources recommend constructive activities for recess time that can assuage those fears (Johnstone, Munn, & Edwards, 1992; Roland & Munthe; Ross & Ryan). Solutions to playground problems require tactics developed to deal with abusive behavior on several levels (Ross & Ryan, p. 3). Ross and Ryan recommend several approaches, beginning with helping children relate with each other; restructuring the physical play area as well as playtime activities; setting a school policy with rules and regulations agreed upon by children, teachers, school staff, and parents; and "improving the playground [as] ... a whole school project, involving the whole school community" (p. 3).

One urban primary school in England had each class pattern a patio of flagstone and flower plantings as a cooperative group project for building pride in their school's appearance and in each other. An inner-city school in the United States adapted that idea. The third-graders in this school used recess time to relieve the bleakness of their school's setting by cleaning the schoolyard and decorating the interior corridors with boxes of flowers. These kinds of activities prompt children to channel their energies into proactive experiences during school times that otherwise are spent in random and/or destructive play. But bullying can extend beyond the school day. It needs to be considered a serious issue by school personnel and child counselors everywhere.

Schools need help in setting policies for peace education that thwarts bullying by giving counsel to both the perpetrators and the victims. Children need to have a role in the composition and implementation of such policies. Sanctions need to be clearly worded and consistently applied. If peace education truly begins at home and in schools, child care centers, and neighborhoods, dealing with violence has to be upheld throughout the whole community.

To assist the teacher in counseling children, a wide selection of books (such as Dr. Seuss's *The Butter Battle Book* [1984]) is available for an effective "bibliotherapy" approach to peace education (Luke & Myers, 1994–1995). During class and individual discussions, teachers might listen attentively to children's views on war and violence. With growing concerns about providing safe schools, new publications are appearing that can be used in such discussions. One journal, *Safe Learning*, takes on difficult issues such as gun control, sexual abuse and harassment, hate speech, and fears. This journal proposes positive ways for educators and families to assist children with difficult situations in schools and the community. Likewise, teachers need to model nonviolent and equitable behaviors. For example, during playtime, teachers need to be observant of the kinds of behaviors that are transpiring and respond to skirmishes between children with fairness and encouragement of all sides to state their problems and resolve the situations.

Children frequently depict war and violence in drawings. They should be allowed to describe their illustrations as an opportunity to defuse anxiety caused by exposure to violence and conflicts. Teachers can then prompt the children to illustrate peaceful solutions to the same scenarios.

Programs are emerging that deal with bullying as one of an alarming growing number of dangers facing the young child. Many of these programs are set in a cooperative learning approach to education. Conflict resolution to divisive issues, clashes, taunting, and teasing begins at an early age. In Great Britain, Kidscape is a program specifically designed for two age levels, children aged 3 to 5 and 6 to 11, as well as children with special needs and children for whom English is a second language (Roland & Munthe, 1989, p. 109). According to Roland and Munthe, the program is "designed to protect children from a variety of dangers, including bullying, abduction, getting lost and possible sexual abuse" (p. 109). The program devises a set of lessons that involve activities such as discussion, role playing, puppetry, and storytelling. Each lesson has a specific message, introduced by a story or discussion and followed by either role playing, puppetry, or brainstorming of strategies (p. 109). For international dissemination, the Scottish Council for Research in Education has produced an entire support program to combat violence in schools. This program, *Action Against Bullying*, is an action packet for policymaking as well as a guide to curriculum ideas for working with children, beginning at age 5 (Johnstone et al., 1992). The program outlines specific steps to initiate, write, and implement school policy against violence.

Last, schools and child care centers might start to enlist parents and the community in any effort to promote peace education. Parents and teachers, together, can monitor television viewing and ban programs that prompt violence and can eliminate the kinds of toys that invite aggressive behavior, replacing them with play experiences and games that model cooperation and bonding.

Violence and the Media

Through the group Action for Children's Television, Peggy Charren spent over 20 years monitoring children's television programming, lobbying Congress, and advocating for nonviolence in children's programs. She recognized that many of the aggressive children's shows were really extended commercials for the TV productions' spin-off toys. The classic examples are GI Joe, followed by the Transformers and superheroes such as the Power Rangers. She is presently retired from her long-time struggle, but her call for nonviolence resonates more today than when she began her campaign. Cable TV, the Internet, video games, and email warrant careful scrutiny by parents, teachers, and the entire community. Debates are being held worldwide about V-chips and other monitoring devices as appropriate means for controlling the media and its impact on children.

Both families and teachers need to be aware of the kinds of images that movies, television, video or computer games, and the Internet use to bombard children. Many violent themes in media productions permeate much of the child's day, causing stress, anxiety, and fear. Children can become increasingly agitated by the violence in the media. Some censorship is prudent. If all violence cannot be banned, families and educators need to monitor the kind of exposure children are experiencing. Many television programs, movies, and videos earmarked for children really contain questionable material, give subtle or not so subtle messages, glorify violence, and condone inappropriate behaviors. Parents should preview such offerings before permitting their children to view any television program or play with any computer software or video games. Local newspapers and parent publications periodically review media, books, and toys. Read these reviews, watch television with your children, and take charge of the remote control.

To counter violence in all forms of media is the work, and the theme of the writings, of Diane Levin, a professor of early childhood education at Wheelock College. In her book *Remote Control Childhood? Combating the Hazards of Media Culture*, she defines the problematic effects media violence has on children and recommends further strategies that both families and educators can try to deal with the problems. Her work is endorsed by the National Association for the Education of Young Children and is published by the organization as a resource for combatting violence in all forms of the media.

Migration and Immigration

The Refugee Question

Children in child care centers and schools are aware that some classmates come from elsewhere. Their dress, language, manner, or appearance sets them apart. Many of these children who appear to be different are recent immigrants to the community; some are refugees. Appreciation, respect, and tolerance for people who are different are important values to foster. To promote such values, children need to know about the refugee experience and empathize with the plight of being a refugee.

Refugees can be victims of war or people seeking asylum from life-threatening political conditions. They seek admission into a new homeland for humanitarian reasons. Some refugees spend years living in refugee camps while having their requests for immigration processed. The Convention on the Rights of the Child protects refugee children by its declaration that each child has a right to a name and nationality. The Women's Commission for Refugee Women and Children is another non-government agency that strives to improve conditions of refugees worldwide through education and advocacy measures; it has published *The Refugee Experience Teaching Guide* (Craig, 1994). The United Nations High Commissioner for Refugees (UNHCR) also produces curriculum materials, such as the booklet *Refugee Children Around the World* (1990), the journals *Refugees* (1996) and *Refugee Children* (n.d.), and the teacher guides *Refugee Experience* and *Teacher's Guide*. In one edition of *Teacher's Guide*, UNHCR set forth a range of curriculum activities that combat xenophobia (the "fear and hatred of foreigners") as well as encourage a spirit of "goodwill" to refugees (United Nations High Commissioner for Refugees, 1994, p. 1).

When teaching young children about such issues as the refugee experience, it is important to provide hopeful models of successful resolutions as a balance to the depiction of despair faced daily by refugees. To counter any sense of futility, children must also recognize the dignity of any people in their triumph over adversity. And to ward off ethnocentric views, children must realize that no one country alone resolves the world's problems. People of all ages and backgrounds in many countries support and assist refugees in self-initiated resolutions.

In all teaching about refugees, teachers should promote personal compassion. Have the children find their voice on the refugee question. Surely, children in your class might well be refugees from Haiti, Rwanda, Somalia, Sri Lanka, Afghanistan, or Lebanon. Ask questions such as what kind of friends would they like to meet at a new school. Have opportunities for all children to share their feelings on having to find a new homeland and a new life. One teacher of deaf and hearing-impaired children found that when she had her children depict their four most important personal events in a circle-of-life drawing, more was revealed than she had been able to learn from any other resource. One deaf Cambodian child pictured war and flight. Deaf from birth, the child had never communicated his background nor any of his feelings until he got involved with this art project. Brainstorming sessions, class discussions, and writings are also appropriate vehicles for children to express their knowledge of refugee experiences and their contributions to help resolve issues.

Bradford College organized a moving experience for school-age children in Great Britain who were studying the effects of World War II as a part of the National Curriculum. The children came to the college dressed as evacuees of 1939 to meet college staff portraying key people in the evacuation movement of children from the war-torn cities to the safer areas in the countryside. They role played historical events, which they studied through research and interviews of people who had been those displaced children. One student shared with the author her grandmother's story of being one such child who was separated from her family, lonely and scared.

The refugee population is growing. To express support for the plight of these people, the United Nations General Assembly designated June 20, 2001, as the first World Refugee Day (United Nations High Commissioner for Refugees, 2001, p. 79). The date was chosen to honor the Organization of African Unity, which since 1974 has hosted over 3.5 million refugees (UN High Commissioner, 2001, p. 79). To illustrate the courage, dignity, and perseverance of refugees, the UNHCR is compiling a roll of prominent persons who were once refugees. They include such recognized figures as the former (and first woman) U.S. secretary of state, Madeleine Albright and the writer Isabel Allende (UN High Commissioner, 2001, p. 79).

Hunger and Poverty

Like children nationwide, many from Massachusetts join with their families in Walk for Hunger, the annual May fund-raiser. Children are aware that many among them go hungry. They can recognize that the hunger issues might belong to their own families, friends, and neighbors as well as children from some distant place. This recognition is important in any discussion of hunger problems to avoid stereotyping and balance the numerous TV images of starving children from Third World nations. While children cannot always appreciate the complexities of the problems that contribute to hunger issues and the accompanying causes of poverty, they can be empowered to contribute to the solutions of the problems.

Environmental study lends itself to a proactive approach of identifying ways to protect the environment and to preserve resources through study of land and water management. Such studies cut across disciplines to include the sciences, geography, economics, and mathematics. Particular attention to these studies is the focus of special days such as Earth Day and World Food Day. Worthwhile as such special-day endeavors are, they should not be just annual happenings; rather, efforts to conserve and share resources need to be a part of a daily pattern. Agencies such as the UN Food and

Agriculture Organization and the Inter-Faith Hunger Appeal Office on Education sponsor programs and publish a wealth of materials on curricula that inform teachers of the issues and provide appropriate approaches for children.

When studying hunger and poverty issues, it is important to conduct fair comparisons of different countries, lifestyles, diets, and nutrition. Wealthy nations do not necessarily support the most nutritious diet. Hunger and poverty are universal problems. Children can grapple with finding solutions to expanding food supply, improving storage and transportation, promoting fair exporting practices, and predicting adverse weather conditions. Recycling projects, water resource research studies, and local food drives are proactive activities for children. They can also participate in producing foods, cooking, monitoring daily meals, trying foods from other cultures, recognizing certain allergies to foods, and appreciating cultural food taboos. With the guidance of their teachers and school dieticians, children can take responsibility in writing school lunch and snack policies. Resources for these study projects can include local food growers, the Environmental Protection Agency, local water resource agencies, and local TV meteorologists. Surely, more can be done with the traditional kindergarten and primary school farm unit, plant and seeds unit, play store, and housekeeping learning centers to connect children to actual life experiences around food production and consumption.

This young French child is making a choice in his village's cooperative store, which sells mainly products of its region of France.

As a cautionary note in setting up work stations, learning centers, and art and play activities in a preschool or primary class, we encourage teachers to think about the use of food. Often, teachers substitute dry pasta or rice for sand in sand tables or instant pudding for finger paints in art projects. From our perspective, it seems a questionable practice to use food for play while other children are starving and hungry. The message is in the medium.

Consumption

Most children and youth in Sweden, especially if they are city dwellers, belong to the second or third generation of a consumption society. Everything can be bought. Money is the universal key. To shop is perhaps the main leisure activity, a pleasure in itself (Gelelius & Millwood, n.d., p. 24).

We could substitute any of the industrialized nations for Sweden on this issue. Surely, children of prosperous countries are living in consumption societies. Teachers frequently express their dismay about the overabundance of possessions their students have or want, as they recognize their responsibility to encourage children to become informed consumers. The popular press recognized the problem of retailers' pitch and marketing strategies to hook even the youngest child into being a consummate consumer (Leonhardt & Kerwin, 1997).

Real-life consumer experiences can be the vehicles for teaching economics and environmental studies. Creating new approaches or ideas for producing products, recycling programs, and critical analysis of advertisements are viable lessons in economics, as well as reading, math, and science. The interconnectedness of the global economy is complex, but young children can appreciate some of the factors that contribute to the world's economy.

Children's play stores can be real learning centers for recycling toys and outgrown clothing. Exchange and bartering processes could be explored, as well as sharing and recycling. The usual transportation unit done in prekindergarten through grade 3 needs to be broadened to study (perhaps through scientific experiments) transport of foods, water, and agricultural goods in a safe and adequate manner. Children could then appreciate that everyone benefits from shipping and receiving vital foodstuffs in the global exchange of consumer goods.

Exchanges are popular with children. Using computer networks (such as Scholastic Network), children can exchange through the World Wide Web. One approved program, the South African Black Doll Project, invites schools to volunteer their efforts to send black dolls to children in South African townships (Scholastic Network, 1995). In exchange projects, children acknowledge and are duly impressed by the ingenuity of their counterparts in other countries. Children from many nations often build their own toys from recycled wires and bottle tops. In Kenya, toy animals are structured from clay, straw, or dried banana skins. Dolls made of used burlap bags charm children from Haiti to Bangladesh. Papier-mâché toys made by children can be found in Japan, Mexico, Malaysia, and Singapore. Shells, stones, pinecones, and other things from nature are used in games worldwide. Using goods from nature helps children connect their play to their habitat and the world's environment as well as each other.

Many educators have already discovered the plethora of art and construction supplies that recycled materials provide. Some communities have established cooperative banks of recyclable materials for teaching. The message to children who use these materials counters that of the "throw away" society. Recycled and recyclable materials not only help children become more cognizant of how things can be used for multiple purposes, they also prompt youngsters to think of creative uses for things. Children can be motivated to establish their own recycling banks in their classroom, school, or center.

Sustaining the Environment

Growing out of the issues of consumption are the concerns about sustaining the world's environment. Throughout the book, sustaining the environment has been infused as one of the twelve principles of global education. Preservation of the environment for future generations is upheld and implied in many issues discussed. But it is fitting here to cite specific environmental concerns.

Unbridled consumption on the part of one segment of the world's population impacts the whole world's population and the future conditions of the planet. When natural resources are depleted to maintain the consumption and lifestyles of the highly developed nations, it becomes necessary to look at this lifestyle's effect on the physical world. When there is a population explosion in one part of the world, the effects on resources need to be considered. The impact of industry, war, or natural and accidental disasters on the environment is an issue for study in a global education curriculum.

Along with other agencies and organizations, the Population Reference Bureau (PRB) in Washington, D.C. has researched the world population's effect on the environment. In doing so, PRB has posed three questions, namely:

How do humans use the environment?

How do humans impact the environment?

When does human activity change the environment?

(Crews & Stauffer, 1997)

The bureau findings are dire. They cite that humans use the environment as:

"a resource bank" for raw materials, resources and energy;

"a habitat" of greater space than other "living species";

"a sink for wastes" (Crews & Stauffer)

Factors that impact the environment include a world "population" that is growing, an "economic growth" with living standards of increased wealth and consumption, a "technological change" that determines new resources, and "political-economic systems" that control "who has access to resources and how the resources are used" (Crews & Stauffer, 1997). "Resource depletion", and "pollution" threaten the environment and

Three young boys enjoying the beauty of their world.

cause crises but "innovations" can result to reverse the damages. (Crews & Stauffer). To meet the challenges for a sustainable environment, educators, parents, and political leaders need to reach a consensus to reverse detrimental practices, to define responsible uses of the environment, to develop innovative technologies, to write protective laws, and to enforce policies that are responsible for the environment worldwide. Education for these proactive goals begins early in the child's life with study of the issues through the approaches outlined in the global education curriculum.

Equity Issues

Equity issues are embedded in a complex web of cultural, social, economic, and political causes. Such issues are evident in education, the workplace, government bodies, and home environments. Attitudes that foster prejudice and stereotyping promote practices that treat people unfairly. These attitudes are formed at an early age, as soon as preschoolers begin to ask, "Who am I?" (Derman-Sparks, 1992, p. 117). Equity issues, as discussed in previous chapters, involve gender, race, socioeconomic class, culture, ethnicity, and nationality.

To grapple with inequity issues, you must be confident about yourself, accepting your own identity, before you can be open to the worth and appreciation of others. However, a sense of arrogance and superiority, the trademark of the bigot, can also be the attitude of well-intentioned do-gooders who concern themselves with remedying inequities by touting their own, "better," practices. To avoid this pitfall, teachers and parents must reflect on themselves while becoming knowledgeable about the world as they examine how and what they teach young children and as they lobby for the equitable rights of all.

Access to Technology

In any recent discussion among economists, political scientists, or business leaders, a common theme emerges: to be productive and successful in the world economy one must be computer literate and updated in the latest form of technology. Yet educators recognize the discrepancies in access to that technology among children globally. Even in preschool programs and child care settings, inequities exist. Very young children who come from homes where computers are available are growing up computer literate. These children benefit from environments not only where books are read and read to them but where family members routinely "play" with them on a computer or model the uses of technology in their daily lives. These homes value the printed word in many forms. Children from these homes can be at a distinct advantage to others should the school not provide adequate experiences using technology.

Many schools around the globe have no computers or, at best, utilize outdated, antiquated models. For years, Seymour Papert, who developed the LOGO language at MIT, has pleaded for a computer for each child. He portrays the computer as analogous to any writing implement such as a pen or pencil. Just as one pencil or pen per school or class of 20 children would restrict writing and learning, such a ratio of computers to students can be inhibiting to the writing and learning processes (Papert, 1993).

Computers can function as "assistive technology" for the child with special needs (U.S. Department of Education, 2000). Technology can help children with disabilities in their communications in writing and reading, make classroom instruction available beyond the confines of the school, and be adaptive for the child who has a mobility or sensory impairment.

The U.S. Department of Education is funding programs to compensate for inequity in technology. Support for distance learning to schools, community centers, child care facilities, and homes is available through Star School Grants. Massachusetts Corporation for Educational Telecommunications (MCET, also called Mass Interaction) has been the recipient of such funding for developing multiple forms of state of the arts technology that include the use of television, satellite, videoconferencing, video on demand, asynchronous transfer mode (ATM), and the Internet as tools to improve literacy and numeracy skills (MCET, 1999, p. 93). Two of their productions are distance learning programs that address an intergenerational audience of parents, family members, educators, and children to forge home-school-community partnerships for promoting literacy skills in preschool and school age children. Initially, the programs were presented nationwide in two series, "Taking the First Steps: Parents as Teachers" for the preschool level and "Building Bridges for Excellence in the Early Grades: A Home/School Partnership" for the elementary school years. Using local cable television and educational stations along with Mass Interaction's network, the series were designed to research the impact that technology has on the teaching of literacy. The results are yet to be determined, but immediate feedback indicated that television was a viable technology for outreach (Breitborde & Swiniarski, 2001).

The shows were live and interactive, with phone calls received from coast to coast. The programs continue to be replayed on television stations and are available through videotapes for community-, school-, and home-based programs. The series focus on three themes—family culture in teaching and learning, the home as a learning environment, and family and community values. Many video clips were produced that depict a multicultural and international population of children and families engaged in activities at home, in schools and child care centers, and in communities worldwide. "The programs reached out to families in their homes to strengthen their knowledge and ability to foster literacy development in ways that honor diverse cultures and lifestyles" (Breitborde & Swiniarski, 2001).

As another outreach to families, the U. S. Department of Education has updated its free publication *Parents' Guide to the Internet*. The book is designed to help parents know how and where to access the Internet while "safeguarding" children from "its potential hazards" (U.S. Department of Education, 2000). Specific information contained in the guide includes:

- Identifying community locations that offer free Internet access
- Making sense of computer and Internet terminology
- Searching for information on-line
- Protecting children from offensive material
- Using technology to benefit children with special needs
- Finding family-friendly Internet sites
- Selecting a home computer
- Choosing an Internet service provider (ISP) or on-line service (U. S. Department of Education, 2000)

To compensate for discrepancies between affluent communities and deprived areas, many companies and individuals have made direct contributions and offered moneys, grants, and equipment. This philanthropy reflects the sciences' and businesses' concerns about the role technology will continue to play in all transnational endeavors, although it does not close the gaps in technology opportunities that exist among communities, schools, and workplaces.

Organizations also provide compensatory programs to promote equity in the availability and use of technology. National Geographic Society (NGS) produced materials and a handbook, *Geography & Technology: Think the World of Your Community* for dissemination in the schools during November 1999 for NGS's annual Geography Awareness Week. The NGS state alliances offer free workshops to teachers on geographic information systems (GIS). The Northeast Global Education Center has provided professional development opportunities for teachers to learn how to use GIS in their classrooms, as well as school-based programs for the children to learn how to interpret remote sensing images.

Schools and teachers also recognize that creative and competent people with skills in technology will drive the economy. They want to provide equal opportunity to all their children to explore the outer limits of technology. Some schools have as their mission to "equip all students with skills and tools, both academic and interpersonal, that are essential for a dynamic and rapidly changing world" (Adamo, 1996). One second-grade teacher is joining with her elementary public school colleagues to fulfill that mission by "connecting children to the world through technology" in her classroom (Adamo). She not only uses technology in her daily teaching but advocates and promotes it at conferences and symposia with other teachers. A former Washington, DC teacher of the year, Dr. Donna Graham-Harris has used the platforms available to her during her award ceremony at the White House and at speaking engagements around the country to encourage access and computer competency for all children (Graham-Harris, 1995). Such efforts need to have universal support and replication.

Model Programs

To establish model prejudice-free early childhood programs, administrators and teachers need to carefully examine their behaviors to determine whether they promote unintentional and subtle biases. Care has to be taken not to favor one group of children over another, restrict boys and girls to defined roles, limit possibilities for exceptional children, or contain a sharing of ideas or professional development through parochial readings or restricted exchanges.

The following questions are helpful in evaluating any program:

Do we treat all children fairly?

Are learning expectations the same for boys and girls?

Are girls and boys equally encouraged?

Do all children have equal access to activities and equipment?

Do the teaching materials reflect the needs of a diverse and inclusive population of children?

Do the teaching materials reflect an accurate representation of the world's cultures?

Are the children exposed to music, art, literature, play, foods, languages, and lifestyles both like and different from their own in the context of daily experiences?

Does the staff stretch itself to read professional materials published in another language or from another country?

Does the school have an equity policy?

Does the staff advocate for children and their families?

Are exceptional children included in all activities?

What provisions are made to accommodate all learners' needs?

In this section, we describe programs that provide equitable educational opportunities for children of all social classes and cultures and curricula that reflect the principles of global education.

Rainbow's End

Peter is 2 years old. He and Dad go off to school together each morning. Dad's day is spent in the geography department of a large midwestern university, Southern Illinois University, working as a graduate student on water and land resource issues. Peter attends the university's toddlers' program with other age mates from a diverse cross-section of the world. The center's population is reflected aptly in its name, Rainbow's End. The staff and children constitute a rainbow coalition of races, cultures, nationalities, and languages. The center is a global village where children and staff from all corners of the world join to form a family and community that is sensitive to all. Differences are recognized and appreciated. Friendships, formed early in life, bond children and adults around universal mutual concerns and needs. The director of the center has put into place a school policy reflecting the philosophy of the anti-bias curriculum endorsed by the National Association for the Education of Young Children (Bredekamp & Rosegrant, 1992). Hiring practices coincide with the open directives of the university, which is one source the center draws upon for its competently trained staff.

While gender differences exist in dress styles and appearances, all the children are encouraged to play together at similar tasks with all the toys and learning centers at

Friends share a book.

hand. Both boys and girls have ample opportunity to experiment with computers. Stories, selected and read daily to the children, reflect heroes and heroines and different times, places, and peoples.

The power of words is recognized. People's national dress is "clothing," not "costumes." While children are playing with cars and trucks, it is noted that drivers in other parts of the world drive on "another side," not "the wrong side." All people dwell in "homes," not "shacks."

The staff and center are open to the families they serve. Communication is evident. Parents and grandparents are welcome to participate in the day's program. While the center is primarily for the university students, staff, and faculty, it serves as an extended family for all, especially people whose families live a distance away. Children's work, family traditions, favorite toys, and special people are also shared. Visitors, young and old, feel immediately included.

Built on the university campus, the physical plant itself affords easy access to all. It is a purpose-built, one-story facility with attention given to overall design as well as access to inside and outside environments that maximize learning. This is but one center striving to meet the needs of its children to develop skills necessary for life in the global village.

Model World Language Programs

Communication in more than one language is critical for equal access to information and the sharing of ideas. To address this challenge, the state of Michigan has initiated the Model World Languages Programs. These programs open doors once closed by offering "the less commonly taught languages of Arabic, Chinese, Japanese, Korean and Russian," beginning in some communities in grade 2 through grade 12 (Michigan State Board of Education). Ten model programs exist throughout the state, with each program unique in its language offerings and grade range. The language selected is often representative of the population of the community itself. Instruction draws on native speakers from the community, who team teach with the regular school staffs.

Other states are experimenting with innovative practices that promote world languages. One model of bilingual education, which requires both English- and non-English-speaking children to acquire a second language, is known as the Two-Way Program. Usually the two languages are those most spoken in the local community. Presently in Massachusetts, the two languages reflect its linguistic minorities, with the teaching of English and Spanish. One Salem, Massachusetts, program requires English and Spanish from kindergarten to grade 8. This is a public school of choice for the parents and children of an urban community. Somewhat like in an international school, expectations are that the staff and student body speak both English and Spanish throughout the day's instruction. It is hoped that choices of languages will grow to include the state's other linguistically distinct populations as well.

Such models provide alternatives to the movement to eliminate bi-lingual education in preference for a monolingual curriculum. Encouraging all children to think, communicate, and learn in more than one language is not only enriching to cognitive development but to social and personal growth as well. While children in the nations of Europe, Japan, China, India, South Africa, Canada, Lebanon, and Israel, to name a few, learn more than one language in the early years, most children in America wait until the upper elementary grades for study of world languages. Programs such as the Two-Way model offer instruction at an early age, when language is easily acquired and can be used throughout their lives.

Becoming an Advocate for Children

Stand for Children: A Model of Advocacy

Marian Wright Edelman, as director of the Children's Defense Fund, organized a rally in Washington, DC to focus on the inequities among the children of America. Her Stand for Children march on June 1, 1996, brought a record number of participants from all corners of the country and included children themselves. Since young children are a segment of American society that cannot vote, this march gave that constituency a voice and an opportunity to buffer the rhetoric that claims to value America's children as the country's best resource.

According to *Webster's New Collegiate Dictionary* (1953), an advocate is one "to call to one's aid.... [O]ne who defends or espouses any cause." As a Yale-trained lawyer, Ms. Edelman is a model advocate who improves the conditions in the lives of children. Educators, parents, and community leaders join with her efforts to advocate for their own private and public endeavors. The National Association for the Education of Young Children identifies five ways to become a "Children's Champion":

- Speak out on behalf of children.
- Improve the life of one child beyond your own family.
- Hold public officials accountable for a national commitment in actions as well as words.
- Encourage organizations to commit to children and families.
- Urge others to become Children's Champions. (National Association for the Education of Young Children, 1996, p. 56).

You as an educator can be an advocate. First, you might identify some issue pertinent to your children or experiences in your school's community that can improve children's lives. Then, to set your community's agenda, a feasibility study needs to be made. This study could be an inventory of the assets and support available. All segments of the community have to be approached for a vested interest in the endeavor. With data from your studies, you have some documentation to launch a campaign that could legislate your issues to a broader audience in state mandates, curriculum reform measures, and frameworks. Teachers' stories of success in advocacy for children's rights can be case study models for you in writing and following through on your action research project.

Case Study and Action Research

Model case study and action research project outlines are tools that help you, the professional, define your issue, formulate your goals and objectives, identify your resources, map your strategies, and assess and determine the success of your efforts. According to Amy Driscoll, case studies are not intended to find the "right answers"; rather, they help professionals "develop a repertoire of approaches and responses" (1995, p. vii). Case studies lead teachers to identify problems that are "subtle, multi-faceted, ongoing and sometimes insolvable" (Driscoll, p. vii). Once you identify your issues, problems, or curriculum changes in your case study, your course of action can be attempted. Get parents involved. Scott Thompson (1996) claims, "Parent-teacher action research not only redefines the who and how of research: it also creates a participatory, ongoing process for school change" (p. 72).

Sample case study and action research outlines are provided in this text for your examination and implementation (see Figures 9.1 and 9.2). As detailed earlier in this chapter, the advocacy efforts of Dr. Donna Graham-Harris and Jennifer Adamo to expand access to technology for all children are included in typical teachers' stories of how practitioners can make a difference. These two teachers set technology policies in their schools, implemented the policies in daily classroom teaching, encouraged other teachers to become computer crusaders, and enlisted support from a forum outside the schools.

Summary

In this chapter we outlined major issues facing the educational establishment for teaching life skills for the global village. Identification and discussion of the issues, realistic

---

Identification of Issue: Identify a problem or change in the curriculum you want to address in your Early Childhood Program.

Analysis of the Issue: Who are the key players? How do their roles impact the issue? How do they impede or permit the changes necessary? What environmental factors restrict the necessary changes? What kinds of adaptations need to be made? What kinds of materials (resources) would enhance the curriculum changes necessary for addressing the issue? How should these materials be made available to your children? What safety factors, physical and social barriers, and environmental arrangements need to be considered to ensure that no child is excluded from use of these materials?

What kinds of activities permit your children some autonomy in the decision making process of resolving this issue?

What kinds of changes in behavior need to be made by your staff, the children, their families, and the community?

Assessment and Evaluation: What authentic approaches to assessment of learning can you use? What outcomes define the success of your study?

Resources: What resources have you used to do this case study?

Figure 9.1   Case Study Format

Topic: Indicate what you are going to research, establish, evaluate, or implement.

Rationale and Goals: Indicate your reasons for the project and expected outcomes you hope to accomplish.

Literature Search: What indicators do you have that the plan is feasible? Do you have any data supporting this project? Did you do a needs assessment or examine other models?

Methodology: What are your data sources? How are you going to implement your plan? Where and with whom? What is your time table?

Assessments: How are you going to evaluate the success of your project?

Conclusions: What are your actual outcomes? What new insights and experiences were the results of this undertaking? (You can summarize this information in graphic or statistical representations when appropriate.)

Resources: Include all documentation of your study in a complete bibliography.

Figure 9.2   Action Research Plan

curriculum approaches, resolutions, and existing model programs were defined and examined. Each community has a responsibility to face these issues and resolve to advocate for solutions that ensure that all children live in a safe, protective, and accepting environment, with a proper nutritional daily diet and adequate housing. Each society should guarantee equal and equitable educational opportunities that maximize every child's potential to be a fulfilled and contributing member of society.

Case study and action research approaches provide advocacy routes to define the most compelling issues and identify possible solutions to pressing problems. Community and family involvement is necessary for any participatory democratic undertaking. The Stand for Children march and the teacher stories of two practitioners opening access to technology for all children are model case studies of action research. Globally literate teachers can advocate successfully on issues with the support of families and the community at large.

Reflection Questions

1. Survey the technology needs of the children you teach. Where in your community is computer access free and open to all families?
2. What kind of measures would your center or school need to adapt in an institutional policy to ensure equal education opportunities free of gender, racial, ethnic, and linguistic bias?
3. How might you advocate for a safe and protective environment for the children in your community? for children worldwide?

References

Adamo, J. (1996). *Connecting children to the world through technology.* Unpublished presentations at the Symposium on the Rights of the Child at Salem State College, Massachusetts, and at the Technology Conference on Globalizing Your Classroom Using the New Technology at Bridgewater State College, Massachusetts, for the Bay State Centers for Global Education.

Bredekamp, S., & Rosegrant, T. (1992). *Reaching potentials: Appropriate curriculum and assessment for young children: Vol. 1.* Washington, DC: National Association for the Education of Young Children.

Breitborde, M., & Swiniarski, L. (2001). *Family education and community power: New structure for new visions in the education village.* Paper written for the Oxford Conference on Education and Development, Oxford University, UK.

Byrne, B. (1993). *Coping with bullying in schools.* Dublin: Columba Press.

Carlsson-Paige, N., & Levin, D. (1990). *Who's calling the shots?* Philadelphia: New Society Publishers.

Craig, A. (1994). *The refugee experience teaching guide.* New York: Women's Commission for Refugee Women and Children.

Crews, K., & Stauffer, C. (1997). *World population and the environment: A data sheet from the population reference bureau.* Washington, DC: Population Reference Bureau.

Derman-Spraks, L. (1992). Reaching potentials: Through antibias, multicultural curriculum. In S. Bredekamp & T. Rosegrant (Eds.), *Reaching potentials: Appropriate curriculum and assessment for young children: Vol. 1.* Washington, DC: National Association for the Education of Young Children.

Driscoll, A. (1995). *Cases in early childhood education.* Boston: Allyn & Bacon.

Finlay, B., & Johnson, C. (Eds.). (1994). *The state of America's children yearbook.* Washington, DC: Children's Defense Fund.

Gelelius, H., & Millwood, D. (n.d.). *I want more.* Stockholm, Sweden: National Swedish Board for Consumer Policies and Swedish International Development Authority.

Graham-Harris, D. (1995). *Using the computer's international highway.* Unpublished Endowed Lecture for the Mary Procopio Lecture Series at Salem State College, Massachusetts.

Johnstone, M., Munn, P., & Edwards, L. (1992). *Action against bullying: A support pack for schools.* Edinburgh, Scotland: Scottish Council for Research in Education.

Law, N. (1973). *Children and war: A position paper.* Washington, DC: Association for Childhood Education International.

Leonhardt, D., & Kerwin, K. (1997, June 30). Hey kid, buy this. *Business Week,* pp. 62–67.

Levin, D. (1998). *Remote control childhood: Combatting the hazards of media culture.* Washington, DC: National Association for the Education of Young Children.

Luke, J., & Myers, C. (1994–1995). Toward peace: Using literature to aid conflict resolution. *Childhood Education, 71*(2), 66–69.

Massachusetts Corporation for Educational Telecommunications. (1999). *Mass learn pike.* Cambridge, MA: Author.

Michigan State Board of Education. *Michigan model world languages programs.* (Flyer published by the state of Michigan, n.d.).

National Association for the Education of Young Children. (1996). Stand for children. *Young Children, 51*(5), 53–56.

National Geographic Society. (1989). *National Geographic Kids Network.* Washington, DC: National Geographic Society Video Production.

Papert, S. (1993). *The children's machine: Rethinking school in the age of the computer.* New York: Basic Books.

Rapone, A. (1996). Articulating a vision: Guatemalan women refugees and communitarian development. *Hunger Teach Net, 6*(4), 13–14.

Rohrer, J. (1996). "We interrupt this program to show you a bombing." Children and schools respond to televised war. *Childhood Education, 72*(4), 201–205.

Roland, E., & Munthe, E. (Eds.). (1989). *Bullying: An international perspective.* London: David Fulton.

Ross, C., & Ryan, A. (1991). *"Can I stay in today miss?" Improving the school playground.* Stoke-on-Trent, UK: Trentham Books.

Scholastic Network. (1995). *South African Black Doll Project.* New York: Scholastic.

Seuss, Dr. (1984). *The butter battle book.* New York: Random House.

Thompson, S. (1996). How action research can put teachers and parents on the same team. *Educational Horizons, 74*(2), 70–76.

United Nations Children's Fund. (1996). *The state of the world's children: Official summary.* New York: Author.

United Nations High Commissioner for Refugees. (n.d.). *Refugee children.*

United Nations High Commissioner for Refugees. (1990). *Refugee children around the world.* Geneva, Switzerland: Author.

United Nations High Commissioner for Refugees. (1994). *Combatting hate and destruction: Overcome xenophobia. Teacher's guide.* New York: Scholastic.

United Nations High Commissioner for Refugees. (1996). *Refugees, 106*(4).

United Nations High Commissioner for Refugees & Clark, J. (2001). "Observing the first world refugee day", *Social Education, 65*(2), 78–87.

U.S. Department of Education. (2000). *Parent's guide to the Internet.* Washington, DC: Author.

Webster's New Collegiate Dictionary. (1953). Springfield, MA: G. & C. Merriam.

Websites

Equal Access to Software and Information: *http://www.isc.rit/~easi*

The Eric Clearinghouse on Disabilities and Gifted Education: *http://ericec.org*

Federal Emergency Management Agency: *www.fema.gov*

National Geographic Society: *www.nationalgeographic.com*

Population Reference Bureau: *http://prb.org/prb*

U. S. Department of Education: *http://www.ed.gov/pubs/edpubs.html*

Introduction to Themes: Putting Theory into Practice

In this chapter we present for the reader's review some ideas that translate theory into the practical world of the classroom. Previous chapters in this book have provided theory, research, and a broad overview of issues related to educating children in and about the world. In Chapter 10 we demonstrate that teachers informed by this overview and concerned about global issues can indeed incorporate global teaching into their classrooms and centers for young children. These practices can enhance the standards required in state and national mandated curricula.

Global education is more a matter of modifying existing curricula to incorporate broader perspectives, multiple points of view, and globally relevant themes than a matter of adding new curricula. We encourage our readers to review their own lessons and units, following the 12 principles proposed in Chapter 1 and revisited in our Conclusion to see what changes they might make. The activities suggested in this chapter may give you some ideas; we hope you will adapt them to your curricula as you see fit.

The activities described here have been field-tested. We have organized them into broad curriculum themes that reflect the growing understanding of young children with respect to themselves and others. The activities may be either used as stand-alone experiences or linked to other themes, concepts, and skills related to particular teaching contexts. For example, the activity entitled "Nuts" included under the theme "Unity and Diversity: We Are Alike and Different" might be used either as part of a science unit on plant characteristics or as part of the teaching of process writing.

We invite teachers to modify these activities as the needs of their children and communities dictate. No activity should be followed as a recipe. Since learning is constructivist—that is, since children make meaning built on their own experiences—teachers need to build curricula on what is already meaningful to children and within their grasp. The globally aware teacher is a socially aware teacher, whose curriculum not only is based on but also addresses, and even invites the class to participate in, the local community and larger world issues. We encourage you, then, to adapt our ideas to the conditions particular to your teaching and to what is meaningful and important to your children.

Cultural Awareness: Learning About Ourselves and Others

Name Stories (based on a project at Kamehameha preschools, Honolulu, Hawaii)

One simple way of introducing children to the idea that people of different cultures have common needs that are met in different ways is to have them research the origins of their own names. Naming is a universal practice with variations that depend on culture, geography, fashion, and other factors. Asking children to find out (or asking parents to share) the origin of their names will reveal interesting similarities and differences.

Names may originate to honor family members living or dead, the day or circumstances of birth, or ethnic traditions. For example, children of Hawaiian ancestry are given a Hawaiian middle name, chosen after their birth, often in consultation with a local religious figure. Hawaiian names are long and interesting, conveying a story within the name (e.g., one's name might be "Kapaulehuanapalilahilahiokaala," meaning "lehua flower blooming on the ridges of Mt. Kaala"). Some Native Americans obtained new names following a notable feat or event occurring at puberty. Miwok Indians of California are named for natural things; the name "Iskemu," for example, means "water running through the dry creek." Among Vietnamese, one's surname is given first, followed by one's given name. Jewish people are named after an important deceased relative. Many African American parents give their children African names in a conscious effort not to continue to pass down the names of slave owners. Tibetan names refer to the day of one's birth (e.g., someone named Nyama was born on a Sunday).

An inquiry into their name origins will reinforce in children the idea that differences among people are interesting, as well as remind them of the link to their own ancestors and culture. The project is also a good way to involve families in their children's school. Teachers can ask family members to share with young children how their names were chosen, perhaps sending along a form for parents to complete. Teachers can then edit and format the name stories and create a class "Name Book" illustrated with photographs of the children as babies and additional drawings.

Venn Diagrams

Venn diagrams, originally representing mathematical sets and subsets, are excellent graphic tools to help children visualize characteristics unique to each and those shared with others. The overlapping circles provide room for listing characteristics unique to each "set" and the characteristics they share. Two students might talk about all the ways they are different from each other ("I have black hair, yours is red"; "I live with my grandmother, you live with your dad"; "I live in a trailer, you live in an apartment"; "I celebrate Kwanzaa, you celebrate Chanukah") and all the ways they are the same ("We both love ice cream"; "We both have pets"; "We both have brown skin"; "We both like chocolate ice cream"). You might narrow the range of discussion to themes like "Things We Like to Do" or "All About Our Families." Venn diagrams can be used to compare such elements as two characters in a story, two animals, two holidays, two kinds of trees, two versions of a folktale (e.g., the tale of Red Riding Hood compared with the story *Lon Po Po* [Young, 1989]), and two seasons of the year. The conceptual goal is to recognize that there is unity and diversity in nature and human life.

Sense of Place

Everyone has places that have special meaning to them. One's special place may be under a tree in the side yard, in the kitchen of grandmother's apartment, at a cabin in the woods, on one's front porch steps, or down by the pond in the evening. This activity is designed to convey the idea that a sense of place is universal and important to

"What I want to be is an artist that draws people's dreams."

one's identity and, perhaps, one's roots and that these places come in all forms—city and country, near and far, ordinary and exotic.

You might introduce the activity with poetry or literature that provides strong descriptions of setting. Two excellent examples are Nikki Giovanni's poem *Knoxville, Tennessee* (1994) and Cynthia Rylant's book *When I Was Young in the Mountains* (1985); these examples have the advantage of providing views of the same mountain setting written from two different perspectives, that of a black poet and that of a white prose writer. A Venn diagram can graphically display the memories these writers share and the differences between their experiences.

Ask the children to think of all the places that they especially like because they do special things there or have special memories, or just because they like that place and return to it again and again. Use examples of your own special places, reinforcing the idea that these places do not have to be exotic or extraordinary. (I like to use the examples of my favorite corner of the living room sofa, where I sit and read the newspaper at the end of the day, and my mother's kitchen table, where we gather to talk after every holiday dinner.) Older children should make a list of these places, putting them in a word cache or word bank.

Next, ask the children to choose one of these places and think of (or list) all the smells that are there and words to describe these smells, then all the sounds, then all the textures ("What things are there to touch in your place?" "How do things feel?"), tastes, and, finally, sights. Leaving sights to the end helps children focus on the other, less obvious senses associated with their special places. Again, older children may make word caches of these sense-related words and phrases.

Having been guided to remember images and words associated with their special places, the children now have a rich collection of language to describe their places, either through drawing or through writing. We suggest that, rather than writing a whole story, children should write a description of the setting, perhaps to accompany a picture. The emphasis should be on the place itself, not the activities associated with it.

Final processing of this activity should include an involved discussion comparing special places, underscoring how different our special places are from others' while acknowledging that having a special place is universal to the human experience. Teachers might end the activity by showing pictures of children in other parts of the nation and the world set in different physical environments and guiding children's hypothesizing about what kinds of special places these other children might have.

Music may be added to this activity. Many folksongs relate to special places. For example, sea chanteys sung by fishermen evoke strong images of maritime life; we have used this music to enhance the "Sense of Place" activity with children who live in coastal Massachusetts.

Neighborhood Walkabout

Although children may walk daily in their neighborhoods or in the neighborhood of their school or child care center, a "walkabout" guided by a teacher can be a new learning experience. For this activity, have in mind goals related to cultural diversity, the many ways people live and the variety of activities they engage in, the ways people adapt to their environments, and the ways they create environments for themselves. Ask children to think about, draw, or write answers to questions such as the following:

Who lives here?

What kinds of activities are people doing? What are they talking about?

How do people create buildings and spaces to help them live?

What are the buildings made of? Why are they made that way?

How close together are they spaced? Why might that be?

What do you smell?

What languages do you hear? What sounds? (You might ask them to be silent for two minutes to pay attention to sounds and then try to recall everything they heard.)

What do the signs on buildings tell you about this neighborhood? You might give children time to draw or fill in an observation chart during the walkabout itself, so that their images are captured quickly. Older children may conduct research to address some of the hypotheses they made in answer to the questions above. For example, the economic history of the town might have dictated where people built houses; in a fishing community, houses might be close together and near the waterfront, unlike houses in a town with a farming history. The presence of languages other than English might be part of the neighborhood's immigration history.

It helps to have a camera to record the images children want to take back with them. A digital camera will help create a multimedia presentation. We suggest some sort of display (a bulletin board, an illustrated chart story, a class book) to strengthen children's understanding of different lifestyles and to foster discussion.

Follow this visit with another walkabout in a different kind of neighborhood, perhaps ethnically different, so that children can see differences in human activity, language, culture, occupations and ways of life, and physical surroundings.

Heritage Museum: Where I Come From

Enlist family help in sharing one or two artifacts that represent children's cultural or ethnic heritage. These might include cookbooks or foods, items of dress, invitations to family celebrations, pictures of homelands, playthings, examples of native languages. Children should be able to explain how those artifacts are used in their cultures. You should find out ahead of time which cultures will be represented so that you can build your own knowledge of that culture through background research. Have on hand books and maps as resources for information, and ask families to send in explanations if necessary. To extend the sharing activity, children and teacher can arrange a mini-museum display of the artifacts with a few sentences of explanation. Finally, children should be asked what they learned about someone else's culture that they didn't know, what they learned about their own, and what questions they have. You might compile the information in a class book, or, by taking pictures of the artifacts with a digital camera and adding dictated or written explanations, create a computer presentation of the material.

Mrs. Kolat, a Holocaust survivor, embraces a young friend.

It is important to be sensitive to the fact that some children and their families may not know their cultural heritage or be willing to share it. Other children may live with foster families or be adopted. In activities such as this, teachers should present alternatives such as the option to choose a culture that a child is interested in rather than his or her own. A child may be paired with an adult in the school or child care center who will share his or her culture with that child.

There are many children's books whose themes relate to the topic of cultural heritage. Among them are Chamreoun Yin's *In My Heart I Am a Dancer*, about a male Cambodian traditional dancer and his culture.

Tangram Stories

The tangram, consisting of seven shapes fitted to form a square, originates in Chinese literature and art. Introduce the children to the tangram and encourage them to make designs and pictures using some or all of the seven shapes. Read to them *Grandfather Tang's Story* (Tompert, 1990), which presents the tangram tradition and adaptations. Give them examples of traditional figures using the seven tangrams (e.g., "standing man," "sitting man," "duck," "teapot") and have them try to replicate these figures using their own tangrams. Then ask them to create their own figures.

Tangrams were used to tell stories, usually with moral messages. Ask children to invent their own stories using the figures they have formed. This is a good activity to strengthen sequencing, patterning, and spatial relations skills, as well as imaginative storytelling and speaking skills. Children might work together as partners or create independently.

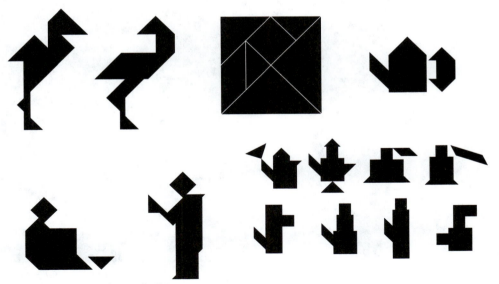

Figure 10.1 Traditional Chinese tangram patterns

Pack My Bag

Using the five themes of geography—location, place, interaction, movement, and region—children will collect information about and analyze their own communities. Help them locate their home addresses on a local map. Take them to city hall and the local Chamber of Commerce and other information offices to gather information about local business and industries, historic sites, and natural and cultural landmarks. Work with the students to collect documents representing their city/town, such as the city shield, old maps, public relations pamphlets, books, photographs, and postcards. Create a "Big Book" containing these materials, including a brochure designed by the children. Pack the Big Book into a bag along with additional artifacts and send the bag to a community in another part of the nation or the world. Ask that they pack a similar bag in return. The end result is a hands-on experience providing children with a greater understanding of their own community as well as similarities and differences with others. This project can be adapted to children of any age level from preschool to elementary school.

Pack My Bag: Using Technology   Using technology, have the class design a webpage about their community or a special event or person from their community. Connect with a school in another community or country to share projects. The children can post photos of their community, write stories, share biographies, and follow up

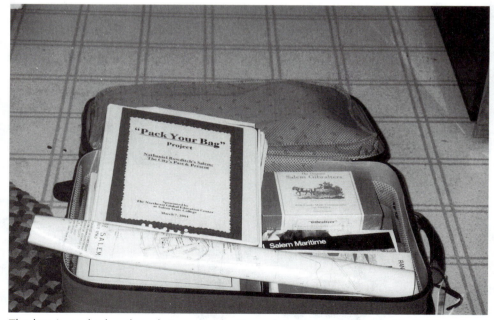

The bag is packed and ready to go to the Brussels International School in Belgium from Horace Mann School in Salem, Massachusetts.

with a bag or box of artifacts from their community. This project is better suited to children in grades 3 and up.

Unity and Diversity: We Are Alike and Different

Building Bridges

Read Philemon Sturges and Giles Laroche's beautifully illustrated book, *Bridges Are to Cross* (1998), which takes the reader on a journey around the world and across its many bridges. The book speaks to the metaphor of the bridge that connects people not only physically but in other ways (Sturges and Laroche). Children could follow up by building bridges with blocks or recycled materials, using the illustrations as inspiration. The children could then brainstorm about the many ways people can build bridges with each other by sharing values, lifestyles, and dreams. Then create a bulletin board of a bridge of their ideas.

Making Books

Become familiar with the different ways "books" have been created in different cultures using different materials. A good reference is *Multicultural Books to Make and Share* (Gaylord, 1994). Use these different forms and materials as they are appropriate for different kinds of stories. An Asian leaf-pattern book or a scroll might be a good way to display a story with a clearly defined sequence of events. Children may construct these various book forms as graphic aids to help them understand the structures of stories they've read or heard or as ways to display their own individual or group story creations. Make sure to tell them about the origins of these book formats and discuss why particular materials were used in the cultures these formats represent.

Nuts

This activity shows that nature demonstrates the principles of unity and diversity. Choose several kinds of nuts: walnuts, pecans, almonds, and so on (or small apples or popcorn). Organize children into four-member groups. Each group receives four of the same kind of nut to distribute to each member. Without talking, children carefully observe and "memorize" their nuts. Tell them they will have to remember what their nut looks like later on. Ask older children to take notes, listing unique characteristics of their nut ("Write down the things that may make your nut different from someone else's"). Ask each group to put their nuts in a central bowl ("mixed nuts"), mix them up, and then try to find their own nut again. For older children, ask them to use their notes to write a paragraph describing their nut to help someone else identify it. Have the groups exchange nuts (e.g., the walnut group now has the almonds) and the written descriptions. Each member of the new groups must read a description and try to identify the nut it describes. This is a good activity to reinforce observing, note taking, and descriptive writing skills. Remember to hold a final discussion, drawing from the children the conclusion that nature provides us with examples of unity and diversity. No two nuts are exactly alike. Provided no one has a nut allergy, the children might enjoy eating the teaching materials at the end of this activity.

Family Pictures

A simple display of family pictures provides a meaningful demonstration of unity and diversity in family life. Ask families to send in pictures of family members, including parents, siblings, cousins, and grandparents. Tell them that anyone who is considered "family" may be included. Hawaiian families, for example, often include friends and neighbors. The only rule is that each child should be able to tell you who these people are. Read to children a book such as *All Kinds of Families* (Simon, 1976) or view the award-winning video *That's a Family* from the Women's Educational Media to strengthen their understanding that there are many varieties of families. Include in your discussion family types such as foster families, adoptive families, grandparent-headed families, only children, children who have two mothers or two fathers, and other alternatives. Share with them your own family structure, especially if it is different from the traditional two-parent "ideal." Ask them to help you define what is a *family* (e.g., "a circle of people who love you"). Arrange a bulletin board display entitled "All Kinds of Families." Ask children over the course of several days to share with the class who is in their family. A follow-up activity might involve making a class book of drawings and simple sentences, individual books about "My Family," or Venn diagrams comparing and contrasting family types. Older children might study traditional family patterns in different cultures, including family structures, adults' and children's roles, and rites of passage.

Migration and Immigration

People and animals travel great distances to move to new homes for many reasons. Some animals migrate seasonally; some people (e.g., migrant farmworkers, those who cross national borders to seek temporary work) do the same. Others move from their homelands never to return because of conditions of famine, war, or oppression. Several good books describe the experience of immigration, including *A Long Way to a New Land* (Sandin, 1981), *Coming to America: The Kids' Book About Immigration* (Fassler & Danforth, 1993) and *Who Belongs Here?* (Knight, 1993). The classic Robert McCloskey story, *Make Way for Ducklings* (1941), tells of migration and the search for a new home. Ask children to watch for great groups of flying birds who seem to be on their way to a new home, and discuss the reasons for their seasonal journey. What were the difficulties that Mr. and Mrs. Mallard faced in adjusting to their new home in the Boston Public Garden? List with the children's help some problems that new immigrants might face (e.g., learning a new language, finding a place to live, finding a new job, using a new kind of money, making friends). Encourage immigrant children in the room to share their experiences and difficulties adjusting to a new homeland. (Be sensitive to the needs of refugee children who may not want to recall their families' traumatic move and who may therefore need privacy.)

Coming to America: The Kids' Book About Immigration has an interactive format; readers are asked to write or draw their responses to questions such as

- "Have you ever moved?"
- "What do you like about your new home?"
- "Do you miss anything about your old home?"

Ask the children, "If your family had to move to a new land, do you think you would be able to take everything in your house with you?" This will lead them to the understanding that sometimes things (and people) must be left behind. Ask them to pretend they are emigrating and that they may take three things with them other than clothing. What would these three things be, and why would they choose them?

Older children can research the immigration and migration history of their communities. Who founded the community? What groups migrated there, for what purpose? What were some significant experiences of these different groups? How did they each contribute to the development of the community? Children can examine town records, view old pictures, contact local ethnic organizations and historical societies, and conduct oral history interviews. A sample curriculum unit on Gloucester, Massachusetts, immigrant fishing families can be found in Breitborde, 2001.

A House Is a House for Me

Everyone needs a home, but that home looks different depending on who you are, what you need, and in what land you live. Show children pictures of homes, both urban and rural, in various countries. Discuss what materials these homes are made of and why. Discuss what it might be like to live there, how many people might share the home, and what might be the benefits of these kinds of houses. *A House Is a House for Me* (Hoberman, 1978) is an entertaining book reinforcing the unity principle that everyone has a home and the diversity concept that homes come in all varieties. When comparing "American" homes with homes of other lands, be careful to provide information that is representative and accurate. Most Africans, for example, do not live in mud huts; Inuit (Eskimos) no longer live in igloos. Traditional Native American homes varied greatly among regions and tribal groups, depending on climate and economy; many contemporary Indians have both modern and traditional homes. Within every country, including the United States, there are great differences in styles of housing.

Birthday Spectrum

This simple kinesthetic activity makes it visually clear that people are both the same and different. Ask groups of approximately 10 children to tell each other when their birthdays are and to arrange themselves in a line representing the annual chronology of the birthdays in the group, with the child having the earliest birthday (e.g., January) at one end and the child with the latest birthday (e.g., December) at the other end. To accomplish this, children will have to speak to each other, planning and working together to arrange the spectrum. This is a good activity for practice with sequencing, communication, and cooperation.

Discussion should reinforce the idea that we all have a birthday (although some cultures and some religions do not celebrate them) but that these birthdays range throughout the year. Children might discuss the advantages and disadvantages of having birthdays at different times of the year. Finally, share with the children information on how various cultures determine birthdays (e.g., Zoroastrians celebrate two birthdays: their date of birth and their name day; Vietnamese celebrate on the date of the new moon closest to their actual birth date).

Monopoly

The game of Monopoly comes in some 32 different national versions. These games can be ordered through toy stores or bookstores or directly by contacting the Parker Brothers division of Hasbro Toys. This game can be used in many ways to help children learn concepts in most curriculum areas. For example, in the movement theme of geography as well as the similarities/differences theme of global education, it provides children with a wealth of information about languages, locations, money, property values, and more. For economics and math study, use the money exchange charts from local newspapers to construct math activities relating to converting currencies of various nations. Have a Monopoly Olympics. Guide students to appreciate that children around the world engage in similar forms of play. Help older children understand that toy manufacturing is one example of a global business venture.

Older children might enjoy creating a local version of Monopoly based on their own town or region, its landmarks, and its economy. For children of age 8 and up, there is a Monopoly version that is designed for the players to make their own game with the help of a personal computer. Constructing the game in this fashion integrates technology into the learning process, while encouraging students to apply the knowledge they have about their own community in a meaningful experience.

As a lesson in conservation of the environment, Monopoly also has a National Parks version. This format can help teach children key concepts in learning about ways government agencies work to manage, sustain, protect and preserve our land and sea.

Proverbs

Proverbs are universal vehicles for inculcating cultural principles and moral edicts. A collection of proverbs from various cultures will reveal common themes. The following proverbs are offered as examples:

"Talk does not cook rice." (China)

"No matter how long the night, the day is sure to come." (Congo)

"One camel does not make fun of the other camel's hump." (Guinea)

"Don't carry coals to Newcastle." (England)

"He who knows others is wise; he who knows himself is enlightened." (China)

"Know thyself." (Greece) [Socrates]

"To thine own self be true." (England) [Shakespeare]

"Knowledge is always better than riches." (Ashanti, Ghana)

"When you follow the path of your father, you learn to walk like him." (Ashanti, Ghana)

"One falsehood spoils a thousand truths." (Ashanti, Ghana)

"You do not teach the paths of the forest to an old gorilla." (Congo)

"The most beautiful fig may contain a worm." (Africa)

It is fun and an exercise in critical thinking to try to come up with the "American" version of these proverbs. For example, many of us might say, "Actions speak louder than words," "It's always darkest before the dawn," or "The apple never falls far from the tree," instead of some of the above proverbs that convey the same messages. Older children can discuss why the universal message is expressed in particular ways (e.g., why are gorillas, coal, and rice used as examples?). They might create fables to explain the origin of one of the proverbs. You and the children can collect examples of proverbs (or superstitions) over the course of a month and display them on a bulletin board or in an illustrated book. To reinforce sight-word skills, proverbs can be duplicated as sentence strips or cut up into words for unscrambling (cloze) activities.

World Religions

Some of the social studies standards require the teaching about the religions of the world (Massachusetts Department of Education, 1997, p. 59). *Sacred Places* (Sturges & Laroche, 2000) introduces children to the religions of the world through its illustrations of special places that people visit to celebrate, meditate, and share their understanding of the meaning of life. The book covers five major belief systems. After you read the book to children, each child could research where these religions began and where they are practiced now in the world. Create a map similar to the one at the end of the book to summarize the class's findings.

Toys Around the World

Toys are the universals of childhood. Collect toys from around the world to show children their similarities and differences, as well as help them to build concepts by categorizing types of playthings. Family and community members can contribute toys for special exhibits. Museum shops and libraries often loan out such collections. Because the toy industry is international, teachers can send for catalogs from different companies around the globe. Have children create collages of pictures of toys from around the world or make posters illustrating the many versions of types of toys (e.g., seriation toys, dolls, transportation toys, masks, puppets). Have them select a toy from another land and create a story, a game, or directions to accompany it.

Alphabet Books

Like toys, alphabet books are ubiquitous. Children can gain an appreciation of the different forms an alphabet can take, as well as information about different cultures as represented in the objects associated with each letter or symbol of the alphabet. They learn, for example, that not all reading is ordered left to right, that the same letters take on different appearances in different cultures, and that many alphabets consist of letters that are quite different from the ones we know in English. Children can compare and contrast these books and alphabets. They can use the pictures as clues to hypothesize about life in that culture. It is helpful to ask speakers of these languages to share the language and review the books with the children. Some interesting alphabet books from a variety of cultures are *Ashanti to Zulu* (Musgrove, 1976), *Jambo Means Hello* (Feelings & Feelings, 1974), *A Peaceable Kingdom* (Provensen & Provensen, 1978), *A Is for Africa* (Onyefulu, 1993), *Say It in Hawaiian* (Wren & Maile, 1992b), the *Cherokee A-B-C Coloring Book* (Pennington, 1994), *A is for Asia* (Chin-Lee, 1997), and *Gathering the Sun: An Alphabet Book in Spanish and English* (Ada & Silva, 1997).

Counting Books: Math Around the World

Math is a universal language but spoken in different "tongues." Children everywhere count. Compile a collection of counting books from different cultures, comparing number systems and pictures representing them. As with alphabet books, pictures provide cues for constructing hypotheses about life in other lands. Research and share with children how math is used differently in different countries. What things are counted? Using what tools? For example, the abacus is still used in many nations. Refer also to global sources of mathematical knowledge, including contributions from the non-Western world. While our numbers have Arabic origins and constitute a base-10 system, other peoples' number systems are different. Inuit tribes of Canada, for example, traditionally used a base-20 system of counting, in reference to the 10 fingers and 10 toes of the human body.

Some counting books demonstrating multicultural/multinational content include the series *Count Your Way Through …* (Haskins, 1987a, 1987b, 1987c), *1-2-3 Counting Locally* (Wren & Maile, 1992a), *Les Nombres* (Bradbury, 1983), and *One Woolly Wombat* (Trinca & Argent, 1995).

Claudia Zaslavsky has collected math lessons and activities building on cultural traditions with applications to community/world problems (see "References" at the end of this chapter).

Street Games Around the World

Especially as American children are increasingly confined indoors, in structured settings, or in front of the television, childhood educators might look for opportunities to play games that allow them to move around and perhaps go outdoors. Several source books describe games that are played in different cultures. The best provide background information on the origins of the games and what function they might have in educating young children of that culture. A review of many games from many cultures will also reveal to teachers and children similarities and universalities in game themes, goals, strategies, and movements; once again, we suggest that teachers and child care workers reinforce with children the idea of unity across diversity. Two good reference books are Barbarash's *Multicultural Games* (1997) and Johnson's *String Games from Around the World* (1996).

Making Music

Music has been called the universal language. Certainly, all cultures make music, originally using locally available materials to express the joys, sadnesses, needs, and desires of life and to mark its turning points. Exposing children to the rich variety of musical forms in the world and to the variety in traditional instruments will help them learn to expect and respect differences. The December 1992 issue of *Faces*, entitled "Making Music," includes articles on music around the world, from Bolivia to Cambodia, Japan, and the Dominican Republic. Obtain recordings of, for example, Jewish klezmer bands, merengue music, Irish jigs, and Italian opera. Help the children listen for the sounds of different instruments: Indian sitars, Italian organs, Cambodian dulcimers. Play also examples of American regional music: Appalachian fiddling, Cajun zydeco, slave and work songs, Woody Guthrie's and Huddie Ledbetter's depression-era songs, and gospel. (The Smithsonian Museum has available taped collections of American music at nominal cost.) Lead children to compare bluegrass with Scottish and Irish music, merengue with salsa, Chicago blues with slave songs and spirituals, to see similarities and common roots. Children can experiment with making their own musical instruments with the help of the "Making Music" issue of *Faces* and Anne Pellowski's *Hidden Stories in Plants* (1990). Some ideas for handmade instruments include a bucket guitar, a washboard, spoons, a glass harmonica (invented by Benjamin Franklin), and a rainstick. Students might also experiment with producing different pitches, tones, and rhythms.

Collecting Things

Collecting gives children a sense of control over their world and helps them effect some order. Encourage children to bring in collections from home, or start them on collecting objects of interest to them. Sharing collections during circle time provides many learning opportunities.

Collected coins are symbolic representations of different countries. Ask older children to find the comparative value of coins in the world market by looking at the financial pages of the newspaper. Have them locate the national origins of the coins on the world map.

Stamps offer images of national themes and icons and are often works of art. Children can classify the stamps, making living graphs of the different regions of the world. The U.S. Postal Service has a variety of materials, study packets, and posters to assist teachers who want to use stamps to connect children to the world. All countries have similar packets; in England, Postman Pat books teach children about communicating by mail and the entire network of the postal world.

Collections of postcards offer wonderful examples of the landscapes, people, architecture, historical landmarks, and art of different countries. Children can classify, graph, locate, and study the images on postcards and can send postcards from their own communities to other places around the globe.

Collecting objects from nature helps children recognize the diversity in the physical world and the beauty that is inherent in our habitats. Observation and classification activities help children identify their objects and learn about what makes up the natural world. Encourage them to describe what they see, feel, and smell as they hold and touch the objects.

Multiple Perspectives: We Have Many Points of View

The True Story of the Three Pigs

There is always more than one side to a story. An important message in multicultural/global education is the idea that people have different perceptions, memories, and understandings of the same event. Getting children to see the other side will help them learn empathy and eventually resolve conflicts with their peers. A good book that illustrates the other side is *The True Story of the Three Pigs* (Scieszka, 1995), which offers a funny and poignant wolf's version of the tale. Any simple, often told tale of good and bad offers opportunities for retelling.

To reinforce the idea that different people have different perceptions, you can use reverse role play. Create a simulated argument between two friends (this might be taken from literature). Have two children play the roles of each character, standing in paper footsteps representing that character. Then have the two children reverse roles, standing in the other character's footsteps and expressing that character's feelings and perspective. Discuss with the children that sometimes people have very different points of view, depending on their needs or past experiences.

Landscapes

One concrete way to expose children to the idea that people (and other creatures) see things from different perspectives is to ask children to describe their immediate setting from different points of view. For example, ask them to look around at their classroom and describe what they see. Then ask them to imagine they are an ant crawling on the floor, and ask them to describe the room from the ant's point of view. Third, ask them to imagine that same ant on the ceiling over their heads. How would the ant describe what it sees? Teachers might encourage children to draw a picture of the same part of the room from different points of view and arrange three walls of drawings:

- "I see ... "
- "The ant on the floor sees ... "
- "The ant on the ceiling sees ... "

My Mother Is the Most Beautiful Woman in the World

My Mother Is the Most Beautiful Woman in the World (Reynher in Butler, Jordan, & Rotert, 1987) tells of a young girl who is separated from her mother as they work diligently in the fields around their village. For help she frantically looks to the other workers, who do not recognize her and ask, "What does your mother look like?" "She is the most beautiful woman in the world," the little girl replies. The sympathetic villagers send for all the women in the region acknowledged to be village beauties, but she rejects one after the other: "She is not my mother. My mother is the most beautiful woman in the world." Suddenly, over the hill comes a humpbacked, hook-nosed, toothless, chubby old woman, who, on seeing the little girl, cries out, "There you are! I was frantic with worry!" The little girl, wrapped in her mother's arms, looks out at the stunned villagers and says, "See? I told you my mother is the most beautiful woman in the world!" This Ukranian story sweetly illustrates that beauty is in the eye of the beholder and, more, that we have our own point of view about what is precious and lovely.

A Cartographer's View of the World

To many native Bostonians, their hometown is fondly called "the hub of the universe." For them, the "West" is anywhere you cannot see or smell the Atlantic Ocean. In their egocentrism, most young children are developmentally as ethnocentric as these adults who cling to their parochial image of the world. To counter this tendency, mapping activities can help sensitize children to other views.

A map is an abstract representation of reality. Generally, children younger than 7 need more concrete or iconic representations for early mapping experiences. Young children might make maps from recycled construction materials that provide a three-dimensional representation. A good first book for the young cartographer is *As the Crow Flies* (Hartman, 1991). This picture book clearly illustrates how we might see the world from many points of view as it introduces the youngster to aerial cartography.

Teachers might help children with good spatial understanding make a collection of maps from a variety of countries. National airline carriers are good resources and will place their home countries at the center of the world. Airline maps display all travel as emanating from their hub. Have the children note the different focal places and think about why they are differently portrayed.

Guide children to look at the compass rose on a map. Most modern maps depict the rose pointing upward to the north. Turn the compass rose around and discuss, for example, how the world might look to someone from Australia. What countries would be then considered "down under" the equator? Maps from Australia show the compass rose pointing upward to the South, which gives even adults a cultural jolt.

Your map collection might include different kinds of maps of the same place; for example, air photo maps, remote sensing maps, demographic maps, topography maps, political maps, railroad maps, and road maps. Help children contrast these different representations. Invite a cartographer to help them interpret the maps. Local and state community planning departments employ cartographers, as do universities with community planning programs. A word of caution—geographic information system (GIS) is best suited for children in upper primary school. It is appropriate to expose younger children to the technology, but they have difficulty understanding the remote sensing interpretations.

Find old maps of the children's community and encourage children to locate familiar addresses. The children can determine whether their school or home address existed in earlier times. If it doesn't appear, ask what they think might have been there instead.

Children can map their international address. Have them divide a paper into four parts, representing each line of their address. In the first section, they might draw a map of their street; in the second, their street within the community; in the third, their community within their state or province; in the fourth, their state or province within their nation. If homeless children are in your class, substitute the school address in place of the home.

Map puzzles allow children to piece their world together. We suggest you use large floor maps or draw maps on the pavement of the playground, guiding children to walk from place to place. You might design an adaptation of a hopscotch game to reinforce the names and locations of different countries or states. This experience develops a sense of place in a kinesthetic manner appropriate to young children's learning.

Globes come in many formats. The traditional globe is tilted to show the world's axis; inflated globes can be tossed about; room-size globes allow children to walk into them; soft, stuffed globes are ones that children can hold and care for. All these provide different sensorial, kinesthetic, and cognitive experiences of the world. These formats of globes are particularly suitable for very young children. Let them "hug the world" as a symbolic way to protect it.

What Time Is It?

Like space, time is a concept that emerges later in children's development. Young children gain a sense of personal time through having routines and repeating patterns; therefore, time concepts should be taught in connection with the children's personal life.

Daily calendar time might be extended to introduce children to the ways different cultures note the passage of time. You can introduce, for example, the Jewish and Chinese calendars and discuss with children the differently calculated year (e.g., the Jewish calendar is much older than our Christian-based one) and the lunar bases of many calendars. Help children keep track of their personal celebrations, family and national holidays, and international events to encourage them to see patterns, cycles, similarities, and differences among their experiences.

Telling time is different depending on where you are. Books such as Ellen Kandoian's *Under the Sun* (1987) show children different perspectives on time. Telling time in more than one language helps children recognize that all people need to mark the passing of time. Make sure to include Braille and sign languages in this activity.

With your help, children can collect instruments that measure time (e.g., old and new clocks and watches, sundials, hourglasses, and cooking timers). Set the clocks at times representing cities in different zones around the world. Play the game "If it is noon in Boston, it must be _____ in _____." Good follow-up readings for this experience are Marilyn Singer's *Nine O'Clock Lullaby* (1992) and Mitsumasa Anno's *All in a Day* (Anno et al., 1990).

We can use our own bodies to calculate the passing of time. Help children to see where their bodies cast shadows at different times of the day and different seasons of the year. They can mark these changes by putting stakes in the ground, drawing their shadows, and recording their observations.

Color Box

This activity allows children to see the world through a spectrum of colors. Have the children look at their environment through the lens of yellow, green, red, and blue transparencies. They can note the ways one place can appear different through these different lenses. Tape the transparencies to a window so that the children can make their observations and record on their own at different times of day. Store the transparencies near the window in a "Color Box" and have the children change the taped transparencies daily. Giles Laroche's delightfully illustrated book *The Color Box* (Dodds, 1992) takes children with a frisky monkey on a journey through many different habitats depicted in each color of the rainbow.

Peacekeeping: We Are a Community

Crow Boy (Yashina, 1965) is a classic Caldecott award winner about a boy who is ostracized by classmates who do not bother to learn why he is different from them. During the course of the story, the other children learn to appreciate his abilities, understand the conditions of his life, and learn acceptance, tolerance, and shame for their past name calling. *Crow Boy* is a gentle book with an important human relations message about prejudice, stereotyping, unkindness, and the potential for turning negative behaviors into positive ones.

The Knight and the Dragon

Tomie De Paola's story *The Knight and the Dragon* (1980) pits a reluctant knight against a reluctant dragon. Both assume that they should learn to conduct themselves according to socially accepted roles, that of a brave, combative knight and a fierce, fire-breathing dragon. The two practice for the big fight with the aid of library books, but each fails miserably to conquer the other. The helpful librarian resolves the conflict peacefully and creatively by offering them books to help them start a cooperative business (a barbecue restaurant) based on pooling their talents. This is one of many books that reinforce the theme that physical conflict is destructive and sometimes silly and that cooperation can be more helpful to both sides than competition.

Anger Brainstorm

Many children come to school having learned limited and destructive ways to express anger. Their home and neighborhood role models may have taught them that a natural response to anger is hitting, swearing, drinking, driving fast, slamming doors, or withdrawing. Most children's repertoires of anger-handling skills are limited to what they have seen their parents, siblings, relatives, and neighbors do. Anger management, or impulse control, is a major problem in children's behavior both within and outside the classroom.

The ability to find ways to handle and express anger constructively is prerequisite to discussing differences of opinion, resolving conflicts, and solving problems using reason. Teaching children positive ways of expressing anger is well worth classroom time because it both enhances the immediate peace and gives children long-term strategies for managing their own behavior.

A simple exercise, based on one described by William Kreidler (1984), that can expand children's repertoire of anger management skills is an "anger brainstorm." In this activity, the teacher guides children to list all the ways people act out anger—for example, pounding pillows, hitting someone, being quiet. Children may act out their suggestions (within limits, of course). Following the brainstorm activity, children discuss what behaviors are always positive outlets for anger, what behaviors are never appropriate, and what behaviors might be appropriate depending on the situation. The benefits of this simple activity are several. For one, children learn that everyone gets angry and that anger is a natural emotion, neither good nor bad. Hearing others' ideas about expressions of anger also exposes children to possibilities other than the ones they see at home. Finally, the categorizing of appropriate and inappropriate responses reinforces critical thinking. To reinforce positive responses, children might role play teacher-designed conflict skits or illustrate examples.

Passing Objects

Creative drama provides children with opportunities to practice skills in planning, hypothesizing, problem solving, communicating, and cooperating as they exercise their natural inclination to fantasize. Children who might not excel at traditional reading, writing, and math may well prove to be excellent at kinesthetic or spatial self-expression or at creative interpretation. A simple group exercise using movement allows children to express themselves nonverbally, think creatively, respond to others, and solve the problem of interpreting without words.

Seat children in a circle and tell them they are going to pretend to pass an object around the circle from hand to hand. You will tell them what the object is and change it from time to time. They are to use no words, only their hands, facial expressions, and bodies to show what the object is, and they have to decide how this object should be handled. A suggested list of objects includes an egg, an ice cube, a porcupine, a baby kitten, a cotton ball, a sewing needle, and a sticky ball of dough or clay.

Machine Pantomime

A more complex exercise with scientific academic content asks children to work together in groups of three or four to "become" a simple machine, perhaps an eggbeater, a washing machine, or a vacuum cleaner. Children may need to observe a simple machine first before they attempt to interpret it kinesthetically. Encourage each group to take the time to discuss how the machine works, what its major parts are, and how they function together and to plan who will act out what part of the machine and when. Teachers of older children might use this activity to introduce or reinforce a unit of study on simple machines and their principles of operation. Depending on the children's cognitive and social level, you may need to guide each group through its decision making. In more independent groups, you might observe which children take the lead in suggesting roles for others and which ones follow. You may decide you need to intervene gently to help the children interact with respect for each other's ideas or to help individual children interpret their "parts."

Social Action: We Can Help

Activities in this section aim at teaching children that they have a responsibility (and the ability) to contribute to the welfare of the earth and its people. Research on the subject of children's resiliency (their ability to overcome difficult life situations) shows that a sense of efficacy is crucial. Children need to know they are capable beings at the same time that they know adults are taking care of them in ways they cannot take care of themselves. It is important that they know adults are helping to solve the problems in their lives and in the world; it is also important for them to know that they are capable of solving some problems, can contribute to the welfare of others, and can achieve some success. Because they are young, they need to see concrete results of their efforts. This means that, whatever the social action you guide them toward, they need to experience results. These can be in the form of communication from those they have helped or in that of actually seeing a quantified material outcome. The following activities are designed to give children opportunities to give of themselves to the earth, to each other, and to those in need.

Caring for the Earth

Giving children responsibility for a small piece of the earth conveys to them the sense that they are trustworthy and effective actors in the world. It helps to have available a patch of land for gardening or landscaping, large enough for several children to work on by using a rotating scheme, or large enough to be divided into small "cooperatives." It is important that whatever children plant be easy to grow, be likely to thrive, and grow fairly quickly, so that they can see the results of their work as soon as possible.

Children need to experience success to sustain their sense of efficacy and responsibility. Give them (guided) choices as much as possible in what to grow and where. Taking care of their piece of the earth also means keeping it clean, well maintained, and healthy. Weeding, watering, feeding, trimming, and the like offer opportunities for learning knowledge and skills in science, math, and art.

Other activities, experiments, and explorations that draw on Native American tales and sensibilities to nature can be found in two books by Caduto and Bruchac, *Keepers of the Earth* and *Keepers of Life*. Several websites offer ideas for activities and lessons related to preservation of the earth's resources (see "Websites" at the end of this chapter).

Sustainable Seas

Borrowing from the project of deep water exploration launched in 1998 by the National Geographic Society, the National Oceanic and Atmospheric Administration, and the Richard & Rhoda Goldman Fund, have your class explore resources to find out ways aquanauts, marine science, and the fishing industry are trying to preserve the seas. Have the children learn about sea life and how they can cooperate with these worldwide conservation efforts.

Recycling

Children can relate to the need to be careful not to use up the world's natural resources and not to waste what could be used again. Make the school or child care center recycling program a teachable moment: help children to learn to sort materials, and follow the recycled materials to a recycling center to see what happens to them. Brainstorm with children how various containers and scrap materials could be used again in the classroom. If they come up with the ideas, they will remember the importance of the concept of respecting the materials of the earth.

Caring for the Classroom

Teaching children to care for the physical environment of the classroom reinforces their sense of efficacy. It also teaches them that objects have forms, functions, and appropriate storage places. For children to feel that the classroom or child care center is theirs as well as the teacher's, they must be given responsibility and some choice in keeping it manageable and safe and keeping the objects within it clean and in good repair. When a new object or new display develops, for example, you might discuss with children where and how they think it should be placed rather than make the decision by yourself.

Nel Noddings, in *The Challenge to Care in Schools* (1992), offers suggestions for teaching children to care for their human-made world not only as opportunities for social action but also for academic learning. She suggests that we discuss with children why we use particular objects and show them examples from other times and other cultures where different objects have been used for the same function. For example, understanding the need for writing utensils and knowing how to care for them can extend into learning about other kinds of writing implements used in other times, in other cultures, or for other functions. While most American schools and child care centers are enclosed buildings with rooms furnished with tables and chairs, in other countries (e.g., Malawi [Breitborde, 1997]) much schooling takes place in the open air under trees, because there is a lack of buildings but also because the climate allows it. Noddings reminds us that Maria Montessori (1966) believed strongly in the psychic, cognitive, and social value of carefully teaching children how to use and care for objects properly and the potential for enhancing children's sense of responsibility and efficacy contained in these experiences.

Reminding us also of Dewey's contention that children love to make things, Noddings suggests that children be given ample opportunity to create. Making and repairing things will enhance children's problem solving and creativity while they learn preservation, conservation, and thrift.

Dividing up the work of taking care of the classroom or center might be done with reference to children's particular interests or talents, with some tasks given to individuals and others to groups. Giving artistic children the task of caring for art materials, giving logically/mathematically oriented children responsibility for computers or board games, and giving the readers responsibility for keeping the books neat and orderly will make sense to them, although some rotating exposure to different kinds of tasks is also necessary.

Caring for Each Other

Many teachers help children contribute to making a group card, story, or book to be sent home to an ill child. In homes where electronic mail is available, children in the classroom or child care center can communicate daily with an at-home mate. A speaker-phone in the classroom is also helpful for daily contact.

New arrivals at the center should be partnered with a "buddy," who takes responsibility to introduce the newcomer to the rest of the group, explain routines, and engage the newcomer in projects and play. Buddies are especially important when the new arrival is an immigrant or a child who speaks little or no English. At the Ford Elementary School in Lynn, Massachusetts, waves of immigrants have arrived from different countries during the past 10 years. During the first wave, European American children who had been born and raised in Lynn helped new classmates from the Dominican Republic by sitting near them and making sure they had all necessary materials, by translating, and by taking care to involve them in playground activities. A few years later, these Dominican children and their white classmates did the same for new Cambodian immigrants. In the past two years, the Ford School has welcomed children from Somalia. Teachers reminded the other children how they felt when they had first arrived and how important it was to feel befriended. The Somalians have lunchroom partners, playground buddies, and seatmates. Teachers spend time in classroom meetings discussing the newcomers' problems and talents and thanking children for their kindness.

Caring for the Community

Children can share their time, helping to collect toys for drives such as Toys for Tots and to bag food for food banks. We suggest that these activities become regular routines to reinforce the idea that sharing good fortune with others is an ongoing responsibility.

Children can also share their talents by displaying art or writing and performing music and drama in community settings, hospitals, and child care centers and schools in other communities. They might make posters that encourage social causes such as protection of the environment. Children can be persuasive advocates.

Adopting Grandparents   One way of strengthening children's habit of caring for others is to use opportunities for intergenerational activities. We feel it is important for children to look beyond their own "kind" (whether it be people of their own culture or their own age group) to relate to, listen to, and learn from people older and younger. Elders as a group enjoy the chance to interact with children and to teach them, provided the interaction is guided by teachers and limited to elders' abilities. Ways to involve children with elders include performances at nursing homes, read-alouds in assisted living settings and community centers, interviews and oral histories (for older children), pet shows, and homework or tutorial sessions. The best projects are those that provide for two-way giving, so that both the children and the elders feel they are contributing to the other group. For example, children might draw pictures of the stories the elders read to them as thank-you souvenirs. If children give a performance at a nursing home, perhaps a resident might introduce them, or perhaps the residents can respond with their own performance (e.g., poetry reading).

Summary

The activities described in this chapter are a few examples of ways to expand the curriculum of a school or child care center to bring in the world and its multiple perspectives. They can be incorporated to meet the criteria of any standards-based classroom required by state or national frameworks. We suggest that you consult the extensive list of resources for teachers, students, and parents in the appendixes of this book, all of which offer many opportunities to do the same. We recommend that you keep in mind the basic principles of global education and the guidelines provided in the Conclusion as you design your activities. The medium of teaching should reinforce the message: activities should engage all children; respect their own experiences and build from them; be integral and important to the curriculum rather than apart from it; incorporate the teaching of basic skills of literacy, numeracy, and critical thinking, teaching effective communication and positive social interaction as they teach content and academic skills; and provide balanced and accurate information that celebrates rather than degrades all cultures.

Finally, global education is interesting and fun. We hope you learn and enjoy yourself as much as we know your children will.

References

Ada, A. F., & Silva, S. (1997). *Gathering the sun: An alphabet book in Spanish and English*. New York: Lothrop, Lee & Shepard.

Anno, M. (Coll.), & Carle, E., Briggs, R., Popov, N., Hayashi, A., Calvi, G., et al. (1990). *All in a day*. New York: Putnam Publishing Group.

Barbarash, L. (1997). *Multicultural games*. Champaign, IL: Human Kinetics.

Bradbury, L. (1983). *Les nombres*. Loughborough (Leicestershire), England: Ladybird Books.

Breitborde, M-L. (1997, February). Personal conversation with Grace Chombo, Eastern Education Research Association annual conference, Hilton Head, SC.

Breitborde, M-L. (2001). *An "adventure" in learning: Curriculum unit V, Immigration to Gloucester*. Gloucester, MA: Gloucester Adventure.

Burns Knight, M., & Melnicove, M. (2000). *Africa is not a country*. Brookfield, CT: Millbrook Press.

Butler, F., Jordan, A. D., & Rotert, R. (1987). *The wide world all around: An anthology of children's literature*. New York: Longman.

Caduto, M., & Bruchac, J. (1993). *Keepers of the earth: Native American stories and activities for children*. Golden, CO: Fulcrum.

Caduto, M., & Bruchac, J. (1997). *Keepers of life: Discovering plants through Native American stories and earth activities for children*. Golden, CO: Fulcrum.

Chin-Lee, C. (1997). *A is for Asia*. New York: Orchard Books.

De Paola, T. (1980). *The knight and the dragon*. New York: G.P. Putnam's Sons.

Dodds, D., & Laroche, G. (Illus.). (1992). *The color box*. Boston: Little, Brown.

Fassler, D., & Danforth, K. (1993). *Coming to America: The kids' book about immigration*. Burlington, VT: Waterfront Books.

Feelings, M., & Feelings, T. (1974). *Jambo means hello: Swahili alphabet book*. New York: Dial Press.

Gaylord, S. K. (1994). *Multicultural books to make and share*. Jefferson, MO: Scholastic, Inc.

Giovanni, N. (1994). *Knoxville, Tennessee*. New York: Scholastic.

Hartman, G. (1991). *As the crow flies*. New York: Macmillan.

Haskins, J. (1987a). *Count your way through the Arab world*. Minneapolis, MN: Carolrhoda Books.

Haskins, J. (1987b). *Count your way through China*. Minneapolis, MN: Carolrhoda Books.

Haskins, J. (1987c). *Count your way through Russia*. Minneapolis, MN: Carolrhoda Books.

Hoberman, M. A. (1978). *A house is a house for me*. New York: Viking Penguin.

Johnson, A. (1996). *String games from around the world*. Palo Alto, CA: Klutz Press.

Kandoian, E. (1987). *Under the sun*. New York: G.P. Putnam's Sons.

Knight, M. B. (1993). *Who belongs here?* Gardiner, ME: Tilbury House.

Kreidler, W. (1984). *Creative conflict resolution*. Glenview, IL: Scott, Foresman.

Make your own Monopoly. (1998). Itasca, IL: TDC Games.

Making music. (1992, December). *Faces, IX* (4).

Massachusetts Department of Education. (1997). *History and social science curriculum frameworks*. Malden, MA.: Author.

McCloskey, R. (1941). *Make way for ducklings*. New York: Viking.

Montessori, M. (1966). *The secret of childhood*. New York: Ballantine.

Musgrove, M. (1976). *Ashanti to Zulu: African traditions*. New York: Dial Press.

National Geographic Society. (1999). *Sustainable Seas Expeditions* [teacher workshops flyer]. Washington D.C.: National Geographic Society.

Noddings, N. (1992). *The challenge to care in schools*. New York: Teachers College Press.

Onyefulu, I. (1993). *A is for Africa*. New York: Cobblehill Books.

Pellowski, A. (1990). *Hidden stories in plants*. New York: Macmillan.

Pennington, D. (1994). *Cherokee A-B-C coloring book*. Cherokee, NC: Cherokee Publications.

Provensen, A., & Provensen, M. (1978). *A peaceable kingdom: The Shaker abecedarius*. New York: Viking Press.

Rylant, C. (1985). *When I was young in the mountains*. New York: Dutton.

Sandin, J. (1981). *A long way to a new land*. New York: Harper & Row.

Scieszka, J. (1995). *The true story of the three pigs*. New York: NAL Dutton.

Simon, N. (1976). *All kinds of families*. Morton Grove, IL: Albert Whitman.

Singer, M. (1992). *Nine o'clock lullaby*. New York: Harper Trophy.

Sturges, P., & Laroche, G. (Illus.). (1998). *Bridges are to cross*. New York: G.P. Putnam's Sons.

Sturges, P., & Laroche, G. (Illus.). (2000). *Sacred places*. New York: G.P. Putnam's Sons.

Tompert, A. (1990). *Grandfather Tang's story*. New York: Crown.

Trinca, R., & Argent, I. (1995). *One woolly wombat*. Norwood, South Australia: Omnibus Books.

Women's Educational Media. (2000). *That's a family* [video]. San Francisco: Author.

Wren & Maile. (1992a). *1-2-3 counting locally*. Honolulu, HI: Bess Press.

Wren & Maile. (1992b). *Say it in Hawaiian: Pri-a-pa (alphabet)*. Honolulu, HI: Bess Press.

Yashina, T. (1965). *Crow boy*. New York: Scholastic.

Yin, C. (1996). *In my heart I am a dancer*. Philadelphia: Philadelphia Folklore Project.

Young, E. (1990). *Lon Po Po*. New York: Scholastic.

Zaslavsky, C. (1996). *The multicultural math classroom: Bringing in the world*. Portsmouth, NH: Heinemann.

Websites:

Africa (website accompanies video series): *www.pbs.org/wnet/africa, www.pbskids.org/africa*

AskERIC (teacher-developed lesson plans): *www.askeric.org*

Center for Global Environmental Education at Hamline University: *www.cgee.hamline/edu*

Earthwatch Global Classroom: *www.earthwatch.org/ed/home.html*

National Association for Environmental Education: *www.eelink.net*

Oxfam Global Curriculum: *www.oxfam.org*

Philadelphia Folklore Project: *www.folkloreproject.org*

Conclusion

The future of the world depends on us.

Introduction

Teachers of young children understandably focus their attention on the welfare and learning of individual children. American teachers especially are concerned that children develop into unique and capable human beings and see themselves that way. Even to achieve these essentially individualistic goals, however, teachers must appreciate the world the child is born into and understand that child's place in the world. We don't need to verbally transfer our larger understandings of self-in-world to young children who have neither the experience nor the cognitive capacity to comprehend them, but having them ourselves gives us a certain attitude, perspective, and set of values that we will inevitably communicate to students in our teaching. The best way for teachers to appreciate the world in its entirety and complexity is to have firsthand experience of cultures and places different from our own. We suggest that travel to other places, whether it be in neighborhoods across town or countries across the ocean, is time well spent in personal and professional development. (And we suggest that if readers do travel, they not confine their observations to landmarks nor their interaction to tour guides.) Short of being able to provide to our readers firsthand experience of new places, new cultures, and new perspectives, we hope to have given you information, strategies, and materials that will help to enlarge and inform the scope of your work.

The world of young children no longer ends with the boundaries of their neighborhoods, if it ever did. New communications technologies, mass media, and a shrinking, increasingly interdependent planet of nations make it impossible to assume that our children's lives are determined only by local events. A child's community at the turn of the 21st century is the world. We adults cannot ignore the plight of children in Pakistan or Honduras who stitch the soccer balls our American children play with; nor can we ignore the plight of the overindulged, overprotected upper-middle-class child in America who may not know the joy of a difficult job well done or a hardship overcome or the satisfaction of knowing that he has helped someone else in important ways. We believe that young children are by nature tolerant human beings, curious about and accepting of differences. We suggest that teachers build on these natural impulses and fuel them with experiences that support children's uniqueness and local lives while linking them to the wonderful diversity of human and physical life on the planet.

We are living in a global age. Businesses, governments, and health, environmental, and social agencies are interdependent. The challenge of this age to us as educators is to prepare ourselves and our students for the complex responsibilities of being simultaneously local, national, and world citizens. Communities are microcosms of the world's people as well as part of global infrastructures. All countries are experiencing changes in their demographics. Because of economic changes, political unrest, and social upheaval, immigration is occurring worldwide. Cultural diversity appears even in places that once were rather homogeneous. One can find Somalians living in the northern regions of Finland and in Lynn, Massachusetts; Vietnamese in Australia and Los Angeles; Haitians in France and Miami; Russians in Israel and Brighton Beach. While these population shifts have different origins, they pose a common challenge to educators faced with providing a curriculum that maintains a standard of excellence while responding to the very different needs of very different children.

We end this book where we began, with recognition of our diverse world, our interconnectedness, and our interdependence. We revisit these challenges with a look at our working definition of global education, described in Chapter 1 as including 12 principles. Woven through these principles of global education are the themes of unity and diversity and of the interrelationship of local and world communities. We would like educators to see the world in every community and, conversely, see every community linked to the world. We would like them to take responsibility to teach to that reciprocal vision. We hope that this book has furnished a few sound arguments to support our goal. We hope we have convinced you that acting locally is acting globally, that teachers cannot in good conscience nor in good educational practice ignore the global implications of curriculum content, academic skills, or the social and moral behavior we would have children learn.

Revisiting the Twelve Principles of Global Education

Global education asks teachers and parents to educate with a world view. Recognizing that global education deals with issues, concerns, attitudes, and process skills that are integral parts of any early childhood curriculum is an important first step for teachers and parents. We review here the 12 principles first mentioned in Chapter 1, which address the broad perspectives and the cross-curricular nature of global education. These principles inform the discussions of theory and practice throughout this book.

1. Global education is basic education.
2. Global education is lifelong learning.
3. Global education is cooperative learning.
4. Global education is inclusive of all.
5. Global education is education for social action.
6. Global education is economic education.
7. Global education involves technology.
8. Global education requires critical and creative thinking.
9. Global education is multicultural.
10. Global education is moral education.
11. Global education supports a sustainable environment.
12. Global education needs a core of globally literate educators.

To be effective, the 12 principles need the involvement of families, educators, and policy makers in implementing their message in homes, communities, schools, and child care centers. To assist in this daunting task of implementation we provide you with some guidelines in the form of questions formulated for each of these principles.

We intend that these guidelines be open-ended and promote discourse and discussion. While they might serve as a kind of checklist for designing and evaluating any early childhood program, the list is not definitive. We invite families and teachers to adapt our suggestions to the context of your own programs and missions and to modify them in developing your unique set of creative criteria.

Guidelines for Implementation

1. *Global education is basic education.*

    1.1   Do the content and materials of the curriculum include attention to information, issues, and concerns related to other nations and to the world as a whole?

    1.2   Does the curriculum provide children with basic literacies, including literacy in world languages, mathematics, and technology?

    1.3   Do those in charge of planning, reviewing, evaluating, implementing, or renewing curriculum- and purchasing-related materials consider global connections?

2. *Global education is lifelong learning.*

    2.1   Does the curriculum offer children joint learning experiences with people of other ages?

    2.2   Do the professional development programs of the school or center provide for the education of adults on global issues, including study, travel, and communication with educators in other parts of the world?

    2.3   Do parents and community folks participate in the life of the school or center, including them as learners, teachers, and decision makers?

3. *Global education is cooperative learning.*

    3.1   Does instructional practice include significant opportunities for children to work together and learn from each other?

    3.2   Are social skills that are requisite to effective cooperation taught directly?

    3.3   Do teachers and parents learn alongside children?

4. *Global education is inclusive of all.*

    4.1   Do school or center policies respect differences in family style (e.g., scheduling of parent conferences, documents written in native languages)?

    4.2   Does the instructional organization of children provide for regular interaction of heterogeneous groups?

    4.3   Is access to the materials of instruction and curriculum content equitable across all learners?

5. *Global education is education for social action.*

    5.1   Does the curriculum provide children with opportunities for community service?

    5.2   Do teachers and administrators advocate for local, national, and global concerns?

5.3   Are children taught about the efforts of adults in improving local, national, and world conditions?

6. *Global education is economic education.*

6.1   Does the curriculum include economic literacy for children?

6.2   Do purchasers of school or center items consider the implications of purchases on the lives and welfare of people in the local, national, and global community?

6.3   Are children and staff encouraged to use resources wisely?

7. *Global education involves technology.*

7.1   Do children have equal access to new technologies for learning?

7.2   Is technology used to enhance communication among peoples of the world?

7.3   Is technology used to improve instruction for children with special learning problems?

8. *Global education requires critical and creative thinking.*

8.1   Are children encouraged to analyze, synthesize, and evaluate information?

8.2   Does the curriculum encourage children to pose problems, formulate hypotheses, and try out solutions?

8.3   Are there significant opportunities for children to generate and implement creative ideas and projects?

9. *Global education is multicultural.*

9.1   Does the composition of the student body reflect the cultural composition of the local or regional community?

9.2   Does the curriculum inform children of the richness of their own heritages and instill pride in their cultural backgrounds?

9.3   Are significant efforts made to offer children regular and substantive experiences with children of cultures different from their own?

10. *Global education is moral education.*

10.1   Does the school or center support a climate of mutual respect, caring, and support?

10.2   Are children taught to consider and take responsibility for the impact of their behavior on others?

10.3   Are questions of ethics and morality regularly discussed among children and among the adults in the school or center?

11. *Global education supports a sustainable environment*.

11.1   Does the school or center respect and care for its immediate environment in the daily practices both inside and outside the physical facility?

11.2   Does the curriculum address environmental issues and efforts to sustain and protect the physical world?

11.3   Does the school or center involve the community in projects such as recycling, tree planting, or playground maintenance?

12. *Global education enhances the spirit of teaching and learning.*

> 12.1   Does the professional climate in the school or center respect the unique contributions of each of its staff and children?
>
> 12.2   Are staff members as well as children encouraged to reflect on their educative process?
>
> 12.3   Are staff members along with their students encouraged to ask the challenging questions and pursue their determined solutions?

We suggest that you use these guidelines to help you judge the extent to which the education you are providing is in fact global. You will undoubtedly want to add your own questions to this list. It is important that educators using these guidelines be able to describe how they are implemented. For example, in what ways is a climate of respect evident? What part of the curriculum supports children's learning about their own heritage? How do families participate in decision-making roles? How are social behaviors that are required for effective cooperative learning taught and reinforced? We urge you to consider what these guidelines look like and sound like in your own setting.

Sustaining the Vision

One teacher, even one school, cannot successfully implement global education. By nature, global education is a collaborative endeavor, as it involves many different people with, perhaps, many different interests. Central to the success of any global education program is communication, but communication poses some problems. On one hand, globally literate educators and families, focussed on human welfare around the world, seek to avoid the "Tower of Babel" discourse of rampant individualism. On the other hand, we want to hear the voice of the individual within the voices of many. Global educators face a perennial dilemma in our effort to respect the rights of the individual while implementing the social mandate for a just and civil world community.

But global educators do not face the dilemma or the work alone. Other professionals, including the staff of nongovernmental organizations, civil agencies, and governmental groups, are part of a worldwide effort to educate for world citizenship. They are willing to join with teachers and families to share their expertise and their experiences in engaging in the daunting task of designing communication systems and programs that respect the individual while shaping the social message. Such agencies develop resources and tools that encourage fact finding, mediation, negotiation, and cooperation. We suggest that you consult with agencies to use their documents in your advocacy efforts and global educational practice. We have listed many in Appendix A.

Putting It Together

Our goal in writing this book has been to help teachers educate children to live in a democratic society with an appreciation of local and national needs framed within a world perspective. To achieve that end, we took some risks. We advocated providing global education early in the lives of children. We looked at the state of the world's children and advocated for the protection of their rights as defined by the UN Convention on the Rights of the Child. We identified programs, individuals, and agencies that model exemplary approaches to global education through either effective teaching practice or political advocacy. We introduced guidelines to serve as foundations for developing early childhood global education programs. We shaped a theoretical framework for sound global educational pedagogy that rests on developmentally appropriate practice and responds to the needs of all learning styles and learners. We outlined specific ideas that we feel are examples of the kind of teaching we advocate in formal and informal instruction in homes, schools, and child care facilities. We tried to dispel stereotypes of global education as being a political, one-world approach to schooling by a respectful coverage of an extensive variety of local, national, and international educational models. While we recognize education is political, we tried to avoid a single perspective or philosophy in our consideration of the multifaceted views on education documented throughout the book and defined by our diversity theme in the definition of global education.

In the end, however, we recognize that final responsibility for undertaking the work of global education rests with you. We hope we have provided information, support, guidelines, and options for you to use in your own lifelong journey into learning about your world. We believe the best global educator is a global learner, and we hope you will undertake the journey. We hope you will ask the challenging questions along the way. We encourage you to join us in shaping a positive future for today's children.

The future of the world depends on us.

Appendix A: Resources for Teachers

Books

Baht, M. (1988). *Pueblo stories and storytellers.* Tucson, AZ: Treasure Chest.
  A history and collection of Pueblo folk stories.

Baker, G. C. (1994). *Planning and organizing for multicultural instruction.* Menlo Park, CA: Addison-Wesley.
  Guidebook for multicultural instruction ranging from preparation to teaching strategies.

Barbour, C., & Barbour, N. (2001). *Families, schools, and communities: Building partnerships for educating children.* Upper Saddle River, NJ: Merrill/Prentice Hall.
  This book is focused on the importance of community in the lives of children.

Bartis, P., & Bowman, P. (1994). *A teachers guide to folklife resources for K–12 classrooms.* Washington, DC: American Folklife Center, Library of Congress.
  A list of materials prepared for the classroom by folklorists and other cultural studies specialists.

Bay State Centers for Global Education. (1992). *Global learning: A compilation of sample curricular units and resource information for K–12 teachers.* Boston: Author.

Beaty, J. (1997). *Building bridges with multicultural picture books: For children 3–5.* Upper Saddle River, NJ: Merrill/Prentice Hall.
  Encourages teachers to engage children with multicultural book characters and to help and accept people.

Benson, P. (1986). *Teaching foreign cultures in social studies: Strategies for teaching social studies with a global perspective.* Washington, DC: National Endowment for the Humanities.
  Sections on teaching with a global perspective in Latin America, the Soviet Union, and Western civilization.

Bosma, B. (1987). *Fairy tales, fables, legends, and myths: Using folk literature in your classroom.* New York: Teachers College Press.
  Handbook of imaginative teaching ideas, including more than 50 complete lesson plans. For each lesson, teachers are provided clear and precise explanations of the cultural and historical background and folklore concepts.

Collins, T. H., & Czarra, F. (1991). *Global primer: Skills for a changing world.* Denver, CO: Center for Teaching International Relations.
  Activities for K–9 on themes in global education such as "World Connections," "World Awareness," and map skills.

Davidman, L. (1994). *Teaching with a multicultural perspective: A practical guide.* White Plains, NY: Longman.
  Provides instruments and observation guides to help put multicultural teacher education into practice.

De Cou-Landberg, M. (1994). *The global classroom: A thematic multicultural model for the K–6 & ESL classroom: Vols. 1 and 2.* Reading, MA: Addison Wesley Longman.

Department for Education, Welsh Office, Department of Education, Northern Ireland, Scottish Office. (1995). *Superhighways for education.* London: HMSO Publications Center, P.O. Box 276, London, SW8 5DT.
  Explains technology's multiple uses in and impact on education in the United Kingdom.

Derman-Sparks, L. (1991). *Anti-bias curriculum: Tools for empowering young children.* Washington, DC: National Association for the Education of Young Children.
  Shows adults how to stand up for what's right and how to empower children so they can, too.

Education Department of South Australia. (1988). *Home: Years R–3*. South Australia: Government Printer. ISBN: 0-7243-8044-2.
Developed to assist in the teaching of Aboriginal studies in years R–3.

Embry, L. (1991). *Math around the world*. Carthage, IL: Good Apple.
Math/geography enrichment activities for grades 4–6.

Fu, V., Stremmel, A., & Hill, L. (2002). *Teaching and learning: Collaborative exploration of the Reggio Emilia approach*. Upper Saddle River, NJ: Merrill/ Prentice Hall.
This book looks at implementing the Reggio Emilia approach for American schools.

Gallop, N. (1993). *Science is women's work: Photos and biographies of American women in the sciences*. Windsor, CT: National Women's History Project.
Encourages girls to pursue their interest in science and mathematics.

Gibbs, J. (1994). *Tribes: A new way of learning together*. Santa Rosa, CA: Center Source.
Helps people discover similarities while appreciating their differences.

Gibson, L. (1993). *Making your mark: Fun with Australian art*. Marrickville, N.S.W., Australia: Science Press.
Activity book that focuses on discovering Australia and its art.

Gilliland, H. (1995). *Teaching the Native American* (3rd ed.). Dubuque, IA: Kendall/Hunt.
Practical suggestions and ideas for educators of Native American students.

Gomez, A. (1996). *Crafts of many cultures: Thirty authentic craft projects from around the world*. Jefferson City, MO: Scholastic Professional Books.
Step-by-step guide to creating global art projects.

Gutlohn, L. (Ed.). (1992). *American mosaic: Reading for multicultural literacy*. San Francisco: Macmillan– McGraw Hill.
Stresses the uniqueness of various cultural heritages.

Hammer, R. (1993). *Hidden America: A collection of multicultural stories*. Golden Valley, MN: Place in the Woods.
Features the people, places, and things of importance to four minority subcultures: African Americans, Hispanic Americans, Native Americans, and American women. Short essays and tales.

Harris, V. J. (Ed.). (1992). *Teaching multicultural literature in grades K–8*. Norwood, MA : Christopher-Gordon.
Presents titles, descriptions, and ideas for integrating good books into all subject areas.

Hawke, S. D., & Davis, J. E. (1992). *Seeds of change: The story of cultural exchange after 1492*. Reading, MA: Addison-Wesley.
The events of 1492 began one of the most profound cultural interchanges in history. This book describes the merits and consequences of the introduction of the horse, potato, corn, sugar, and diseases to the Americas.

Hodges, S. (1997). *Celebrating likes and differences*. Everett, MA: Warren Publishing House.
Presents fun and easy theme units for exploring diversity with young children. Turns the study of common objects into a special learning time for young children through themes with built-in opportunities to examine similarities and differences within the classroom and the community. For ages 3–6.

Johnson, D. W., & Johnson, F. P. (1994). *Joining together: Group theory and group skills*. Boston: Allyn & Bacon.
Research theory and activities to promote group effectiveness.

Kiang, P. (1992). *Asian American studies curriculum resource guide (Massachusetts K–12)*. Needham, MA: Massachusetts Asian American Educators Association.
Explores themes in the Asian American experience. A guide for educators of Asian American students.

Miller-Lachman, L. (1992). *Our family, our friends, our world*. New Providence, NJ: R.R. Bowker.
An annotated guide to significant multicultural books for children and teenagers.

Milord, S. (1992). *Hands around the world: Three hundred sixty-five creative ways to build cultural awareness and global respect*. Charlotte, VT: Williamson.
Multicultural activities for grades 1–8.

Ministry of Education. (1992). *Dancing with the pen: The learner as a writer*. Wellington, New Zealand: Learning Media, Ministry of Education, Box 3293.
Written by New Zealand educators, this book is for primary teachers. It aims to develop their understanding of how children learn to write and how teachers can facilitate the process.

Montessori, M. (1966). *The secret of childhood.* New York: Ballantine.
Early childhood classic that provides today's reader insight into the cultural development of children.

Nicholson, H. E. (1993). *Inspirations for geography.* Leamington Spa, Warwickshire, England: Scholastic, Villiers House.
Teacher resource and guide book of geography lessons for elementary grades.

Nieto, S. (1996). *Affirming diversity: The sociopolitical context of multicultural education* (2nd ed.). White Plains, NY: Longman.
Comprehensive framework for intervention strategies for multicultural education, including case studies.

Noddings, N. (1992). *The challenge to care in schools.* New York: Teachers College Press.
Offers a theory-based program of integration of themes of care in personal, social, and environmental topics. Classroom-friendly.

Orlando, L. (1996). *The multicultural gamebook: More than 70 traditional games from 30 countries.* Jefferson City, MO: Scholastic Professional Books.
Complete step-by-step guide for a variety of easy games from 30 different countries.

Peace Child International. (1994). *Rescue mission planet earth: A children's edition of Agenda 21.* New York: Kingfisher Books, Grisewood & Dempsey.
Introduction by Boutros Boutros-Ghali, Secretary-General of the United Nations. Environmental action book written by children of the world; includes a children's activity booklet.

Perry, T., & Fraser, J. W. (Eds.). (1993). *Freedom's plow: Teaching in the multicultural classroom.* New York: Routledge.

Reynolds, D., & Farrell, S. (1996). *Worlds apart? A review of international surveys of educational achievement involving England.* London: Office for Standards in Education.

Scott, S. (1992). *Not better ... not worse ... just different.* Amherst, MA: Human Resource Development Press.
Teaches children to respect and accept one another regardless of learning or physical differences, race, or sex.

Spann, M. B. (1992). *Literature-based multicultural activities: An integrated approach.* New York: Scholastic.
Activities for children ages 5–9.

Steele, P. (1991). *The people atlas.* New York: Oxford University Press.
An atlas of human life that combines a continent-by-continent survey with special detailed sections on food, language, homes, and more. For grades 2–5.

Stull, E. (1994). *Multicultural discovery activities for the elementary grades.* Upper Saddle River, NJ: Center for Applied Research in Education.
More than 50 illustrated folktales recommended by the authors, several folktale collections, indexes, and bibliographic sources. Includes flannel board figures and puppets.

Taylor, C. A. (Ed.). (1993). *Guide to multicultural resources.* Madison, WI: Praxis, Fort Atkinson, WI: Highsmith Press.
A concise directory, mediography, and almanac of current information on multicultural organizations, services, and trends.

Terzian, A. (1993). *The kid's multicultural art book: Art & craft experiences from around the world.* Charlotte, VT: Williamson.
Good range of easy and interesting projects with cultural background added.

Thomas, R. (1995). *Connecting cultures.* New Providence, NJ: R.R. Bowker.
A guide to multicultural literature for children; includes fiction, folktales, and poetry.

Tiedt, P. (1990). *Multicultural teaching: A handbook of activities, information and resources.* Boston: Allyn & Bacon.
Multicultural guide for teachers and future teachers for lessons at all levels.

York, S. (1996). *Roots and wings: Affirming culture in early childhood programs.* Jefferson City, MO: Scholastic.
Comprehensive approach to multicultural education with stress on the importance of culture and rising above prejudice. Includes over 60 hands-on activities.

Zarrillo, J. (1994). *Multicultural literature, multicultural teaching: Units for the elementary grades.* Fort Worth, TX: Harcourt Brace.
Focuses on teaching with multicultural literature in the elementary school classroom.

Zaslavsky, C. (1996). *The multicultural math classroom: Bringing in the world.* Portsmouth, NH: Heinemann.

Mathematics for elementary and middle-grade children based on mathematical systems and materials from around the world.

Multimedia, Curricula, and Software

About the UN: Literacy. Church World Service, Film Library, 28606 Phillips St., P.O. Box 968, Elkhart, IN 46515. (219) 264-3102. An 18-minute video featuring people around the globe participating in literacy programs, gaining skills that enable them to learn about issues vital to their lives.

About the UN: Rights of the child. Church World Service, Film Library, 28606 Phillips St., P.O. Box 968, Elkhart, IN 46515. (219) 264-3102. A 16-minute video reviewing what the world's children are entitled to. An examination of some of the world's children and constructive responses. Suitable for ages junior high to adult.

A different place: The intercultural classroom. Insight Media, 2162 Broadway, New York, NY 10024-6642. (212) 721-6316. Film depicts cultural conflicts in the high school classroom, showing how insensitivity to different styles of communication reinforces negative perceptions between teachers and learners, as well as among students. Experts analyze the vignettes and offer insights into different ways of building a sense of community in the classroom. 2 vols., 37 min. total.

Africa adventure. Mennonite Central Committee, Resource Library, 21 South 12th Street, Box 500, Akron, PA 17501-0500. Available free upon request, borrower pays postage. Multimedia children's project teaches about African life. Program includes a 33-minute video, teacher's guide, audiocassettes of African music, maps, photos, a poster, a book, and brochure.

Africa: Geography mini-unit. (1992). J. E. Moor, Evan-Moor, Monterey, CA. Mini-unit introducing the continent of Africa.

The Africans: Global Africa. Church World Service, Film Library, 28606 Phillips St., P.O. Box 968, Elkhart, IN 46515. (219) 264-3102. A 55-minute video that presents Ali Mazuri's look at the peoples of Africa, including their history and culture. Mention "Educators Guide to Free Videos" when ordering.

The Africans: Legacy of lifestyles. Church World Service, Film Library, 28606 Phillips Street, P.O. Box

968, Elkhart, IN 46515. (219) 264-3102. This 55-minute video contrasts the ideas of romantic gloriana and romantic primitivism from an African perspective. Mention "Educators Guide to Free Videos" when ordering.

The Africans: New conflicts. Church World Service, Film Library, 28606 Phillips St., P.O. Box 968, Elkhart, IN 46515. (219) 264-3102. A 55-minute video presenting Ali Mazuri examining the tensions inherent in the coexistence of three heritages: the traditional African, Islamic, and Christian. Mention "Educators Guide to Free Videos" when ordering.

African tales. Mennonite Central Committee, Resource Library, 21 South 12th Street, Box 500, Akron, PA 17501-0500. Available free upon request, borrower pays postage. A 23-minute video presenting African fables and a child's view of a food market, homes, the village blacksmith, and a church service in Zaire.

Around the world adventures. Instructional Fair, TS Denison, P.O. Box 250, Grand Rapids, MI 49502-0334. (800) 443-2976. Exciting activities, recipes, and patterns for daily life in 10 countries. Includes pertinent information, foreign-word keys, reproducibles, mini-books, passports, and stickers.

Asia: Geography unit. (1992). J. E. Moor, Evan-Moor, Monterey, CA. Unit introducing the continent of Asia.

Asia resource box. Mennonite Central Committee, Resource Library, 21 South 12th St., Box 500, Akron, PA 17501-0500. Available free upon request on a circulation basis, borrower pays postage. Teaches elementary-grade children about Laos and Thailand. The kit includes a teacher's guide, a story cloth, a glove, a book, photos, and a ball and spoon made from bomb casings. Also contains a two-part video about a Lao girl's family farm, school, food, and games and Thailand's refugees, markets, waterways, and cultures. Teaches peacemaking.

Bienvenidos. Instructional Fair, TS Denison, P.O. Box 250, Grand Rapids, MI 49502-0334. (800) 443-2976. Explores the traditions, language, music, dance, art, food, stories, holidays, and customs of Mexico and the Hispanic culture. Organized monthly topics and activities correspond with all areas of the curriculum. Teachers do not need to speak Spanish to use this resource with success. Grades 1–6.

Bridging cultures: A program kit for schools and public libraries. By Barbara Radke Blake and Tom Kruger. Neal-Schuman Publishers. (212) 925-8650. Provides a wealth of resources and tools that bring different cultures to life in lively and fun ways for children. Native American, Asian/Pacific Islander, Hispanic American, and African American cultures are explored in separate chapters, which demonstrate specific folklore themes and provide information on each group. Kit includes audiocassettes, clip art, and instructions for craft projects. For use with children ages 4–10.

Celebrate with a story. Instructional Fair, TS Denison, P.O. Box 250, Grand Rapids, MI 49502-0334. (800) 443-2976. Resource offers original stories, fingerplays, and props to help the storyteller share holidays and multicultural events with young children. Features holidays that celebrate our relationships with each other, our cultures, our natural world, and diverse religions. For early childhood.

Children in El Salvador. Central America Resource Center, Minnesota. Slides. A seven-day unit for grades K–3. Includes 101 slides, tape of music, tape of songs and games in Spanish, tape for the script for the civil war and refugee camp slides. Seven-day lesson plan with activities.

Culture, time, and place. Insight Media, 2162 Broadway, New York, NY 10024-6642. (212) 721-6316. Thirty-minute film explains how language, schooling, and interpersonal relationships are vehicles of acculturation that communicate values, beliefs, attitudes, and expectations to children. Helps children to see themselves as part of a broad cultural network.

Culturgrams. Upstart, W5527 Hwy. 106, P.O. Box 800, Fort Atkinson, WI 53538-0800. (800) 448-5828. Concise four-page booklets focus on the customs and courtesies, people and lifestyles, as well as government and economy of a nation. Designed in loose-leaf format stored in a three-ring binder. Complete set includes 153 countries.

Different and the same: That's us! Church World Service, Film Library, 28606 Phillips Street, P.O. Box 968, Elkhart, IN 46515. (219) 264-3102. Available free to schools, on a circulation basis, borrowers pay postage. A 14-minute video that teaches children to recognize, respect, and celebrate cultural diversity. Suitable for elementary audiences. Men-

tion "Educators Guide to Free Videos" when ordering.

Ethnic arts & facts. P.O. Box 20550, Oakland, CA 94620. Offers "culture kits" from Africa, Mexico, Peru, and Guatemala. The kits include cultural/ historical overviews written by university scholars "who have lived within the culture" and contain authentic traditional artifacts such as masks, baskets, cloth, and musical instruments.

Everybody's beautiful career cutouts. Scholastic Books Clubs, P.O. Box 7503, Jefferson City, MO 65102-7503. Order #12770. Twenty-three cutouts introduce young children to various cultures, trades, professions, ages, and physical challenges. Great to use as part of a community helper or multicultural theme. Resource guide included. Size range 8" to 15" tall.

Everybody's ethnic: An alphabet that embraces cultural diversity. Upstart, W5527 Hwy. 106, P.O. Box 800, Fort Atkinson, WI 53538-0800. (800) 448-5828. Set of four posters is scored and can be cut for display. The set highlights and describes the visual, performing, and culinary arts of a wide variety of cultures.

Folktales of peace. Mennonite Central Committee, Resource Library, 21 South 12th St., Box 500, Akron, PA 17501-0500. Available free upon request on a circulation basis, borrowers pay postage. A 22-minute video in which professional storytellers breathe life into folktales of peace from different cultures. Appropriate for grades K–6. Study questions included.

Grocery store. M. Keyes, YMCA, New York, NY. A role-play simulation in which a diverse group from a multicultural neighborhood meets to resolve a dispute that arises at a local grocery.

Hispanic/Latino culture theme. Upstart, W5527 Hwy. 106, P.O. Box 800, Fort Atkinson, WI 53538-0800. (800) 448-4887. Celebrates Hispanic/Latino culture. Takes readers to colorful South and Central America to explore the lives of ancient civilizations, present-day culture, and endangered animals. Includes a poster, dateline, program guide, and endangered animal bookmarks.

Holidays for children video series. Library Video Company, P.O. Box 1110, Catalogue M-47, Bala Cynwyd, PA 19004. (800) 843-3620. Educational video series explores the symbols, customs, rituals, and folklore underlying major holidays. Shows connections between different cultures. A sample of the holidays includes Elections Day, PowWow, Cinco de Mayo, Ramadan, Kwanzaa, Rosh Hashanah, Yom Kippur, St. Patrick's Day.

Imagination expressDestination: Neighborhood. New Media Schoolhouse Sourcebook, Box 505, Pound Ridge, NY 10576. (888) 843-6674. A CD-ROM activity pack for grades K–6. Students create scenes, then add text, music, sound, dialogue, and narration to spin interactive tales about their daily adventures. Centers on the familiar places in students' lives to provide an inviting environment for storytelling or writing about real-life experience. Published by Edmark for Mac/Win.

Imagination expressDestination: Ocean. New Media Schoolhouse Sourcebook, Box 505, Pound Ridge, NY 10576. (888) 843-6674. A CD-ROM activity pack for grades K–8. Students learn about the oceans as they create interactive stories and movies starring dolphins, bat rays, buried treasure, and undersea divers. They select scenes, then add "stickers," text, sound effects, dialogue, and narration to bring the adventure to life. Published by Edmark for Mac/Win.

International crafts and games. Instructional Fair, TS Denison, P.O. Box 250, Grand Rapids, MI 49502-0334. (800) 443-2976. Captures the spirit of cultural diversity with 100 easy-to-make projects. Grades 1–6.

Multicultural clip art. Instructional Fair, TS Denison, P.O. Box 250, Grand Rapids, MI 49502-0334. (800) 443-2976. Software for Windows or Macintosh. Artwork for each country or continent includes maps, flags, clothing, people, architecture, customs, animals, wildlife, and more. Art can be downloaded into word processing and paint programs.

Multicultural clip art from around the world. (1995). S. Shneck, Scholastic, NY. Clip art activities for juvenile age levels.

Multicultural education. Association for Supervision and Curriculum Development, 1250 North Pitt Street, Alexandria, VA 22314-9718. (800) 933-ASCD. Scenes from pioneering schools show how classroom teachers develop multicultural lessons and how principals create environments that respect different cultures. Includes one 40-minute videotape, facilitator's guide, and the book

Teaching with a Multicultural Perspective: A Practical Guide.

Multicultural games. By Lorraine Barbarash. Human Kinetics, P.O. Box 5076, Champaign, IL 61825-5076. (800) 747-4457. Seventy-five games and activities from 43 cultures on six continents. Each game has two special elements that help students discover other cultures and learn more about their own. A blend of cultural awareness, physical activity, skill practice, and fun.

Multicultural holiday kit. Upstart, W5527 Hwy. 106, P.O. Box 800, Fort Atkinson, WI 53538-0800. (800) 448-4887. Used to promote each holiday individually or in combination to create an international holiday festival. Kit includes four-poster set, 200 bookmarks, a bulletin board decorator, and a program guide.

Multicultural music. Instructional Fair, TS Denison, P.O. Box 250, Grand Rapids, MI 49502-0334. (800) 443-2976. New songs with familiar melodies teach children about unique places in the world. Africa, Australia, Canada, France, Japan, Mexico, the Netherlands, and Poland are each covered in separate chapters. Also features songs in native languages, illustrations, word lists, activities, projects, patterns, and recipes. Book and cassette may be purchased together or separately. Grades pre-K–4.

Multicultural pack. Scholastic Books Clubs, P.O. Box 7503, Jefferson City, MO 65102-7503. Order #12812. Set of four paperback books to introduce students to different cultures. Titles include: *Rise and Shine, Marik-chan!* by Chiyoko Tomioka. Children follow a Japanese girl through her morning routine as she and her family prepare to go to work and school. *Bright Eyes, Brown Skin*, by Cheryl Willis Hudson and Bernadette G. Ford. Rhyming text and soft watercolor illustrations depict an African American boy and girl at school and at play. *Arroz con leche*, by Lulu Delacre. A celebration of Latin American heritage, including 12 enchanting songs and rhymes in both English and Spanish. *The Story of Jumping Mouse*, by John Steptoe. A Native American tale beautifully illustrated in black-and-white drawings. A brave mouse makes a journey to "the far-off land" and makes many sacrifices along the way.

Multicultural tales. New Media Schoolhouse Source-book, Box 505, Pound Ridge, NY 10576. (888) 843-6674. A CD-ROM activity pack for grades 2–6. *The Red Shoes, Jazztime Tale,* and *The Nightingale* are narrated by Ossie Davis and Ruby Dee. A clip art program is included with the software package. Published by Queue for Mac.

Multiple intelligences in the classroom. Insight Media, 2162 Broadway, New York, NY 10024-6642. (212) 721-6316. Profiling a Massachusetts elementary school, this video introduces multiple intelligence theory and defines seven kinds of intelligence. The longer version shows administrators how to imple-ment and support this theory in school. Teacher's version 31 minutes; administrator's version 41 minutes.

The multiple intelligences series. Association for Su-pervision and Curriculum Development, 1250 North Pitt St., Alexandria, VA 22314-9718. (800) 933-ASCD. Scenes from elementary, middle, and high school classrooms show how a multiple intel-ligences approach helps teachers. Includes three 20- to 36-minute videotapes, three facilitators guides, the book *Multiple Intelligences in the Classroom,* and the audiotape *On Multiple Intelli-gences & Education.*

My first amazing world explorer. New Media School-house Sourcebook, Box 505, Pound Ridge, NY 10576. (888) 843-6674. A CD-ROM activity pack for grades K–4. Takes students on trips around the physical and natural world. Through hundreds of narratives, students discover concepts of geo-graphical mapping, travel, time, and distance. Published by DK Multimedia, available for Mac/Win.

Native American leaders program. Upstart, W5527 Hwy. 106, P.O. Box 800, Fort Atkinson, WI 53538-0800. (800) 448-4887. Brings the great Native American leaders from the past into the classroom. Kit includes an eight-poster set, 200 bookmarks, bulletin board decorator, and a resource guide. *Native American Wind Shields* may also be pur-chased to accompany program. The set includes four designs representing the Southwest, North-west, Thunderbird, and Buffalo. Each wind shield represents a Native American tale and includes a historical narrative for storytelling.

Neighborhoods are different (2nd ed.). Britannica Learning Materials, 310 South Michigan Ave., Chicago, IL 60604-9839. (800) 554-9862. Eight-year-old narrators from a variety of ethnic and so-cioeconomic backgrounds give us tours of their neighborhoods. Consultant: Mark Schug, Ph.D., University of Wisconsin. 12 minutes.

Our Native American friends (Apache/Miccosukee/ Eskimo). Britannica Learning Materials, 310 South Michigan Ave., Chicago, IL 60604-9839. (800) 554-9862. Hayden Anderson, an Apache, lives in a modern house on a reservation in Arizona. Richard Sanders lives on a Miccosukee reservation in Florida. Up in the Arctic Circle, Julius Jessup studies his Eskimo heritage at school. 10 minutes.

Pequena the burro (the importance of heritage). Film Archives, Cinema Center, Botsford, CT 06404-0386. (800) 366-1920. Shows students how a look at where they've come from can give them a new perspective on where they can go. When Pequena the burro is feeling ordinary and inadequate, a wise friend reminds her that being a burro is a great gift. With clearer vision of who she is, Pe-quena transforms doubt into determination. She inspires students to do the same. Grades K–4. 14 minutes, color.

Prejudice and discrimination: The unforgettable pen pal. Film Archives, Cinema Center, Botsford, CT 06404-0386. In this video, A.J. and the club mem-bers learn valuable lessons about prejudice and discrimination. Helps kids understand the negative effects prejudice causes and the importance of forming their own opinions about others intelli-gently. Grades K–4. 28 minutes.

Prejudice: Answering children's questions. Insight Me-dia, 2162 Broadway, New York, NY 10024-6642. (212) 721-6316. Peter Jennings hosts an audience of young children and explores prejudice and stereotypes based on race, sex, religion, and dis-ability. 75 minutes.

Quilt of many cultures. Film Comm, 641 North Av-enue, Glendale Heights, IL 60139. (708) 790-3300. Available to schools free upon request, bor-rower pays postage. Book four weeks in advance of desired date. A 34-minute video focusing on the many cultures of Southern India.

Rainbow war. Church World Service, Film Library, 28606 Phillips Street, P.O. Box 968, Elkhart, IN

46515. (219) 264-3102. Available free to schools, on a circulation basis, borrowers pay postage. A 20-minute video that is a delightful allegory about tolerance and good will. Features special effects and stirring music performed by the London Royal Philharmonic Orchestra. Mention "Educators Guide to Free Videos" when ordering.

Rainforest for children video series. Library Video Company, P.O. Box 1110, Catalogue M-47, Bala Cynwyd, PA 19004. (800) 843-3620. Three-volume set, 25 minutes each. Filmed on location in the rainforests of Costa Rica. Offers concise and fun bits of information on indigenous plants, cultures, and animals. Provides children with an appreciation for the value of the rainforests.

Second step: A violence-prevention curriculum. (1992). Committee for Children, Seattle, WA. Teacher's guide with video and posters to reduce aggressive behavior in children ages 9–12. Increases students' levels of social competence.

Time for Horatio (cooperating for a kinder world). Film Archives, Cinema Center, Botsford, CT 06404-0386. (800) 366-1920. Horatio is a kitten who can't understand why everyone is so mean to him until he travels with his friend Oliver to the Greenwich Royal Observatory and learns that the world is running on "mean time." Horatio returns to London with a mission to stop MEAN time and start the world running on KIND time. Horatio's adventures lead him to the very top of Big Ben, where his actions help children imagine a world in which peace and cooperation replace violence and hatred. 19 minutes.

Understanding Asian Americans: A curriculum resource guide. Compiled and edited by Marjorie H. Li and Peter Li. Neal-Schuman Publishers. (212) 925-8650. A complete one-volume resource package. Offers step-by-step instructions for 15 elementary school cross-cultural activities such as origami, calligraphy, and haiku. Sixteen projects for the high school level follow discussions of historical myths, family roles, film portrayals of Asians, etc. A section on incorporating Asian studies into the curriculum offers concrete advice to educators, and extensive bibliography provides sources for information on Asians in the United States and pertinent legislation. For use with children ages 4–9.

Women of hope. Bread and Roses, 330 West 42nd St., New York, NY 10036. (800) 666-1728. A 12-poster set, 64-page bilingual teaching guide, 27-minute video, and "Images of Labor," a 10-poster set featuring original art works on labor themes. Focuses on Latino and African American women.

Yasawa, my island home. Columban Fathers Mission, Mission Education Department, 400 North Calhoun (Bellevue), St. Columbans, NB 68056. Available free to schools upon request on a circulation basis, borrowers pay postage. Request three weeks in advance. This 16-minute video presents a child's life on Fiji where there are no televisions, roads, vehicles, telephones, etc. Suitable for grades K–4.

Periodicals

Aramco World. Aramco Services Company, 9009 West Loop South, Houston TX 77096-1799. Official bimonthly publication of AWAIR.

Childhood Education. Association for Childhood Education International, 11501 Georgia Avenue, Ste. 315, Wheaton, MD 20902. (301) 942-2443. Features articles about classroom practices, issues affecting teachers and children, current research, etc.

Courier: Provoking Thought and Dialogue About the World. Stanley Foundation, 216 Sycamore St., Muscatine, IA 52761-3831. Official publication of the Stanley Foundation, published three times annually.

Development Teach Net. Interfaith Hunger Appeal, 475 Riverside Drive, Ste. 1630, New York, NY 10115-0079. The global education quarterly publication of Interfaith Hunger Appeal.

Equity & Excellence in Education. School of Education, Furcolo Hall, University of Massachusetts, Amherst, MA 01003. The University of Massachusetts School of Education journal.

Lion and the Unicorn. 2715 North Charles Street, Baltimore, MD 21218-4319. (410) 516-6987. Critical journal of books for children. Each issue explores one theme or genre or one aspect of the field of children's literature.

Multicultural Education. Caddo Gap Press, for the National Association for Multicultural Education,

3143 Geary Blvd., Ste. 275, San Francisco, CA 94118. Quarterly publication focusing on multicultural educational issues.

Multicultural Messenger. International Multicultural Education Association, People's Publishing Group, Inc., 230 West Passaic St., Maywood, NJ 07607. Newsletter published 10 times annually. Covers national and international current events from a multicultural perspective.

Multicultural Review: Dedicated to a Better Understanding of Ethnic, Racial and Religious Diversity. Greenwood Publishing Group, Inc., 88 Post Road West, P.O. Box 5007, Westport, CT 06881. Quarterly publication that reviews multicultural publications.

National Geographic. 11555 Darnestown, Gaithersburg, MD 20878. (202) 857-7000. Monthly publication. Focuses on people, flora, and fauna of different global geographic locations and historic epochs.

Rechild: Reggio Children Newsletter. Reggio Children SRL, Via Guido Da Castello 12, 42100 Reggio, Italy. Membership newsletter published in Italian and English.

Rethinking Schools. 1001 East Keefe Ave., Milwaukee, WI 53212. (414) 964-9646. Focuses on elementary and secondary schools. Published by Milwaukee area teachers, goals are to promote educational equity, support multiculturalism and progressive values, and provide a voice for teachers, parents, and students.

School Voices. 79 Leonard St. (Basement), New York, NY 10013. A New York City newspaper for parents, educators, and students that is published by a pro-equality, multiracial network of educators and parents.

Teaching Tolerance. Southern Poverty Law Center, 400 Washington Ave., Montgomery, AL 36104. Biannual publication dedicated to teaching appreciation of diversity. Free to educators.

Young Children. National Association for the Education of Young Children, 1509 16th Street NW, Washington, DC 20036-1426. (202) 232-8777. Professional journal of early childhood education with a scholarly approach to practice, research, and theory.

Organizations

Academic Collective Bargaining Information Service (ACBIS)
University of the District of Columbia Labor Studies, Department of Management and Office Systems, College of Professional Studies
4200 Connecticut Ave. NW, MB 5200
Washington, DC 20008
Phone: (202) 282-3718
Fax: (202) 282-3786

Academy of Educational Development
1875 Connecticut Ave. NW
Washington, DC 20009
Phone: (202) 884-8000
Fax: (202) 884-8400

American Forum for Global Education
45 John St., Ste. 908
New York, NY 10038
Phone: (212) 791-4132

American Indian Institute
University of Oklahoma
555 Constitution Ave., Ste. 237
Norman, OK 73072-7820
Phone: (405) 325-4127
Fax: (405) 325-7757

Arab World and Islamic Resources and School Services
1865 Euclid Avenue, Ste. 4
Berkeley, CA 94709
Phone: (510) 704-0517

Association for Asian Studies
1 Lane Hall
University of Michigan
Ann Arbor, MI 48109
Phone: (313) 665-2490

Association for Childhood Education International
1150 Georgia Ave., Ste. 315
Wheaton, WA 20902
Phone: (301) 942-2443

Association for Multicultural Counseling and
    Development
c/o American Counseling Association
5999 Stevenson Ave.
Alexandria, VA 22304
Phone: (703) 823-9800
Fax: (703) 823-0252

Association for Supervision and Curriculum
    Development
1250 Pitt St. N
Alexandria , VA 22314-1403
Phone: (703) 549-9110

AWAIR
Center for Global Education
Augsburg College
2211 Riverside Ave.
Minneapolis, MN 55454
Phone: (612) 330-1159
Fax: (612) 330-1695

Center for Human Services
7200 Wisconsin Ave., Ste. 600
Bethesda, MD 20814
Phone: (301) 654-8338

Center for Research on Education, Diversity,
    and Excellence (CREDE)
University of California at Santa Cruz
1156 High St.
Santa Cruz, CA 95064
Phone: (408) 459-3501

Center for World Indigenous Studies
c/o John Burrows
P.O. Box 2574
Olympia, WA 98507-2574
Phone: (360) 956-1087
Fax: (360) 956-1087

Children's Creative Response to Conflict Resolution
    Program
521 N. Broadway
Box 271
Nyack, NY 10960
Phone: (914) 353-1796

Children's Museum
Howard East Asian Outreach Program
300 Congress St.
Boston, MA 02210
Phone: (617) 426-6500

China Program
American Council of Learned Societies
228 E. 45th St.
New York City, NY 10017
Clearinghouse for Immigrant Education (CHIME)
100 Boylston St.
Boston, MA 02116
Phone: (617) 357-8507
Fax: (617) 357-9549

Common Destiny Alliance
c/o Dr. Willis D. Hawley
College of Education
University of Maryland
3119 Benjamin Bldg.
College Park, MD 20742-1121
Phone: (415) 864-1169
Fax: (510) 540-0171

Comparative and International Education Society
c/o Institute of International Education
1400 K St. NW
Washington, DC 20005-2403
Phone: (202) 326-7759

Congreso Boricua
Puerto Rican Congress of New Jersey
515 S. Broad St.
Trenton, NJ 08601
Phone: (609) 989-8888

Council for Exceptional Children
1920 Association Dr.
Reston, VA 22091-1589
Phone: (703) 620-3660

Council on International Education Exchange
205 E. 42nd St.
New York, NY 10017-5706
Phone: (212) 661-1414

Council on Interracial Books for Children
1841 Broadway

New York, NY 10023
Phone: (212) 757-5339

Cultural Survival
46 Brattle St.
Cambridge, MA 02138
Phone: (617) 441-5400
Fax: (617) 441-5417

Educational Center for Applied Ekistics
1900 DeKalb Ave. NE
Atlanta, GA 30307
Phone: (404) 378-2219

Educators for Social Responsibility
23 Garden St.
Cambridge, MA 02138
Phone: (617) 492-1764

Equity Institute
6400 Hollis St., Ste. 15
Emoryville, CA 94608
Phone: (415) 658-4577

Five College Center for East Asian Studies
Smith College
8 College Lane
Northhampton, MA 01063

Foundation for Global Community
222 High St.
Palo Alto, CA 94301
Phone: (415) 328-7756

Global Education Associates
475 Riverside Dr., Ste. 1848
New York, NY 10115
Phone: (212) 870-3290
Fax: (212) 870-2729

Global Learning
1018 Stuyvesant Ave.
Union, NJ 07083
Phone: (908) 964-1114
Fax: (908) 964-6335

Global Outreach
P.O. Box 3291
Merrifield, VA 22116-3291

Phone: (703) 385-2995
Fax: (703) 385-2996

Holocaust Resource Center
Kean College of New Jersey
Library, 2nd Floor
Union, NJ 07083
Phone: (908) 527-3049

Institute for Childhood Resources
c/o Dr. Stevanne Auerbach
220 Montgomery St., No. 2811
San Francisco, CA 94104
Phone: (301) 405-2334
Fax: (301) 314-9890

Inter-Faith Hunger Appeal
475 Riverside Dr., Ste. 1630
New York, NY 10115-0079
Phone: (212) 870-2035

International Society for Intercultural Education,
    Training and Research
808 17th St. NW, No. 200
Washington, DC 20006
Phone: (202) 466-7883
Fax: (202) 223-9569

International Youth Foundation
c/o Rick Little
67 West Michigan Ave., Ste. 608
Battle Creek, MI 49017

Japan Society of Boston
22 Batterymarch St.
Boston, MA 02109
Phone: (617) 451-0726

Keizai Koho Center Fellowship
10 Village Lane
Unionville, CT 06085
Phone: (860) 673-8684

Korea Society
950 Third Ave., 8th Floor

New York, NY 10022
Phone: (212) 759-7525
Fax: (212) 759-7530

Multicultural Education Training and Advocacy Inc.
    (META)
240A Elm St., #22
Somerville, MA 02145
Phone: (617) 628-2226
Fax: (617) 628-0322

National Association for Bilingual Education (NABE)
1220 L St. NW, Ste. 605
Washington, DC 20005
Phone: (202) 898-1829
Fax: (202) 789-2866

National Association for the Education of Young
    Children
1509 16th St. NW
Washington, DC 20036
Phone: (202) 232-8777

National Association for Holocaust Education
c/o Dr. Irene Shur
Westchester University
Dept. of History
Westchester, PA 19383
Phone: (610) 436-2789

National Association for Multicultural Education
2101-A N. Rolfe St.
Arlington, VA 22209-1007
Phone: (703) 243-4525

National Association of Counsel for Children
1205 Oneida St.
Denver, CO 80220
Phone: (303) 322-2260

National Coalition of Education Activists
P.O. Box 679
Rhinebeck, NY 12572-0679
Phone: (914) 876-4580
Fax: (914) 876-4580

National Conference of Christians and Jews
71 5th Ave., Ste. 1100

New York, NY 10003-3095
Phone: (212) 206-0006
Fax: (212) 255-6177

National Council for the Social Studies
3501 Newark St. NW
Washington, DC 20001-3167
Phone: (202) 966-7840
Fax: (202) 966-2061

National Geographic Society
1145 17th St. NW
Washington, DC 20036-4688
Phone: (202) 775-6577

National Institute Against Prejudice and Violence
31 South Greene St.
Baltimore, MD 21201
Phone: (410) 328-5170
Fax: (410) 328-7551

National Women's History Project
7738 Bell Rd.
Windsor, CT 95492
Phone: (707) 838-6000

New England Center for Equity Assistance
300 Brickstone Square, Ste. 900
Andover, MA 01810

Northeast Global Education Center
Salem State College
Library Room 316
Salem, MA 01970
Phone: (978) 542-6044
Email: *louise.swiniarski@salemstate.edu*
Website: *http://www.salemstate.edu/ngec/*

Organization for Economic Cooperation
    and Development (OECD)
2, rue Andre Pascal
75775 Paris Cedex, France
Phone: 01 45 24 8200

Oxfam America
26 West St.
Boston, MA 02111-1206
Phone: (617) 482-1211

Quality Education for Minorities Network
1818 N St. NW, Ste. 350
Washington, DC 20036
Phone: (202) 659-1818
Fax: (202) 659-5408

Reggio Children S.R.L.
Via Guido Da Castello, 12
42100 Reggio Emilia, Italy
Phone: 0522/455416
Fax: 0522/455621

Southern Poverty Law Center
P.O. Box 2087
Montgomery, AL 36102
Phone: (334) 264-0286

Stanley Foundation
216 Sycamore St., Ste. 500
Muscatine, IA 52761-3831
Phone: (319) 264-1500
Fax: (319) 264-0864

Swedish Information Service
825 3rd Ave.
New York, NY 10022

Teaching English in Japan Program
Eailham College
Richmond, IN 47373-4095
Phone: (317) 983-1324

UNESCO
5815 Lawton Ave.
Oakland, CA 94618-1510
Phone: (510) 654-4638

UNICEF
3 United Nations Plaza
New York, NY 10017
Phone: (212) 326-7000

Unity-and-Diversity World Council
5521 Grosvenor Blvd.
Los Angeles, CA 90066
Phone: (310) 577-1968
Fax: (310) 390-2192

Up with People
1 International Ct.
Broomfield, CO 80021
Phone: (303) 460-7100
Fax: (303) 438-7302

World Affairs Council
22 Batterymarch St.
Boston, MA 02109
Phone: (617) 482-1740

World Health Organization
Ave. Appia
CH-1211 Geneva 27, Switzerland
Phone: 22 7912111
Fax: 22 7910746

World Organization for Early Childhood Education,
    U.S. National Committee
3620 Foxhunt Dr.
Ann Arbor, MI 48105
Phone: (313) 761-5604

Appendix B: Resources for Children

Books

Aardema, V. (1981). *Bringing the rain to Kapiti Plain.* New York: Dial Books.

Adoff, A. (1973). *Black is brown is tan.* New York: Harper Collins.

Adoff, A. (1982). *All the colors of the race.* New York: Beech Tree Books.

Aleichem, S. (1978). *Hanukah money.* New York: Greenwillow Books.

Aliki. (1976). *Corn is maize: The gift of the Indians.* New York: Harper & Row.

Allan-Meyer, K. (1995). *I have a new friend.* Hauppauge, NY: Barron's.

Anno, M. (Coll.), & Carle, E., Briggs, R., Popov, N., Hayashi, A., Calvi, et al. (1990). *All in a day.* New York: Putnam.

Ashley, B. (1991). *Cleversticks.* New York: Crown.

Bailey, D. (1990a). *Carnival in Trinidad.* Austin, TX: Steck-Vaughn.

Bailey, D. (1990b). *Diwali in India.* Austin, TX: Steck-Vaughn.

Bailey, D. (1990c). *My home in Japan.* Austin, TX: Steck-Vaughn.

Bailey, D. (1990d). *A wedding in Poland.* Austin, TX: Steck-Vaughn.

Bailey, D., & Sproule, A. (1991a). *A festival in Britanny.* Austin, TX: Steck-Vaughn.

Bailey, D., & Sproule, A. (1991b). *My home in Bangladesh.* Austin, TX: Steck-Vaughn.

Bailey, D., & Sproule, A. (1991c). *My home in Brazil.* Austin, TX: Steck-Vaughn.

Bailey, D., & Sproule, A. (1991d). *My home in Ireland.* Austin, TX: Steck-Vaughn.

Bang, M. (1985). *The paper crane.* New York: Greenwillow.

Barton, H., & Knowton, J. (1985). *Maps and globes.* New York: Harper Collins.

Bond, M., & McKee, D. (1986). *Paddington at the palace.* New York: G.P. Putnam's Sons.

Braine, S. (1995). *Drumbeat . . . heartbeat: A celebration of the powwow.* Minneapolis, MN: Lerner.

Brenner, B. (1978). *Wagon wheels.* New York: Harper & Row.

Brenner, B., & Takaya, J. (1996). *Chibi: A true story from Japan.* New York: Clarion.

Brett, J. (1992). *Trouble with trolls.* New York: Putnam & Grosset.

Brimmer, L. D. (1996). *A migrant family.* Minneapolis, MN: Lerner.

Butler, G., & Karetak, J. (1980). *Inuit games.* Rankin Inlet, NWT: Keewaith Inuit Association.

Calhoun, M. (1990). *While I sleep.* New York: Morrow.

Carlstrom, N. W. (1992). *Baby-O.* New York: Little, Brown.

Carrison, M. P. (1987). *Cambodian folk stories.* Rutland, VT: Charles E. Tuttle.

Cherry, L. (1990). *The great kapok tree.* New York: Gulliver.

Chocolate, D. (1992). *My first Kwanzaa book.* New York: Scholastic.

Chocolate, D. (1996). *Kente colors.* New York: Walker.

Christian, R. (1982). *Cooking the Spanish way.* Part of the "Easy Menu Ethnic Cookbooks" series. Minneapolis, MN: Lerner.

Cohen, C. (1988). *The mud pony.* New York: Scholastic.

Cooper, F. (1992). *Imani's gift at Kwanzaa.* Cleveland, OH: Modern Curriculum Press.

Crews, D. (1991). *Big mama's*. New York: Trumpet Club.

Damon, E. (1995). *All kinds of people: A lift-the-flap book*. London: Tango.

De Gerez, T. (1986). *Louhi: Witch of North Farm*. New York: Viking Penguin.

De Paola, T. (1975). *Strega Nona*. London: Prentice-Hall.

De Paola, T. (1980). *The knight and the dragon*. Toronto: General.

De Paola, T. (1983). *The legend of the bluebonnet*. New York: Scholastic.

De Paola, T. (1988). *The legend of the Indian paintbrush*. New York: Scholastic.

Disher, G. (1993). *The bamboo flute*. New York: Ticknor & Fields.

Dooley, N. (1991). *Everybody cooks rice*. Minneapolis, MN: First Avenue Editions.

Dooley, N. (1996). *Everybody bakes bread*. Minneapolis, MN: Lerner.

Dorros, A. (1991). *Abuela*. New York: Dutton.

Dorros, A. (1992). *This is my house*. New York: Scholastic.

Dupre, R. (1993). *Agassu*. Minneapolis, MN: Lerner.

Fassler, D. (1992). *Changing families*. Burlington, VT: Waterfront.

Fassler, D., & Danforth, K. (1993). *Coming to America: The kid's book about immigration*. Burlington, VT: Waterfront.

Feelings, M. (1970). *Zamani goes to market*. New York: Seabury Press.

Feelings, M. (1971). *Moja means one*. New York: Dial.

Feelings, M. (1974). *Jambo means hello*. New York: Dial.

Feeney, S. (1985). *Hawaii is a rainbow*. Honolulu: University of Hawaii Press.

Ferris, J. (1989). *Arctic explorer: The story of Matthew Henson*. Minneapolis, MN: Lerner.

Flack, M., & Wiese, K. (1978). *The story about Ping*. New York: Penguin.

Fox, M. (1983). *Possum magic*. San Diego: Gulliver.

Fox, M. (1988). *Koala Lou*. San Diego: Gulliver.

Friedman, I. R. (1984). *How my parents learned to eat*. Boston: Houghton Mifflin Company.

Fritz, J. (1982). *The good giants and the bad Pukwudgies*. Toronto: General.

Gilman, P. (1992). *Something from nothing*. Ontario: North Winds Press.

Giovanni, N. (1994). *Knoxville, Tennessee*. New York: Scholastic.

Goble, P. (1984). *Buffalo women*. New York: Aladdin.

Greenfield, E. (1991). *Big friend, little friend*. New York: Black Butterfly Children's Books.

Grifalconi, A. (1986). *The village of round and square houses*. Boston: Little, Brown.

Hancock, S. (1983). *Esteban and the ghost*. New York: Dial.

Hartman, G. (1991). *As the crow flies*. New York: Macmillian.

Haskins, J. (1987). *Count your way through China*. Part of the "Count Your Way Books" series. Minneapolis, MN: Lerner.

Hayashi, A. (1991). *Aki and the fox*. New York: Doubleday.

Hebert, M. (1995). *Horatio rides the wind*. Surrey, England: Templar.

Hermes, J. (1995). *The children of Bolivia*. Part of "The World's Children" series. Minneapolis, MN: Carolrhoda.

Hill, E. S. (1990). *Evan's corner*. New York: Viking Penguin.

Hoberman, M. A. (1988). *A house is a house for me*. New York: Puffin Books.

Hodges, M. (1984). *Saint George and the dragon*. New York: Little, Brown.

Honan, M. (1991). *Amazing grace*. New York: Dial Books.

Jasinek, D., & Ryan, P. B. (1990). *A family is a circle of people who love you*. Minneapolis, MN: CompCare.

Johnson, A. (1990). *When I am old with you*. New York: Orchard.

Johnson, A. (1991). *One of three*. New York: Orchard Books.

Johnson, A. (1996). *String games from around the world*. Palo Alto, CA: Klutz Press.

Johnston, T., & De Paola, T. (1985). *The quilt story*. Hong Kong: South China Printing.

Joosse, B. (1991). *Mama do you love me?* New York: Scholastic.

Kandoian, E. (1987). *Under the sun*. New York: G.P. Putnam's Sons.

Keller, H. (1992). *Island baby*. New York: Greenwillow.

Kissinger, K. (1994). *All the colors we are*. St. Paul, MN: Redleaf Press.

Knight, M. B. (1992). *Talking walls*. Gardiner, ME: Tilbury House.

Knight, M. B. (1993). *Who belongs here?* Gardiner, ME: Tilbury House.

Knutson, B. (1991). *How the guinea fowl got her spots: A Swahili tale of friendship*. Minneapolis, MN: Lerner.

Krensky, S. (1987). *Who really discovered America?* New York: Scholastic.

Leder, J. M. (1996). *A Russian Jewish family*. Part of the "Journey Between Two Worlds" series. Minneapolis, MN: Lerner.

Lenski, L. (1987). *Sing a song of people*. Boston: Little, Brown.

Levine, E. (1990). *I hate English*. New York: Scholastic.

Lewin, H. (1983–1994). *Jafta collection*. A six-book series. Minneapolis, MN: Lerner.

Lewis, T. P. (1971). *Hill of fire*. New York: Harper & Row.

Lofts, P. (1987). *Warnayarra: The rainbow snake*. Melbourne, Australia: Ashton Scholastic.

Louie, A. (1982). *Yeh Shen: A Cinderella story from China*. New York: Philomel.

Lowery, L. (1996). *Wilma Mankiller*. Minneapolis, MN: Lerner.

MacLachlan, P. (1980). *Through Grampa's eyes*. New York: Harper & Row.

Margolies, B. (1990). *Rehema's journey*. New York: Scholastic.

Martin, B., & Archambault, J. (1987). *Knots on a counting rope*. New York: Trumpet Club.

McCloskey, R. (1941). *Make way for ducklings*. New York: Viking.

McDermott, G. (1972). *Anansi the spider*. New York: Scholastic.

McGovern, A. (1972). *If you lived with the Sioux Indians*. New York: Scholastic.

McKissack, P. C. (1992). *A million fish … more or less*. New York: Alfred A. Knopf/Borzoi.

Meltzer, M. (1992). *The amazing potato*. New York: HarperCollins.

Menzel, P. (1994). *Material world: A global portrait*. San Francisco: Sierra Club.

Merrill, J. (Adapter). (1992). *The girl who loved caterpillars: A twelfth-century tale from Japan*. New York: Philomel.

Miles, M. (1971). *Annie and the old house*. Boston: Little, Brown.

Mitchell, B. (1986). *Shoes for everyone: A story about Jan Matzeliger*. Minneapolis, MN: Carolrhoda.

Monjo, F. N. (1970). *The drinking gourd: A story of the Underground Railroad*. New York: Harper Trophy.

Morris, A. (1989a). *Bread, bread, bread*. New York: Lothrop, Lee, & Shepard.

Morris, A. (1989b). *Hats, hats, hats*. New York: Lothrop, Lee, & Shepard.

Mosel, A. (1968). *Tikki Tikki Tembo*. New York: Holt.

Musgrove, M. (1980). *Ashanti to Zulu*. New York: Dial.

Nunes, S. (1992). *To find the way*. Honolulu: University of Hawaii.

O'Connor, B. (1993). *Mammolina: A story about Maria Montessori*. Minneapolis, MN: Lerner.

O'Connor, K. O. (1992). *Dan Thuy's new life in America*. Minneapolis, MN: Lerner.

Orr, K. (1996). *Story of a dolphin*. Minneapolis, MN: Lerner.

Peel, J. (1992). *Where in America is Carmen Sandiego?* New York: Golden.

Pellowski, A. (1990) *Hidden stories in plants*. New York: Macmillan.

Pennington, D. (1994). *Cherokee A-B-C coloring book*. Cherokee, NC: Cherokee Publications.

Peters, R. M. (1992). *Clambake: A Wampanoag tradition*. Minneapolis, MN: Lerner.

Polacco, P. (1992). *Mrs. Katz and Tush*. New York: Bantam.

Porter, A. P. (1995). *Kwanzaa*. Minneapolis, MN: Lerner.

Prokofiev, S., & Carlson, M. (Trans.) (1988). *Peter and the wolf*. New York: Viking Penguin.

Provensen, A., & Provensen, M. (1978). *A peaceable kingdom: The Shaker abecedarius*. New York: Penguin.

Regguinti, G. (1992). *The sacred harvest: Ojibway wild rice gathering*. Minneapolis, MN: Lerner.

Ringgold, F. (1992). *Aunt Harriet's underground railroad in the sky*. New York: Scholastic.

Roe, E. (1991). *Con mi hermano/With my brother*. New York: Bradbury Press.

Roessel, M. (1995). *Songs from the loom: A Navajo girl learns to weave*. Minneapolis, MN: Lerner.

Rohmer, H. (1989). *Uncle Nacho's hat*. San Francisco: Interprint.

Rylant, C. (1982). *When I was young in the mountains*. New York: E. P. Dutton.

Sadora, R. (1979). *Ben's trumpet*. New York: Scholastic.

Sage, J. (1991). *The little band*. New York: McElderry.

Samton, S. W. (1991). *Jenny's journey*. New York: Viking Penguin.

Sandin, J. (1981). *The long way to a new land*. New York: Harper & Row.

Santrey, L. (1983). *Young Frederick Douglass: Fight for freedom*. Mahwah, NJ: Troll Associates.

Say, A. (1991). *Tree of cranes*. Boston: Houghton Mifflin.

Schoberle, C. (1990). *Esmerelda and the pet parade*. New York: Simon and Schuster.

Scieszka, J. (1991). *The frog prince, continued*. New York: Viking Penguin.

Scieszka, J. (1995). *The true story of the three pigs*. New York: NAL Dutton.

Scott, A. H. (1992). *On mother's lap*. Boston: Clarion.

Seuss, Dr. (1984). *The butter battle book*. New York: Random House.

Shalant, P. (1988). *Look what we've brought you from Vietnam*. New York: Simon & Schuster.

Shelby, A. (1990). *We keep a store*. Chicago: Orchard Books.

Shulevitz, U. (1973). *The magician*. New York: Macmillan.

Simon, N. (1976). *All kinds of families*. Morton Grove, IL: Albert Whitman.

Singer, M. (1992). *Nine o'clock lullaby*. New York: Harper Trophy.

Sloat, R., & Sloan, T. (1993). *The hungry giant of the tundra*. New York: Dutton.

Smalls-Hector, I. (1992). *Jonathan and his mommy*. New York: Little, Brown.

Spier, P. (1980). *People*. New York: Doubleday.

Steig, W. (1983). *Amos & Boris*. New York: Penguin.

Steptoe, J. (1987). *Mufaro's beautiful daughters*. New York: Lothrop, Lee, & Shepard.

Stoutenburg, A. (1987). *American tall tales*. New York: Penguin.

Surat, M. M. (1983). *Angel child, dragon child*. Milwaukee, WI: Raintree.

Swamp, Chief J. (1995). *Giving thanks: A Native American good morning message*. New York: Lee & Low.

Thompson, V. L. (1966). *Hawaiian myths of the earth, sea, and sky*. Honolulu: University of Hawaii Press.

Tompert, A. (1990). *Grandfather Tang's story*. New York: Crown.

Trân-Khánh-Tuyêt. (1987). *The little weaver of Thai-Yen village*. San Francisco: Children's Books Press.

Wren & Maile. (1992). *Say it in Hawaiian: Pi-a-pa (alphabet)*. Honolulu: Bess Press.

Periodicals

Chickadee. Young Naturalist Foundation, 179 John Street, Ste. 500, Toronto, Ontario M5T 3 G5 Canada, (416) 971-5275. For 3- to 9-year-olds. Each issue features photographs and illustrations, stories, games, puzzles, crafts, and a pull-out.

Cobblestone: The History Magazine for Young People. 20 Grove St., Peterborough, NH 03458. Monthly publication focusing on history in a manner understandable to young people.

The Daybreak Star Indian Reader. United Indians of All Tribes Foundation, 1945 Yale Place E., Seattle, WA 98102. (206) 325-0070. A 24-page magazine featuring accurate information about Native Americans and their cultures.

Faces: The Magazine About People. Cobblestone Publishing, Inc., 20 Grove St., Peterborough, NH 03458. Monthly publication focusing on human experiences encompassing all cultures.

Harambee. (Just Us Books). A newspaper for young readers published six times a year, focusing on the African American experience. Contains information, articles, photographs, learning activities, book lists, interviews, word lists, and the Captain Africa comic strip adventure.

Kids Discover. 170 Fifth Ave., New York, NY 10010. Published 10 times per year. Each issue is dedicated to a particular element: a geographic location (e.g., Australia), a historic epoch (e.g., ancient Greece), a historical figure (e.g., Abraham Lincoln), a natural phenomenon (e.g., tornadoes), and so on.

National Geographic World. National Geographic Society, 11555 Darnestown, Gaithersburg, MD 20878. (202) 857-7000. Features factual stories on outdoor adventure, natural history, geography, sports, science, and history for children ages 8–13.

Quest. Peter Li Education Group, 330 Progress Rd., Dayton, OH 45439. A reading and writing magazine for elementary school children featuring puzzles, games, and seasonal stories designed to enrich the cultural awareness of readers.

Skipping Stones: A Multicultural Children's Quarterly. P.O. Box 3939, Eugene, OR 97403. (503) 342-4956. A multilingual, environmental awareness magazine designed to let children from diverse backgrounds share their experiences, cultures, languages, and creative expressions.

Stone Soup. Children's Art Foundation, P.O. Box 83, Santa Cruz, CA 95063. (408) 426-5557. Stories, poems, reviews, and art by children up to age 13. Activity guide bound to each issue.

Tapori. Fourth World Movement, 7600 Willow Hill Dr., Landover, MD 20785. (310) 336-0092. Gives disadvantaged children a means of expression and gives other children a means to learn about poverty, to communicate, and to show their friendship.

Zillions. 101 Truman Ave., Yonkers, NY 10703. (800) 288-7898. Evaluates toys, games, food, and other products kids use and provides advice on consumer and lifestyle problems kids face.

Multimedia

Abiyoyo. Reading Rainbow, GPN, P.O. Box 80669, Lincoln, NE 68501-0669. (800) 228-4630. A story song retold and sung by its author, Pete Seeger, based on a South African lullaby and folk story. A boy and his father come up with a plan to save the townspeople from a giant, Abiyoyo.

African tales. Mennonite Central Committee, Resource Library, 21 South 12th St., Box 500, Akron, PA 17501-0500. Available free to schools on a circulation basis, borrower pays postage. African fables and a child's view of food, a market, homes, the village blacksmith, and a church service in Zaire/Congo. 23 minutes.

Amazing Grace. Weston Woods, 389 Newtown Tpke., Weston, CT 06883-9989. (800) 243-5020. Narrated by Alfre Woodard. A 10-minute film or video. Grace is not discouraged by her classmates from trying out for Peter Pan in the school play because she is a black girl. Encourages discussion on themes of heroism, self-esteem, theater, and African Americans.

American cultures for children video series. Library Video Company, P.O. Box 1110, Bala Cynwyd, PA 19004. (800) 843-3620. Twelve-volume set; each video is 25 minutes and is appropriate for grades

K–4. All titles are closed-captioned for the hearing impaired. This series helps children to understand the diversity of their classrooms, neighborhoods, and country by introducing them to each culture through a variety of fun and fast-paced educational segments that focus on everyday life for children in other countries as well as in America. Cultures include: African American, Arab American, Chinese American, Irish American, and Vietnamese American.

Arthur's eyes. Reading Rainbow, GPN, P.O. Box 80669, Lincoln, NE 68501-0669. (800) 228-4630. A boy initially shy about wearing glasses gets into some awkward scrapes. The program deals with another kind of blindness, the kind that sees past the color of a person's skin to the real person underneath.

Berlioz the bear. Reading Rainbow, GPN, P.O. Box 80669, Lincoln, NE 68501-0669. (800) 228-4630. Berlioz the bear and his fellow musicians are due to play for the town ball when their bandwagon becomes stuck in a hole in the road. Host LeVar Burton goes on a musical journey through New York City, meeting many musicians who call the streets their stage.

The blue dashiki (Jeffrey and his city neighbors). Film Archives, Cinema Center, Botsford, CT 06404-0386. (800) 366-1920. This award-winning program follows a boy who wants to earn money to buy the dashiki he has seen in a local African import shop. The urban flavor of the black community is vividly captured without narration or dialogue. 14 minutes.

Families of India. Library Video Company, P.O. Box 1110, Bala Cynwyd, CA 19004. (800) 843-3620 Explores live-action urban and rural daily life in Northern India through a child's point of view by spending a day with two families who share everything from Indian food, clothing, and housing to religion and schools. 30 minutes. Telly Award Winner.

Hail to mail. Reading Rainbow, GPN, P.O. Box 80669, Lincoln, NE 68501-0669. (800) 228-4630. A certified letter is followed in a humorous journey to its intended recipient. The simple act of mailing a letter becomes a trip spanning the entire world in an effort to get the mail on time.

Hill of fire. Reading Rainbow, GPN, P.O. Box 80669, Lincoln, NE 68501-0669. (800) 228-4630. Based on a true story about the Paricutín volcano in Mexico, a volcano erupts in a poor farmer's corn field. Host LeVar Burton visits Volcano National Park in Hawaii and describes volcanic processes and lava.

How to make an apple pie and see the world. Reading Rainbow, GPN, P.O. Box 80669, Lincoln, NE 68501-0669. (800) 228-4630. The reader is led around the world to gather the ingredients for making an apple pie. The program helps to explain that dreams come true from hard work and a lot of effort.

In the month of Kislev. Weston Woods, 389 Newtown Tpke., Weston, CT 06883-9989. (800) 243-5020. A 13-minute film or video for ages 4–8 narrated by Theodore Bikel. Tells the story of Hanukkah in the oral tradition with wit, accompanied by authentic klezmer music.

Japanese boy: The story of Taro. Film Archives, Cinema Center, Botsford, CT 06404-0386. (800) 366-1920. The life of a Japanese boy at home and school reveals the attitudes, customs, and problems of a Japanese farm family. 20 minutes.

Knots on a counting rope. Reading Rainbow, GPN, P.O. Box 80669, Lincoln, NE 68501-0669. (800) 228-4630. A Native American tale about Boy-Strength-of-Blue-Horses and his grandfather reminiscing about the boy's birth, his first horse, and his first horse race, where he faces his greatest challenge: his blindness. This program emphasizes courage and facing the things that frighten us.

Little Big Mouse. Between the Lions. Get Wild About Reading. (2001). WGBH and Sirius Thinking Executive Producers Ltd. Boston, MA. (800) 949-8670. This is a story about how little creatures can perform big tasks.

The magic school bus inside the earth. Reading Rainbow, GPN, P.O. Box 80669, Lincoln, NE 68501-0669. (800) 228-4630. A hilarious adventure follows a quirky teacher, Ms. Fizzle, and her students on a field trip they'll never forget. They learn first-hand about the different kinds of rocks and the formation of the earth.

Mexican boy: The story of Pablo. Film Archives, Cinema Center, Botsford, CT 06404-0386. (800) 366-1920. A Mexican boy tells how he worked to make a wish come true, then found he had to choose between his wish and his family's happiness. 22 minutes.

My little island. Reading Rainbow, GPN, P.O. Box 80669, Lincoln, NE 68501-0669. (800) 228-4630. A young boy takes his best friend to visit the little Caribbean island of Montserrat, where he was born.

Notable women paper dolls in full color. T. Tierney (Illus.). (1989). Toronto: General.

Our Hispano-American friends: Cuban American/Mexican American/Puerto Rican American. Film Archives, Cinema Center, Botsford, CT 06404-0386. (800) 366-1920. Cuban-born Ilen Casasus describes her favorite foods from Miami's "Little Havana." Rosa Maria Portillo practices a Mexican dance in East Los Angeles. And Noel Seda lives in New York City, where street markets offer products from his home island, Puerto Rico. 10 minutes.

People. Library Video Company, P.O. Box 1110, Catalogue M-47, Bala Cynwyd, PA 19004. (800) 843-3620. Hume Cronyn and James Earl Jones narrate Peter Spier's magical book that celebrates the beauty of diversity of individuals and cultures around the world. 55 minutes.

Rechenka's eggs. Reading Rainbow, GPN, P.O. Box 80669, Lincoln, NE 68501-0669. (800) 228-4630. Hosted by author Patricia Polacco. She demonstrates the traditional Ukrainian egg-painting art and shares how she got the idea for the story.

Stories from the black tradition. Film Archives, Cinema Center, Botsford, CT 06404-0386. (800) 366-1920. For grades K–4. In color, a collection of five stories on video: *A Story–A Story, Mufaro's Beautiful Daughters, Why Mosquitoes Buzz in People's Ears, The Village of Round and Square Houses*, and *Goggles*. 52 minutes.

Appendix C: Internet Resources

African American/African Studies
Located at the University of Pennsylvania
Address: http://www.library.upenn.edu
> This thorough and in-depth Gopher server covers an extensive amount of information on African studies. It includes information at the University of Pennsylvania, elsewhere in the United States, Africa, and elsewhere. Of special note is the K–12 African studies directory, which includes curriculum materials for the classroom. Lesson plans and classroom activities are listed. African recipes and many graphic files in GIF format.

AIESEC United States
Student organization
Address: http://www.us.aiesec.org
> A highly proactive international student organization in 85 countries dedicated to global leadership development and cultural understanding.

American Association of Colleges for Teacher Education (AACTE)
Homepage
Address: http://www.aacte.org
> Organization supports programs in teacher education, multicultural education, and international education; leadership and development; networking; professional and women's issues; and school reform.

Balch Institute for Ethnic Studies
Homepage
Address: http://www.balchinstitute.org
> A multicultural library, archive, museum, and education center. Educational programs include school group visits and diversity workshops.

Chapter 1.2 Information Collection
Address: http://www.xs4all.nl/~swanson/history/chapter0102.html
> An excellent resource for interactive history projects for children and teachers around the world, this site includes a multicultural calendar for holidays and electronic field trips.

Citykids Online
Homepage
Address: http://www.citykids.com/
> A multicultural organization dedicated to the survival, education, and self-expression of today's youth.

Comparative and Global Studies in Education
Located at Immaculate Heart College Center
Address: http://www.gse.buffalo.edu/DC/CCGSE/ccgse.htm
> Offers programs dealing with feminist spirituality and global studies and outreach programs for schools.

Global Schoolhouse
A member of Microsoft's Connected Learning Community
Address: http://www.gsh.org/
> Brings Internet resources and classroom projects to the educational community.

Global SchoolNet Foundation
Homepage
Address: http://www.globalschoolnet.org
> Nonprofit corporation and contributor to the design, culture, and content of educational networking using the Internet in the classroom.

Juniper Learning
Homepage
Address: http://www.juniperlearning.com/
   An educational development company offering cross-curricular, multicultural, hands-on programs for K–12 teachers and their young students.

KIDLINK: Global Networking for Youth 10–15
Located at KIDLINK's organizational headquarters
Address: http://www.kidlink.org/
   Grassroots project aimed at getting as many children as possible involved in a global dialog.

Most Foreign Countries, U.S. Dept. of State Background Notes on Foreign Countries
Located at the University of Pennsylvania
Address: http://www.state.gov/r/pa/bgn/
   This resource covers most countries of the world with up-to-date and complete information helpful to students doing in-depth research. For each country, information about the following topics is provided: people, flag, history, education, geography, natural resources, agriculture, industry, trade, economy, government, names of principal government officials, relations with the United States, etc.

Multicultural Book Review
Homepage
Address: http://www.isomedia.com/homes/jmele/homepage.html

This effort by graduate students in Seattle University's master in teaching program attempts to build a canon of quality multicultural books for K–12 educators. Submit your own review or read what's already here in this massive list of publications.

Multicultural Pavilion
Located at the University of Virginia
Address: http://curry.edschool.virginia.edu/go/multicultural/
   A resource for educators, with links to other related sites, providing reviews of multicultural kids' media and a newsgroup.

National Multicultural Institute
Homepage
Address: http://www.nmci.org/nmci/
   Organization engaged in developing multicultural and cross-cultural awareness through diversity training workshops, conferences, and educational resource materials.

San Jose Elementary
Homepage
Address: http://www.world.std.com/~mkjg/
   Pre-K–5 Florida's first multiple intelligence school, with multicultural programs featuring English for speakers of other languages (ESOL).

Appendix D: Resources for Parents

The child in the family and the community, by Janet Gonzalez-Mena. Columbus, OH: Merrill Prentice Hall. 2002.

This book relates to children from birth to age 8 as they develop with their families and in multicultural communities.

Cooking the Spanish way. Part of the "Easy Menu Ethnic Cookbooks" series, by Rebecca Christian. Minneapolis, MN: Lerner. 1982.

Count your way through China. Part of the "Count Your Way Books" series, by Jim Haskins. Minneapolis, MN: Lerner. 1987.

Crafts of many cultures: Thirty authentic craft projects from around the world, by A. Gomez. Jefferson City, MO: Scholastic. 1996.

Step-by-step guide to creating global art projects.

Faces: The magazine about people. Cobblestone Publishing, 20 Grove St., Peterborough, NH 03458.

Monthly publication focusing on human experiences encompassing all cultures.

The games of Africa. World Almanac Education, 15355 Neo Parkway, Cleveland, OH 44128-3147. (800) 321-1149.

Introduces five of Africa's most popular games, which have been played for thousands of years and are still played today. Included is a playing board for mancala, colorful playing pieces, and a 48-page book with easy instructions and information on where the games originated.

GeoSafari talking globe. From Educational Insights. World Almanac Education, 15355 Neo Parkway, Cleveland, OH 44128-3147. (800) 321-1149.

With over 10,000 questions programmed into sophisticated speech technology, and the GeoSafari quiz style, the Talking Globe will be the center of attention in classrooms or at home. The globe provides an instant reference source for thousands of spoken questions. Up to four players or teams can play the fun, fast-paced quiz game. The friendly voice, flashing lights, and sounds congratulate and motivate all along the way.

Gifts, by Jo Ellen Bogart. World Almanac Education, 15355 Neo Parkway, Cleveland, OH 44128-3147. (800) 321-1149.

In lyrical verse and plasticine illustrations, this is the story of Granma's trip around the world and the beautiful and unusual gifts she brings her granddaughter. Through these, she learns all about the world and gains an enthusiasm for different cultures. Grades pre-K–2.

Grandloving: Making memories with your grandchild, by Sue Johnson & Julie Carlson. Fairview Press, 2450 Riverside Ave. South, Minneapolis, MN: PS 024 0604.

Households headed by grandparents are increasing in number internationally. This book contains many ideas for grandparents to share with their grandchildren and tips for helping the development of the youngsters in their lives.

Hands-on geography, by Susan Buckley and Elspeth Leacock. World Almanac Education, 15355 Neo Parkway, Cleveland, OH 44128-3147. (800) 321-1149.

Helps develop early geography skills through activities. Topics covered include maps, seasons, directions, and more.

Hidden America: A collection of multicultural stories, by R. Hammer. Golden Valley, MN: Place in the Woods. 1993.

Features the people, places, and things of importance to four minority subcultures: African American, Hispanic American, Native American, and American women. Short essays and tales.

How to make an apple pie and see the world, by Marjorie Priceman. World Almanac Education, 15355 Neo Parkway, Cleveland, OH 44128-3147. (800) 321-1149.

From the jungles of Sri Lanka to the apple orchards of Vermont, travel with the energetic little baker in this silly adventure story/cookbook spoof, complete with real recipe for apple pie. Grades K–3.

International crafts and games. Instructional Fair, TS Denison, P.O. Box 250, Grand Rapids, MI 49502-0334. (800) 443-2976.

Captures the spirit of cultural diversity with 100 easy-to-make projects. Grades 1–6.

Kachina dancers, by S & S Crafts. World Almanac Education, 15355 Neo Parkway, Cleveland, OH 44128-3147. (800) 321-1149.

Kids learn about ancient Indian tradition with this hands-on project. Kit includes precut heads and bodies, construction paper, feathers, nontoxic glue, elastic cord, tracing paper, paper fasteners, and easy-to-follow instructions. Grades 1–6.

Kids discover. 170 Fifth Ave., New York, NY 10010.

Periodical published 10 times per year. Each issue is dedicated to a particular geographic location globally (e.g., Australia), a historic epoch (e.g., ancient Greece), a historical figure, a natural phenomenon, etc.

Multicultural clip art. Instructional Fair, TS Denison, P.O. Box 250, Grand Rapids, MI 49502-0334. (800) 443-2976. Software for Windows or Macintosh.

Artwork for each country or continent includes maps, flags, clothing, people, architecture, customs, animals, wildlife, and more. Art can be downloaded into word processing and paint programs.

Multicultural games, by Lorraine Barbarash. Human Kinetics, P.O. Box 5076, Champaign, IL 61825-5076. (800) 747-4457.

Seventy-five games and activities from 43 cultures on six continents. Each game has two special elements that help children discover other cultures and learn more about their own. A blend of cultural awareness, physical activity, skill practice, and fun.

My first amazing world explorer. DK Multimedia, New Media Schoolhouse Sourcebook, Box 505, Pound Ridge, NY 10576. (888) 843-6674.

A CD-ROM activity pack for grades K–4. Takes children on trips around the physical and natural world. Through hundreds of narratives, children discover concepts of geographic mapping, travel, time, and distance. Available for Mac/Win.

Our family, our friends, our world: An annotated guide to significant multicultural books for children and teenagers, by Lyn Miller-Lachman. New Providence: Bower.

This book offers critical evaluations of fiction and nonfiction for children from K to grade 12.

Somewhere in the world right now, by Stacey Schuett. World Almanac Education, 15355 Neo Parkway, Cleveland, OH 44128-3147. (800) 321-1149.

A delightful book filled with lush paintings and a multitude of maps that show children how many different things are going on in the world at the same time. This takes the mystery out of time zones while showing the richness of the experiences of peoples of the world. Grades K–4.

Uncle Goose Toys: 2000 Catalog. Grand Rapids, MI: Uncle Goose Toys. Website: www.unclegoose.com.

A colorful catalog of traditional early childhood toys going back to the *gifts and occupations* of Froebel. A good guide for quality play equipment that has proven successful with youngsters over the years.

World GEO puzzle, by National Geographic Curiosity Kits. World Almanac Education, 15355 Neo Parkway, Cleveland, OH 44128-3147. (800) 321-1149.

Children color printed continent stickers, then peel and affix them to the sides of 12 3/4" cubes to create six different geo puzzles. A poster to color is included, which provides hundreds of fascinating cultural and geographical facts. Grades 1–6.

Index